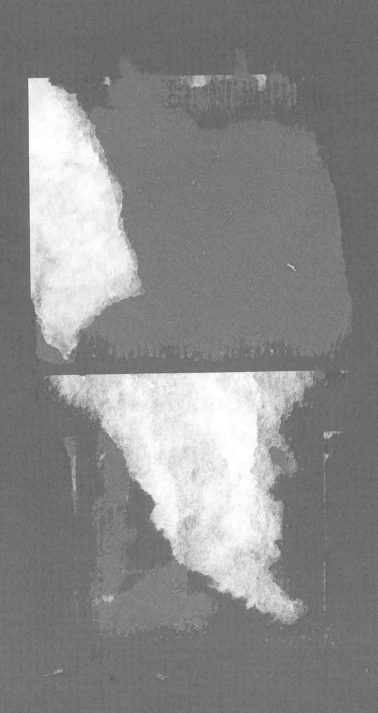

STANFORD WHITE'S NEW YORK

STANFORD WHITE'S NEW YORK

DAVID

GARRARD

LOWE

DOUBLEDAY

NEW YORK LONDON TORONTO

SYDNEY AUCKLAND

ALSO BY DAVID GARRARD LOWE

LOST CHICAGO

CHICAGO INTERIORS

ON PREVIOUS PAGE:

The special excitement of a great urban commercial thoroughfare is captured in this view down Fifth Avenue from Thirty-seventh Street. Not a little of this sophisticated ambience is due to Stanford White's magnificent Tiffany Building, left, which the architect created between 1903 and 1906. The date of the photograph is May 10, 1917, and the flags have been put out to mark the recent entry of the United States into the First World War.

PUBLISHED BY DOUBLEDAY
a division of Bantam Doubleday Dell Publishing Group, Inc.
666 Fifth Avenue, New York, New York 10103

DOUBLEDAY and the portrayal of an anchor
with a dolphin are trademarks of Doubleday,
a division of Bantam Doubleday Dell Publishing Group, Inc.

Book design by Marysarah Quinn

Library of Congress Cataloging-in-Publication Data
Lowe, David,
 Stanford White's New York / David Garrard Lowe. — 1st ed.
  p. cm.
  1. Architecture, Modern—19th century—New York (N.Y.)
 2. Architecture—New York (N.Y.) 3. New York (N.Y.)—Buildings,
structures, etc. 4. White, Stanford, 1853-1906—Criticism and
interpretation. I. Title.
 N6535.N5L69 1992
 720'.92—dc20   *91-43257*
                CIP

ISBN 0-385-26016-4

For
Florence Codman
with memories of books and conversation

CONTENTS

ACKNOWLEDGMENTS

Any list of acknowledgments for *Stanford White's New York* must begin with Sally Forbes. She was present at the birth of the idea for this book and was an integral part of the project until publication. Along the way, Sally's profound knowledge of picture research and her good judgment added immeasurably to the visual aspect of this work. But there was no aspect in which she was not involved, including reading and making suggestions regarding the text, commenting on the captions, checking facts, and correcting my spelling.

In the process of writing this book I was magnificently aided by Peter and Robert White, grandsons of Stanford White, and by Robert's wife, Claire. Their generous sharing with me of albums of photographs, clippings, family recollections, and the unpublished manuscript of Lawrence Grant White's memoirs were an invaluable contribution to this endeavor. The privilege they extended to me of visiting Stanford White's country house, Box Hill, was precious.

James H. Burke brought to the proofreading of the manuscript and the captions his uncompromising concern for the subtle usages of the English language, as well as his wide-ranging knowledge of American history.

My research for the text and my collecting of illustrative materials for this volume were conducted, not only in New York, but also in Boston, Newport, Paris, and Washington. In New York much of this research was carried on at the New York Public Library. The staff was invariably helpful. I would like to thank in particular David B. Combs, Harriet Burdock, and Marie Aroldi of the Art Room and Barbara Hillman of the Local History and Genealogy Room. I would also like to thank Wayne Furman, Administrator of Special Collections, who permitted me to use the Frederick Lewis Allen Room where much of this book was written. The Avery architectural library of Columbia University was an important source of material for this project. I would like to acknowledge the help of Angela Giral, the Librarian; Herbert Mitchell; Janet Parks, Curator of Drawings; Ted Gachot; and Victoria Weiner. The collections of the New York Historical Society proved also to be important repositories of material relating to Stanford White. Wendy Shadwell, Curator of Prints; Dale Neighbors, Assistant Curator of Photography; and Mary Beth Betts, Associate Curator of Architectural Collections, all aided my research with their knowledge and their concern. The New York Society Library was a treasure trove of books on New York City.

In Boston, the staff of the Boston Public Library was unfailingly helpful. I would particularly like to mention Wendy Gogel, Karen Shafts, and Allison Cook of the Print Department. At the Boston Athenaeum, Rodney Armstrong, the Director, gave me access to that institution's superb collections. In the Print Room, Harry Katz readily shared with me his profound knowledge of Richardson's Boston work. I would also like to thank William Bradford Osgood, who provided me with the introduction to the rich resources of The Bostonian Society.

In Newport, my research at the Redwood Library was facilitated by Richard L. Champlin, the Librarian. I would also like to thank Judanne P. Hamidzada, Assistant Curator of the International Tennis Hall of Fame, housed in the Casino, and the staff of the Newport Historical Society. A special word of thanks must go to Eileen and John Slocum, who did much to smooth the way in my research in Newport.

In Paris, my study of the city at the time of Stanford White's first visit was wonderfully aided by Madame Melle Comminges of the archives of Roger-Viollet.

In Washington, my work at the Library of Congress was expedited by the staff of the Prints and Photographic Division.

Not a little of the texture of this book is the result of information and pictorial material provided by individuals connected with institutions associated with Stanford White's life and work. I would like to mention Father Donald Goodness, Rector of the Church of the Ascension; Patrick J. Cunniff, General Manager of The Brook; Meredith Collins of Brown Brothers; Roger Friedman, Librarian of the Century Association; Anne F. Cox, Archivist of the Colony Club; Katharine Gottlieb of the Cultural Services of the French Embassy; Dr. Morris Saffron, Historian of the Harmonie Club; the late Paul Porzelt, Historian of the Metropolitan Club; Melodye Moore, Manager of the Mills Mansion; Father Paul Robichaud, C.S.P., Archivist of the Paulist Fathers; Ray Wemmlinger, Librarian of the Players Club; John Dryfhout, Curator of the Saint-Gaudens National Historic Site; Lisa Weilbacker, Curator of the Seventh Regiment Armory; and Robert Yearwood, Sexton of Trinity Church, Boston.

The writing of this book has been helped in many ways by a host of friends and acquaintances. Among them are the late Donald P. Gurney, Christabel Gough, Elspeth Hart, Joan K. Davidson, Walker Cain, John Gachot, William L. Vance, Frank Hall, Elizabeth Hawes, Gloria Deak, Sean Sculley, Anthony C. Wood, Arthur Satz, John R. Gilman, Charles Pierce, James W. Guedry, John Cadenhead, Carter Manny, James F. McCollom, Jason Selch, Malcolm Scheer, Francis King, Donald Gaynor, Esther Bubley, Stuart Preston, and Ann Burton.

This list would not be complete without my thanks to Carl D. Brandt, who first saw here the makings of a book and never lost faith in it. I would also like to express my appreciation of Bruce Tracy of Doubleday, who did much to guide and direct this work to publication. Finally, I wish to thank my editor, Jacqueline Onassis, who was there at the beginning and whose taste, understanding, and wise words helped me to stay the course.

The goal was New York. Boston and Philadelphia civilly refused to be interested in Western money, but New York was less coy . . .
                    —THOMAS BEER, *The Mauve Decade*

. . . upon a night like this, and under this graceful tower, uplifting its loveliness into the azure air and topped by a Diana fairer than that of the Ephesians smiling down upon gardens more beautiful than any ever hanging in Babylon, there is no need for me to present any defense of the Empire City . . .
                    —BRANDER MATTHEWS, *Vignettes of Manhattan*

CHAPTER 1

BORN IN NEW YORK

"Stanford White," *The Nation* proclaimed magisterially on July 5, 1906, "offered the tragic spectacle of a taste gradually adjusting itself to that of its market . . . His career . . . is that of a magnificent condottiere in architecture, who won brilliant skirmishes, but avoided the laborious operations of sieges and great campaigns." White's life, the magazine concluded, illustrated "the frittering away of genius."

"Stanford White's relation to the merchant class and to the swell mob was of a personal, galvanic kind," John Jay Chapman wrote in *Vanity Fair* the same month. "He excited them, he buffaloed them, he met them on all sides at once, in sport, pleasure, antiquities, furniture, decoration, bibelots, office buildings, country houses, and exhibitions. He was the greatest designer that this country has ever produced."

These polarities of opinion regarding Stanford White's personality and production followed hard upon his sensational murder in the roof garden atop one of his supreme creations by an irrational

Stanford White's father, Richard Grant White, in an 1850s photograph by Mathew Brady. The architect inherited many of his physical characteristics, including his red hair and his height of more than 6 feet, from his writer father.

Pittsburgh millionaire, the husband of a woman with whom White had had a liaison before her marriage. The manner of White's death threw his life in high relief upon the wall of the public's imagination. The voices which followed that death at Madison Square Garden on a warm June evening unequivocally reveal America's uneasy relationship with urbanity, with high art, and with New York City.

"He deserved it," was the self-satisfied explanation of the thirty-five-year-old murderer, Harry K. Thaw.

"Give him hell," his former friend and patron James Gordon Bennett, editor and publisher of the New York *Herald*, dictated to his reporters.

"Mr. White's picturesqueness became the expression of the lust of the flesh and the lust of the eye and the pride of life," announced the New York *Times* on Thursday, June 28, 1906.

The legend of the boulevardier architect slain by an outraged spouse has kept *The Girl in the Red Velvet Swing* in perpetual motion for almost a century and provided a rock-candy quarry to be mined by writers such as E. L. Doctorow, in *Ragtime*, to satisfy the public's literary sweet tooth.

But if one is seeking the true center of this complex being it would be difficult to find a better delineation than that of the distinguished architectural historian Thomas E. Tallmadge: "Once I crossed the ocean with him, and on several occasions when a draftsman I have seen him with his peer, Daniel H. Burnham, laughing, talking, gesticulating—a huge man, six feet three inches in height with a great mustache and bristling red hair; radiating energy and magnetism like a broadcasting station . . ." And then: "Stanford was a child of New York culture and sophistication."

White's broadcasting station energy, his enthusiasm, his willingness to attempt the seemingly impossible were indeed quintessentially "New York." For parallels to his symbiotic relationship with the city one must look to Fiorello La Guardia and George Gershwin. New York was the stream in which Stanford White swam; like parentheses, the city opened and closed his life.

The critics have always been there. White's Corinthian-column-caged Knickerbocker Trust Company at the northwest corner of Fifth Avenue and Thirty-fourth Street could well have been the object of Louis Sullivan's withering wit in *Kindergarten Chats*: "I am going to insist that the banker wear a toga, sandals, and conduct his business in the venerated Latin tongue. . . . I do not relish Roman-temple banks."

And in the early editions of his *Life and Times of H. H. Richardson*, the critic Henry-Russell Hitchcock dismisses White's classical buildings as manifestations of design depravity: "Only in that minor early work [the Farragut pedestal] did White show a creative power comparable to Richardson's."

But for the New Yorker, for the discerning traveler in the city, White's presence flashes out like the dazzling panache of the Hudson's palisades or the broad river's unstoppable surge to the sea. It flashes out from the unexpected majesty of the tall fluted columns decorating the Bowery Savings Bank on the Bowery at Grand Street; it flashes out in the richly rosetted interior of the Gould Library of what was New York University in the Bronx; it flashes out from the precise marble elegance of Fifth Avenue's Metropolitan Club; it flashes out from the Venetian-inspired façade of Joseph Pulitzer's mansion, which lends to banal East Seventy-third Street a touch of the glamour of the Grand Canal. Stanford White's presence, though, is perhaps most perfectly felt on a hot New York summer Sunday afternoon when the triple portal of St. Bartholomew's Church, facing a momentarily autoless Park Avenue, miraculously transports the viewer across the Atlantic to some dusty slumbering village in Provence or even to Byzantium.

The creator of these urban masterpieces was born November 9, 1853, on East Tenth Street near Manhattan's second-oldest place of worship, St. Mark's Church in-the-Bowery. The block is virtually unchanged, a respectable middle-class enclave of red brick and limestone, of high stoops and Greek Revival cornices. In the 1850s the neighborhood was respectable but not fashionable, for it stood on the borders of the great seething caldron of the Bowery. In the year of White's birth, no fewer than fifty-two taverns lined the Bowery along with some twenty-seven oyster houses.

White was the second son of Richard Grant White, a music and drama critic for newspapers such as *The Morning Courier and New-York Enquirer* and the editor of an important twelve-volume edition of Shakespeare's plays. Stanford's only sibling, Richard Mansfield White, had been born two years earlier. In all, Richard Grant White was the author of some seventy books, the production of a man eager for status and recognition. White's books are full of that delight in the surprising word or gesture that was to character-ize his son. "The Star-Spangled Banner" gets short shrift in his *National Hymns*, published in 1861:

> In fact, only the choral lines of this song have brought it into general favor:
>
>> "And the star-spangled banner in triumph shall wave
>> O'er the land of the free and the home of the brave."
>
> But even in regard to this, who cannot but wish that the spangles could be taken out, and a good honest flag be substituted for the banner.

Richard White knew early fame and in 1846 appeared in a series of ironic portraits of Gothamites in the New York *Tribune*:

> At the next table, in an attitude of listless self-complacency, sits a tall, striking-looking man, with a ruddy beard and mustache.... Although still under twenty-five, he is evidently a thorough-bred man of the world—an epicure, an amateur, a dilettante, a gallant, a critic, almost a coxcomb.... That is Richard Grant White, the musical critic of a morning paper.

In this column there are curious forecasts of some of the views later expressed about Stanford White. Like his son, Richard White drew attention on the pavements of New York. One of the reasons—and this delighted him—was that he was often mistaken for an English-man. "I was born too far West," he wrote. And during his one trip abroad, naturally to England, in 1876, the London *Spectator* observed that Richard White was "altogether the most accomplished and the best bred man that America has sent to England within the present generation . . . not at all our idea of a Yankee."

Beneath Richard Grant White's studied peacockery was the reality of a desperately disappointed being. The Whites had been persons of some consequence since that day in 1632 when John White had settled in Cambridge, Massachusetts, and quickly become a selectman of the town. Richard was the son of a once-rich father, a New York merchant who owned clipper ships. But in 1842, when Richard was twenty, his father had been ruined by the advent of steam-driven paddle wheelers. Richard Grant White never adjusted to this change in his circumstances.

Richard White's constant complaint was that America was not yet civilized, that it had neither refinement nor, more importantly, an aristocracy. His books are often an attempt to correct these deficiencies. In his eccentrically brilliant *Words and Their Uses*, which Houghton Mifflin published in 1870 and kept in print for more than thirty years, the author makes his intention very clear: "A tendency to slang, to colloquial inelegancies, and even vulgarities, is the besetting sin, we, as Americans, have specially to guard and to struggle against."

The senior White's passion to build a grander, more elegant America with words would be curiously transmogrified in the life of his son, who would gloriously transfigure America with marble, bronze, and brick. As the father never designed a house, so the son never wrote a book, yet the force which drove both was the same. There was another impulse Stanford White owed to his father. In 1861, Richard White, in a desperate search for a regular income to support his family, had accepted a post in the New York Custom House and thus began a routine which was, in his words, a "wearing grind." Stanford White's life would be a soaring, dazzling flight away from penurious gentility, away from any whiff of the "wearing grind."

White's mother, Alexina Mease, though born in New York

Richard Mansfield White, the architect's older brother, was a classic case of failure. "Dick," as he was called by the family, spent his time unsuccessfully prospecting for gold and silver in the West while living off of the generosity of his younger brother.

Alexina Mease White, Stanford White's mother, retained throughout her life something of the aura of the faded gentility of her South Carolina background. White was devoted to her and even on his honeymoon began his letters home with "Dear Mommie."

was from a Charleston, South Carolina, family imbued with that peculiar combination of ephemeral great expectations and literary leanings so typical of the South's antebellum gentry. The plantation promised to Alexina by a bachelor cousin went with the wind in the aftermath of the Civil War, while her sister, who wrote under the nom de plume of "Aunt Fanny," was a popular author of children's books. Richard Grant White and Alexina Mease were married in 1850 and one of Stanford White's first appearances in print was in his mother's volume of verse *Little Folks' Songs*:

> *O, have ye seen my boy Stannie?*
> *Wee toddlin' mannie!*
> *His e'e sae blue, his cheek sae red,*
> *An old straw hat aboon his head,*
> *All torn and tattered.*
>
> *O, have ye seen my boy Stannie?*
> *Wee busy mannie!*
> *Aye trottin' roun' the garden lot,*
> *Wi' wheelbarrow, spade and waterin' pot,*
> *All bent and battered.*

Stanford White would continue, for the rest of his lifetime, to play the character delineated in these Burnsian lines, always "toddlin'," always "trottin' roun'." And the artistic, bohemian milieu of his early years was to leave an indelible stamp upon him which, in later years, would reveal itself at unexpected times and places. White, for instance, after his first success, spent enormous sums on suits from London tailors such as Hill Brothers, on gloves and cravats from the Parisian furnisher Charvet, and on shirts from the prestigious New York firm of Kaskel & Kaskel, but all this costly finery could be quickly cast aside, as Elizabeth Lehr humorously recalled when describing a dinner at Sherry's in *"King Lehr" and the Gilded Age*:

> Every table would be taken. People whose names stood at the very summit of the social peak, ambitious climbers who wanted to boast

of having dined at the next table to them, distinguished foreigners visiting New York, the cream of fashionable Bohemia.

To the last category belonged Stanford White, the famous architect. Outrageously badly dressed, his untidy shock of red hair looking as though it had not had a comb passed through it for a week, he was not in the least embarrassed as he sat surrounded by some of the most elegant women in New York. A genius and an artist to his finger-tips he was quite indifferent to his appearance. Once he arrived very late for dinner at Mrs. Oelrichs' house and slipped into his seat when everyone else was half-way through dinner. . . . "It never takes me more than five minutes to dress," he remarked. "So I should imagine," said Mrs. Oelrichs rather coldly. . . . "But then just look at your idea of dressing!" He had merely flung on a dinner jacket over his ordinary morning trousers, and had not even taken the trouble to change his shirt.

It was White, though, who had designed for Tessie Oelrichs Newport's one flawless French pavilion.

The fashionable bohemianism of Stanford White's youth is a key to understanding not only his own character but the eclectic character of his patrons and some of his most intriguing commissions, ranging from his pro bono work at that actors' sanctum, the Players Club, to his creation of the exclusive German-Jewish Harmonie Club. In an era when thespians were shunned by polite society and conventional Fifth Avenue sanctuaries advised the relatives of dead theatre folk attempting to arrange a funeral to "try the little church around the corner where they do that sort of thing," White's father was a friend of the noted impresarios William Niblo and James Wallack; frequented that hive of painters, the Studio Building on West Tenth Street; and played the cello on the musical evenings he organized dedicated to Mozart and Beethoven. In the 1890s scuttlebutt had it that Stanford White was the only fashionable man in New York who went to the opera because he wanted to hear the music.

There was a nervous fragility, though, to the respectable bohemianism of the White family's existence. A generation before the architect's birth the neighborhood just south of Tenth Street, stretching from Art Street—now Astor Place—down Lafayette Place, to Bond, had been one of New York's most modish quarters. After the construction in 1830 of Seth Geer's becolumned Greek Revival row, La Grange Terrace, on Astor Place, the district became the home of Irving Van Wart, with whom his cousin Washington Irving often stayed; of New York's Civil War governor Edwin D. Morgan, a future Stanford White patron; of John Jacob Astor II, grandson of the family fortune founder; and of Franklin Hughes Delano, who in 1844 gave the wedding breakfast for one President of the United States, John Tyler, and who, in time, would become the great-uncle of another. But by the time of Stanford White's birth, the haut monde, defined by Charles Astor Bristed in *The Upper Ten Thousand*, published in 1852, as made up of "daintily arrayed men who spend half their income on their persons, and shrink from the touch of a woollen glove," and "delicate and lovely women who wear the finest furs and roll in the most stylish equipages," was moving westward to Washington Square and north to the *terra incognita* of Fifth Avenue above Twenty-third Street. In their place came waves of Irish fleeing the famine which followed the failed potato crops of the 1840s and Germans driven across the Atlantic by the same tuber blight as well as by the consequences of the abortive liberal revolutions of 1848. The Germans, to the discomfiture of Richard White, settled so thickly around St. Mark's in-the-Bowery that the area was soon known as Little Germany, and the important German Club, at Eighth Street and Fourth Avenue, was almost on the family doorstep. This threat to a fragile gentility may explain Richard Grant White's abiding anti-Germanism, which erupted as it did when a Westerner with a Germanic name wrote a letter to *The Morning Courier and New-York Enquirer* dissenting from one of White's theatre reviews and received a reply which included this sentence: "A piece of Teutonic alluvium which the Indo-European migration has deposited upon the plains of Kansas . . ."

The Whites' precarious gentility took on a kind of desperation in the "Flash Years" which followed the close of the Civil War. While Richard White toiled in the United States Revenue Marine

Bureau, New York began a materialistic orgy whose equivalent is found in the Jazz Age of the 1920s and the "Me First" era of the 1980s. Its population, 600,000 in the year of White's birth, now soared to more than a million, and its citizens, never diffident, began to call their metropolis "the Empire City." Nothing better typified this sea change than the street which during Stanford White's career would be New York's Field of the Cloth of Gold, Fifth Avenue. Still an unpaved track above Madison Square in 1850, its desolate upper reaches took on a new incandescence when in 1859 John Jacob Astor III and his younger brother, William Backhouse, used some of the $20,000,000 left to them by their father to build twin mansions in the Ultima Thule lying between Thirty-third and Thirty-fourth streets. Their houses, replete with ballrooms and picture galleries, proclaimed that the big bucks were no longer in Boston or Philadelphia and that New York was about to shed the last vestiges of republican simplicity. Indeed, their father, John Jacob II's manner of dying had underscored that transition. In his last days, the fur trader-cum-real estate magnate had existed solely on the milk of a wet nurse and his flagging circulation had been quickened by his servants tossing him in a blanket.

The Astor brothers did not have to wait long for affluent neighbors, but the one who built just north of them across Thirty-fourth Street raised a few Old Guard eyebrows. Alexander Turney Stewart, who had begun life in America as a poor Irish immigrant, became, through his genius for retailing, many times a millionaire. His six-story, block-square, cast-iron emporium on Broadway between Ninth and Tenth streets employed 200 salespersons and took in more than $10,000 a day. A. T. Stewart's was the place to go for Brussels carpets, heavy silks from Lyon, and the finest of cashmere shawls. To trumpet his transformation, Stewart commissioned the distinguished architect John W. Kellum, the same man who had designed his department store, to create for him one of Fifth Avenue's first true palaces. The white marble mansard-roofed exterior expressed longings for the parvenu splendor of Second Empire Paris, while the statue-studded interior trumpeted the pinchbeck glories of the General Grant era. The price tag for the deluxe dwelling when it was completed in 1869 was a staggering $3,000,000. A. T. Stewart and the site of his house would play an important role in Stanford White's life and career.

If further proof were needed of the blinding brilliance of the Flash Years, it could be found at the northeast corner of Fifth Avenue and Eighteenth Street. There August Belmont, the American representative of the Rothschilds, and his wife, Caroline, a daughter of the Commodore Matthew Perry who opened Japan to American trade, were astonishing visitors with their private gallery, which boasted a glass dome held up by allegorical figures representing painting, music, architecture, and sculpture. Pride of place was given in the gallery to a vast composition by Rosa Bonheur featuring a phenomenal number of horses, a painting which perfectly suited the taste of the man after whom New York's supreme stakes race would be named. The Belmonts were also setting the pace when it came to dining. No longer would it be enough to offer merely terrapin and tenderloin, for the Belmonts proffered "consommé de volaille," "vol-au-vent à la Toulouse," and "gelées au Madeira," all served on gold at a table which seated 200. No wonder the restaurateur Lorenzo Delmonico dubbed Belmont the "Maecenas of gastronomy." Though Richard Grant White was infuriated by Belmont's anti-Lincoln sentiments during the Civil War and his support for New York's Democratic copperhead governor, Horatio Seymour, August Belmont's assent would make possible a commission for Stanford White which would help to revolutionize taste in the city.

All this quickening brilliance prefigured the birth of a new society. The first faint notes had been sounded just before the Civil War when Mrs. William Colford Schermerhorn had decided to give what had been a forbidden form of entertainment, a costume ball, and instructed her 600 guests to garb themselves in the court costume of the period of Louis XV. The rather grim Schermerhorn mansion at the corner of Lafayette Place and Great Jones Street was bedizened in Versailles style to the point of dressing up the servants in period livery and powdered wigs. It was at this ball that the "German cotillion" was introduced and the old-fashioned schottisches and polkas, suddenly deemed vulgar, were banned. It was only left for Nathaniel Parker Willis, writing in *The Home Journal*—later to become *Town & Country*—to define New York's smart set as those "who keep carriages . . . are subscribers to the opera, go to Grace Church, have a town house and country house, give balls and parties," and for *Etiquette: or, A guide to the usages of Society by Count Alfred D'Orsay*—in reality one Charles William Day—to lodge in selected private libraries, for the foundations to be laid of the world which would be the grist for Stanford White's architectural mill. Already it was possible to discern the general outlines of the extravagant 1890s: the masquerades, the mania for monarchy, the ritualistic figure dances which effectively culled the uninstructed, and the very concept of an exclusive "400."

This lambent landscape is no mere gossamer apparition, but a phenomenon as solid as the Pullman Sleeping Car to an understanding of the United States in the 1870s, 1880s, and 1890s. The phaetons, broughams, and landaus were, in fact, beginning to circle. "Inequality," observed William Dean Howells, who would be the brother-in-law of one of White's partners, "is as dear to the American heart as liberty itself." The American Revolution and the banishing of primogeniture had indeed introduced the specter of egalitarianism, a specter made real in New York State by the tardy acceptance of universal manhood suffrage in 1821 and by the abolition, in 1852, of the perpetual leases which prevented the tenants of the great Hudson River estates from ever becoming landowners. Van Rensselaers, Livingstons, and Jays might briefly wring their collective hands, but all need not be lost. No less a figure than John Adams himself had shown the way when he wrote: "We have one material which actually constitutes an aristocracy that governs the nation. That material is wealth." The Adamses, it is true, had a reputation for being cantankerous, and John Adams's words may make the sensitive shudder, but the society which emerged in the Flash Years after the Civil War was indeed founded upon the new, seemingly inexhaustible wealth flowing from the nation's railroads and banks, mines and stockyards. If these plutocrats were truly the new Medicis—as the architect Richard Morris Hunt dubbed them—then they would need a new Michelangelo. Even the Sun King required Le Vau, Le Brun, and Le Nôtre to make the vision of Versailles a reality.

CHAPTER 2

APPRENTICED TO RICHARDSON

S*tanford White at the beginning of his architectural career. His red hair was said to have stood up as stiffly as the bristles of a paintbrush.*

A curious irony of American architectural history is that one of the preeminent men associated with the Beaux Arts tradition could not afford to attend the institution that gave the tradition its name. Ever since the day in 1846 when Richard Morris Hunt became the first American to enter the architecture section of the Ecole des Beaux-Arts and thus set a new and higher standard for the training of American designers, the school on Paris's Left Bank had been the desired destination for this country's aspiring architects. Formed in 1819 out of the schools of the Académie Royale de Peinture et de Sculpture and the Académie Royale d'Architecture, the Ecole, with its intricate combination of independent ateliers directed by leading architects, and of lectures and monthly competitions requiring either sketches or fully rendered projects of assigned subjects, was the world's greatest training ground for architects. Charging no tuition, the Ecole was open to any male, French or foreign, between fifteen and thirty years of age, who could pass its demanding entrance exams.

OPPOSITE:

B*oston's Parker House on Tremont Street where Stanford White often stayed in the 1870s while working on Trinity Church for Henry Hobson Richardson. The old hotel was replaced by the current Parker House in 1927.*

In 1870, when Stanford White began seriously to think of a career, there was not enough money in the family coffers either to permit him to attend his father's alma mater, New York University, or to support him during the two to four years required to complete a course of studies at the Ecole des Beaux-Arts. One of the clearest indications of the state of the White family finances is the fact that in the fall of 1870 Richard Grant White sold at public auction nearly two-thirds of the almost 6,000 books in his private library. Desperate cash-raising auctions were also to play a part in Stanford White's life. Interestingly, among the volumes of English and American history, Restoration drama, and the latest poetry were books, some illustrated, which could only be described as erotic. These too would play a part in the life of Richard White's son.

White's interest in the Ecole des Beaux-Arts was originally in the painting, not the architecture, section. Even as a child he had drawn surprisingly accomplished pictures, and he was soon producing evocative watercolors of the landscapes he observed on visits to relatives in Orange, New Jersey, and Newburgh, New York. Of particular interest to him were the old houses—English and Dutch Colonial—which still thickly graced the countryside around New York City. White's unrequited passion to be a painter was the cornerstone of his artistic life, giving him the power to visualize architectural problems and to sketch and sketch again until he had found their solution. It was this painterly quality in his presentations which made him such a superb salesman. Rendered in pastels and watercolors on carefully chosen colored papers, Stanford White's drawings of buildings were often the factor which tipped the balance and won his firm a commission.

White's letters home from Europe during his first visit are filled equally with his love of buildings and of paintings; a letter to his mother from Laon in November 1878 is typical: "I found Antwerp almost as antiquated as Bruges. Fairly gorged Rubenses there. Fourteen portraits in one old wainscoted room, and two by Vandyke, were enough to take your breath away." And the twenty-five-year-old would write to his father: ". . . a portrait of Paul

Veronese . . . nearly squeezed tears out of my eyes . . . and Raphael's wax head at Lille . . . the loveliest face ever conceived by man. Architecture seems but poor stuff compared with things like these."

Though Richard Grant White's financial resources might be slim, his years as a writer and intellectual-about-town had led to friendships with most of the city's leading artists. He now took his younger son to meet one of them, John La Farge. Richard Grant White could not have made a more astute choice. La Farge was not only a fine artist; he had also studied in the most prestigious atelier of the painting section of the Ecole des Beaux-Arts, that supervised by the distinguished historical painter Thomas Couture. The interview took place in La Farge's quarters in the Richard Morris Hunt–designed Studio Building. After looking at Stanford White's drawings and watercolors, La Farge announced bluntly that in painting "recognition is slow and remuneration slight."

La Farge spoke from experience, for, after some small successes, he had become discouraged and at the time of the Whites' visit was suffering from the consequences of a nervous breakdown. He was also deeply in debt. Stanford White knew well that there was no possibility of family financial support for a tyro artist until such a time as he achieved a far-from-certain success. La Farge understood this too and, noting the number of houses and charming decorative designs in the teenager's portfolio, suggested that White seek employment in an architect's office. Good draftsmen were always in demand. By that counsel John La Farge unknowingly prepared the setting for his own greatest painting.

Richard White now turned to another friend, Frederick Law Olmsted, the landscape architect, who had just won the competition to design Central Park. Olmsted and White had been acquaintances since the time when White's articles in the London *Spectator* explaining the Union position during the Civil War and Olmsted's *Journeys and Explorations in the Cotton Kingdom: A Traveller's Observations on Cotton and Slavery in the American Slave States*, published in London in 1861, had been important factors in preventing England from coming to the aid of the Confederacy. Olmsted was the first member of the Republican abolitionist network which was to play such a beneficial role in Stanford White's career and it was he who uttered the magic word which was to change forever young White's life: "Richardson."

It is not possible to overestimate Stanford White's good fortune in coming, at the very beginning of his architectural apprenticeship, under the aegis of Henry Hobson Richardson. Richardson's significance for the rising designers of the period was encapsulated in a statement made by the masterly Chicago architect, John Wellborn Root, in the summer of 1890:

> Compare the best of our recent architecture—some of Richardson's designs, for example—with the most pretentious buildings recently erected in Europe. In the American works we find strength and fitness and a certain spontaneity and freshness, as of stately music or a song in green woods.

White was only sixteen when, after showing the sketches La Farge had admired, he was taken into the office of Gambrill & Richardson. The skinny redhead's academy would now be that small but charged space at 6 Hanover Street in lower Manhattan. His master would be the man who was attempting to bring order out of architectural chaos, a rational style out of the kaleidoscopic plethora of sham Gothic castles, Egyptian Revival churches, octagonal Moresque pavilions, and Italianate villas which had sprung up like so many dragons' teeth across America since the demise of the Greek Revival hegemony. The most appropriate appellation for the style of American building when Richardson made his appearance is indeed "Reign of Terror."

Richardson had received all the formal education of which Stanford White had been deprived. A great-grandson of Joseph Priestley, the English religious and political radical and discoverer of oxygen, who had fled to America in 1794, he had been born in 1838 on a Louisiana plantation redolent of everything connoted by the term "antebellum." Educated at Harvard and then at the Ecole des Beaux-Arts, where he was the second American to enter the architecture section, the Southerner had been trapped in Paris by the outbreak of the Civil War. His, though, had been a fortunate exile. During his Paris sojourn, between 1859 and 1865, when he returned to the United States and set up his office in New York, Richardson had worked for Henri Labrouste, the architect of the Sorbonne's Bibliothèque Ste. Geneviève, one of the nineteenth century's seminal structures, and for Jacques-Ignace Hittorff, who had championed the cause of color in classical buildings. From Labrouste, Richardson received reinforcement of the Ecole's insistence that a building have a rational internal plan; from Hittorff, he learned not to fear paint and stained glass and mosaics. Both lessons would be passed on to Stanford White.

Henry Hobson Richardson was not only to be White's professional mentor; he was also to be his social one as well. "Richardson was an excellent companion, but though fond of pleasure and society and always ready for a dinner-party or dancing-party, he never allowed these things to interfere with the serious performance of his work; and many of his friends of that time will remember that he not infrequently returned late to his rooms after a party to finish the night in study; or to his *atelier* when an exhibition of plans or drawings was in preparation." This reminiscence by Joseph Bradlee, a friend from Richardson's Ecole days startlingly prefigures White's own method of work and play in his glory years. But that lay far ahead. In his first letters home when traveling from project to project with his master, the still-callow draftsman expressed unadulterated astonishment at Richardson's gargantuan appetites: "How Richardson can be, I can't tell; for, setting aside all Brandies gin, wines and cigars, he seems to subsist chiefly on boiled tripe."

Among the many close friendships which Stanford White established in Richardson's office was that with Charles Rutan, who would be a prominent member in Richardson's successor firm of Shepley, Rutan & Coolidge. Twenty-five years later Rutan would twit White on his notoriously bad spelling and handwriting, which had led him, whenever possible, to use a typewriter:

> The firm received by mail this morning the enclosed letter which I suppose is signed by you. Since we separated some years ago I have tried to improve my hand-writing, but am afraid you have not but have gone backward in this line. It is too bad we have been separated so long that you have forgotten how to spell my name.

But no friendship of the Richardsonian years was comparable in importance to his closeness to Charles Follen McKim. A twenty-three-year-old Pennsylvanian whose father had been deeply involved in the antislavery movement, McKim, like Richardson, had attended Harvard and then, in the late 1860s, had entered the architecture section of the Ecole des Beaux-Arts, becoming the third American to do so. McKim's professional credo embraced an inviolable tenet which was to have a profound influence on Stanford White and upon the philosophical foundations of their firm. This was the conviction that the city was the center of civilization. McKim had made the difficult choice of leaving Philadelphia, where his family had important connections and where he had been offered a place in the office of Frank Furness, for the more challenging milieu of New York because he agreed with his father that "one is a great provincial town; the other is a metropolitan city." Already as a student at the Ecole, McKim had reveled in Paris's animated life. A letter by him dated August 31, 1868, published in the Auburn, New York, *Morning News*, makes patently clear his delight in the urban scene: "Towards evening the cafés of the *Quartier* begin to light up. A number of these are frequented principally by students and mistresses, and since one is a type of all the rest we can hardly go astray . . . we push along through narrow streets and passages, and finally reach the *Café Estaminet du Sénat*, where already a large number of students are collected. It is a little early yet, but depend upon it, eight o'clock will bring along its quota. We are not disappointed, for one after another a crowd come trooping in." Charles Follen McKim's unequivocal celebration of the city would lift

McKim, Mead & White out of the dominant bucolic tradition of American architecture which runs, like some perennial border, from Thomas Jefferson's Piedmont-sited Charlottesville to Frank Lloyd Wright's bosky Oak Park.

Though Henry Hobson Richardson never denied the value of his Ecole training, he rejected two of the basic formulae of that training: first, the acceptance of all the materials and techniques that the Industrial Revolution had made available to the builder and, second, the acceptance of the classical—that high style which had come down from Greece and Rome to the West through the Renaissance—as the supreme standard of design. McKim's life and work would, in contrast, be dedicated to these two ideals. It was this rational melding of the ancient world of marble and bronze, of the acanthus and the rinceau, with the modern world of iron and glass, of the dynamo and the bolt, which would, in time, make McKim and White supreme. It was this which lay behind McKim's staggering Pennsylvania Station, with its vast marble waiting room summoning up the Baths of Caracalla, while its train shed presented a contemporary glass-and-steel aviary welcoming birds of flight to the restless trains. William A. Boring, who came into the McKim, Mead & White office in 1887, and eventually became head of Columbia's School of Architecture, saw at once how important McKim was to the theoretical foundations of the partnership: "The office had an inspiring atmosphere, due largely to Mr. McKim's ideals."

White had, by chance, landed in the perfect spot for a youth who had not had the advantages of a formal architectural education. "Richardson's office organization paralleled his own educational experience at the *atelier* André of the Ecole des Beaux-Arts in Paris," James F. O'Gorman reports in *H. H. Richardson and His Office*, "... he was the *patron*, his draughtsmen his élèves." Richardson's usual method was to work in bed—he suffered constantly from poor health and would die of Bright's Disease in 1886—embodying his conception of a structure in a pencil and ink sketch often no more than two or three inches square. This architectural idea would then be handed over to a draftsman—a Charles McKim or a Stanford White—upon whose judgment and sympathy Richardson knew that he could rely. In this way he allowed his pupils to work at the very beginning of a commission and to develop the design independently, though the basic conception was always the master's.

Marianna Griswold Van Rensselaer in her invaluable monograph, *Henry Hobson Richardson and His Work*, written shortly after Richardson's death, explains the master's subtle teaching technique:

> "Do what you can with it," Richardson would say, adding, of course, some general counsels and directions . . . Then he would not stand at the pupil's elbow to direct his pencil, and would not speedily correct or criticise him, but would wait until he seemed pretty well started on the road to success, or found himself in a tight place out of which only the master could help him.

And Richardson's manner of helping was never to tell the draftsman what to do, but to direct him to a book or to a portfolio of photographs where he might find the correct solution for himself. Stanford White was, for the rest of his life, to benefit from the priceless gift Richardson gave to all of the truly talented *élèves* in his *atelier*. To quote again from Marianna Van Rensselaer:

> They learned to think for themselves, to design for themselves, to decorate for themselves; . . . they learned to make a building and not merely to make a drawing.

When White entered 6 Hanover Street this technique was being employed on the major commission then in the office, the Brattle Square Church on Boston's Commonwealth Avenue. A Congregational house of worship, the rugged sanctuary with its arched windows marks an important development in Richardson's pilgrimage to his ultimate Auvergnat Romanesque style, but it is the 176-foot-high tower, with its frieze celebrating the sacraments modeled by Bartholdi, which gave to the structure its undeniable

The tower of the Brattle Square Church on Boston's Commonwealth Avenue which Charles McKim was designing when White entered H. H. Richardson's office in 1870. The sculpture is by Bartholdi with the faces of the trumpeting angels modeled after those of Emerson, Hawthorne, and Longfellow.

distinction. McKim was the chief draftsman on the Brattle Square Church and there can be no doubt but that the subtle refinement of its tower came from his faultless eye.

The tremendous success of the Brattle Square Church, combined with Richardson's connections in Boston from his Harvard days, was to provide an opportunity of singular importance to young Stanford White. A building key to any understanding of the cultural history of the United States was about to be created. For White it would seal friendships of inestimable value and give him his first chance to spread his creative wings. For Richardson it would allow him to raise a monument that would proclaim the new order he wished to bring to American architecture. "It would not cost me a bit of trouble to build French buildings that would reach from here to Philadelphia," he had written, "but that is not what I want to do." By "French" Richardson had meant Parisian, for, in fact, he wanted to raise an edifice that would prove his theory that the Romanesque of the South of France had been interrupted by the appearance of the Gothic in the twelfth century and that now, in the second half of the nineteenth, that development could be recommenced.

Trinity Church was the stone-and-mortar manifestation of the new American social reality, a reality that would lay behind every White-designed Newport "cottage" and Fifth Avenue palais, every luxurious clubhouse and costly emporium. Since its settlement in the seventeenth century the religious reality of Boston had been Puritan with all that this implied: the celebration of the intellect over the senses, a cheerful acceptance of discomfort, an infatuation with austerity. Before the Revolution, the Church of England, with its ever so faint whiff of medieval Catholicism, was, to say the least, in bad odor. Anglicans had but three places of worship, Christ Church, better known as Old North; King's Chapel; and Trinity, founded in 1733. Surviving the emptying of Boston of most of its better class of citizens—who were Tories—during the Revolution, Trinity, in 1829, erected a sanctuary which, though the local papers labeled it "Gothic," resembled nothing so much as a crenellated firehouse.

Phillips Brooks, the eloquent and dynamic Episcopal rector who was instrumental in getting the Trinity commission for his friend H. H. Richardson. Brooks became a friend of White, too, and they regularly dined together when White was in Boston. This photograph was made about 1877.

On October 31, 1869, the parish installed as rector a thirty-three-year-old as remarkable as Richardson and White, and the three would produce an edifice which has long been considered one of the ten most important buildings in the United States.

Phillips Brooks was a part of that unanticipated blossoming of Episcopalianism following the Civil War which is inextricably entwined with the arrival of a new high society. After the sour grape juice and three-hour sermons of the Congregationalists and the Dutch Reformed, after the narcoleptic Calvinist warnings of hell-fire, after the long literary essays of the Unitarians, Episcopalianism offered magnificent processions, stately liturgy, and the merest nibble, without the bite, of the Roman Catholicism which upper-class Americans had wistfully viewed in the gorgeous ceremonies of St. Peter's, Rome, and Notre Dame, Paris. It was also, it should not be forgotten, the faith of dukes and viscounts and marquesses and, most importantly, of Queen Victoria herself. Brooks's family—Unitarians a generation before—were part of that tide, moving before a rising sea of wealth and fashion, which carried to Canterbury Lawrences and Lowells, led to the founding of an Anglo-Catholic monastery in Harvard's hometown, transformed Hawthorne's daughter Una into an Episcopal nun, and produced the unexpected apparition of Mrs. Jack Gardiner scrubbing the steps of that hotbed of high ecclesiolatry, the Church of the Advent, on Ash Wednesday. Phillips Brooks's brilliant preaching—his literary gifts are readily evident to anyone familiar with the hymn he wrote in 1867, "O Little Town of Bethlehem"—packed the old Trinity barn. "I could have gotten up and shouted!" a dour Scots theologian declared after hearing a Brooks sermon; and so, even before the great Boston Fire of November 1872 left the old church a charred shell, a limited competition for a new Trinity had been held and Richardson had been declared the winner.

Charles McKim had been in charge of the drawings for the competition, but shortly after the victory had been gained, he had left the office to form his own architectural firm. Now Stanford White, whose beautiful renderings—often presenting a structure in a Constable-like landscape—had quickly made him the cynosure of Hanover Street, was put in charge of the drawings for the plans and details of the prodigious project. A Richardson assistant, Glenn Brown, was to write of the impression White made on a visit to one of the firm's projects in Hartford at this time:

> He came in to the clerk's office, tall, lank, red-haired, freckle-faced, with interest and enthusiasm expressed in every feature and movement. He wanted to see the building, and after a rapid survey of the exterior, left me to make his way to the roof. In a short time he returned all excitement. He wanted paper, a board and water colors. "There's a beautiful sunset," he said, "so bully that I want to get it down." Fortunately I was able to give him just the materials he needed. He hurried off; but in less than an hour came back rejoicing over the beauties he had caught in a very effective sketch, with the stone of one of the corner pinnacles in the foreground. I shall never forget his enthusiasm, his quick grasp of the beauties of a commonplace scene, his facility with brush and pencil.

"We often forgot how young he was," a contractor remembered.

Between 1872 and 1874, when Richardson transferred his office from New York to the Boston suburb of Brookline, Stanford White was, for all practical purposes, Gambrill & Richardson as far as Boston was concerned. Living at the old Parker House on Tremont Street, constantly visiting the construction site on the as yet unnamed Copley Square, and regularly meeting with Robert Treat Paine, the Boston philanthropist who headed the building committee, White was given a precious early taste of independence and of power. But his letters home reveal the still very young man who writes to his mother telling her of a bruised knee, reporting a touch of influenza, and begging for clean shirts. He also announces that he had thought of a way to help his hard-pressed family:

> My dear Mother,
> To think after insuring my life for $3,000 I am here all safe! It's disgraceful.

The image of the vigorous tyro clambering upon the roof to capture a sunset is an appropriate one for Stanford White. With his enormous energy he had already developed the knack of making the most of every hour. While working on Trinity and taking often arduous journeys to other places where the firm had commissions, White still found time to savor the sights of the "Hub of the Universe": Bulfinch's noble State House floating above the Common; the classical eighteenth-century King's Chapel across from his hotel; and the exquisite Boston Museum on Tremont Street, where he sated his prodigious appetite for plays. His letters home are threaded with accounts of meetings with people whose names rustle like golden leaves in these the years of the New England Indian summer: Longfellow, Howells, Charles Eliot Norton.

As Trinity's massive sanctuary rose in Boston's Back Bay, the finicky Flemish tower proposed by Richardson for the crossing proved to be structurally impossible and White devised in its place a self-assured, wonderfully articulated one inspired by that of the cathedral in Salamanca, Spain. Here, above the fortresslike rock of the body of Trinity Church, rises something more ornamented, more detailed, more delicate. White would reprise this riveting act in one of his most sensational New York creations.

The interior of Trinity, Phillips Brooks had determined, would be no milk-toned meetinghouse, but a space that would ring with the new dispensation. "In its colour and splendour," Van Wyck Brooks observed, "it indicated forcibly the break of the Boston mind with its Puritan past." To achieve this, Richardson brought together, under the direction of White's wise adviser, John La Farge, some of the outstanding artists of what would become the American Renaissance: Frank Millet, Kenyon Cox, Francis Lathrop, and Augustus Saint-Gaudens. Some, like Saint-Gaudens and La Farge, White already knew, but the experience of working with them as a team on a project of the magnificence and magnitude of Trinity would imbue the young architect with a standard of artistic excellence that would impart to his New York work, in particular, a magical incandescence.

The "Chief" had quickly perceived that his young draftsman possessed a special gift, an unfailingly correct feel for the right effect in domestic architecture. Richardson, on the contrary, was most at ease, most truly himself with public projects such as the Crane Memorial library in Quincy, Massachusetts, and the majestic Allegheny Country Courthouse complex in Pittsburgh. Richardson's dependence on White's sure sense of the appropriateness of decor and arrangement on a residential scale is exemplified in the Newport house that the firm designed in 1875 for the New York banker William Watts Sherman. With its rich variety of exterior textures, its high, dramatic gables, its towering chimneys, the structure owes much to the English architect Richard Norman Shaw and his fellow Queen Anne Revival devotees. There can be little doubt but that White was responsible for this exterior; the use of broken bits of glass and of bright-colored pebbles embedded in the stucco reveal his painterly signature. The interior, with its woody Shavian living hall, is, without question, also his. Later, after he had left Richardson's employ, White would be invited back to do further work on the Sherman house.

The friendships White made while working in Boston on Trinity were strengthened when he was in New York, where he continued to live with his parents on East Tenth Street. Most of the artists resided not far away, and White's life revolved around Saint-Gaudens's studio on Fourteenth Street; John La Farge's digs in the Studio Building, where guests were waited on by his Japanese valet, Awoki, and given lectures on the current artistic rage, Japanese prints; and at the East Fifteenth Street carriage house of the editor Richard Watson Gilder, for whom White would design an arabesque cover for *Century* magazine. The essence of this aesthetic coterie was the Tile Club, founded with the express purpose of decorating tiles in the manner of the English Arts and Crafts master William De Morgan, famed for his brilliant blue and green glazes. The club eventually found a home in a house at 58½ West Tenth Street where the noted illustrator, Edwin Austin Abbey, had a studio and where there was ample space for uninhibited roistering.

*S*tanford White's drawing of the tower of Trinity Church, which he designed to replace Richardson's earlier, unwieldy version, gave indisputable evidence of taste and genius. Constructed of yellow granite and brown fieldstone and roofed with red tile, the beautifully proportioned structure soared 211 feet above the pavement.

View of Trinity Church across Copley Square in the 1890s, with McKim, Mead & White's Boston Public Library under construction. Standing on man-made land in Back Bay, Trinity's 11-million-pound tower rests on 2,000 wooden piles.

STANFORD WHITE'S NEW YORK

OPPOSITE:

The interior of Trinity was designed so that the congregation would focus on the pulpit, first occupied by Phillips Brooks. Preaching was primary at Trinity and the chancel, seen here shortly after the church was consecrated in 1877, was intentionally austere. The chancel's current rich decoration is a 1938 creation.

The Romanesque architecture of the South of France was the ultimate ideal of H. H. Richardson's office. Photographs, such as this one of the Church at Aulnay-de-Saintonge, were to be found throughout Richardson's studio and helped to heighten White's desire to see Europe.

The dwelling was hidden behind another house, and the approach to the club was tellingly described by Louis Baury in the *Bookman*: First there was a gate which "would swing back in answer to a peculiar ring," then the visitor went down a flight of steps into a "mysteriously black subterranean passage," then down a second flight of steps into a garden, up a wooden staircase, and into a "vast,

The William Watts Sherman house in Newport, Rhode Island, a commission which came to Richardson in 1874, provided White with an opportunity to display his feeling for domestic architecture. The Queen Anne revival dwelling, completed in 1876, the year this photograph was taken, marked Stanford White's debut as a designer in a town which would play an important role in his career.

low-ceilinged room" filled with "genial shouting men." Here White passed rollicking evenings with those who would become his collaborators in bringing a new aesthetic to New York: William Merritt Chase, Edwin Austin Abbey, J. Alden Weir, Elihu Vedder. Each member had a "nom de club." Augustus Saint-Gaudens was "the Saint," and Stanford White was "Builder." David Maitland Armstrong, a club member who would eventually purchase the clubhouse, wrote: "Our dining-room, except for the shelves of china, is not very different from when it was the Tile Club's meeting place, the two white-tiled fireplaces that Stanford White designed being unchanged." Those fireplaces were perhaps White's first New York

work. He would also design the sumptuous *A Book of the Tile Club*, published in 1887, with illustrations by members, including himself. The strong male bonding evident among the Tile Club cliques and the frisson that came from having a secret place of rendezvous were to be continuing and essential elements of Stanford White's social life.

White also remained in close touch with Charles McKim, now married to Anna Bigelow, the sister of a fellow architecture student in Paris, William B. Bigelow. He was often at their house on Washington Street, drawn there by his growing friendship with the architect and by the serious musical evenings presented by Mrs.

In 1886 White designed the handsome A Book of the Tile Club, *with end papers incorporating the symbols associated with the various club members. The architect was originally called "the Beaver," though this was later changed to "the Builder," while Augustus Saint-Gaudens was, not surprisingly, christened "the Saint."*

McKim. Through McKim, White now met the man who one day would be the third partner of New York's most dazzling triumvirate. Seven years older than White, William Rutherford Mead was a handsome Vermonter who had been educated at Amherst College and at Florence's Accademia di Belle Arti. His sister Elinor was married to the novelist and editor of *The Atlantic* William Dean Howells, while his brother, Larkin Mead, was the sculptor responsible for the figure of "Vermont" atop the State House in Montpelier, the structure whose Greek Revival grace first turned Mead toward architecture. In 1872 William Mead had become an assistant to

McKim and thus the historic formation had begun. The Vermonter's first impressions of White were highly favorable:

> Stanford White (the son of Richard Grant White) had entered the office of Gambrill & Richardson as a very young man during the time that Mr. McKim had been with them. He almost immediately showed great talent. . . . In these years he was our close neighbor and became our very intimate friend.

The close neighbor and intimate friend was asked to join McKim, Bigelow, and Mead on what was to become their famous 1877 sketching expedition to the New England towns of Marblehead, Salem, Newburyport, and Portsmouth. This midsummer journey, with its collection of measured drawings of eighteenth-century houses, would be a milestone in the history of the Colonial Revival in America. It would also be an important design resource for White, influencing projects as wide-ranging as the delightful dining-room screen of Kingscote in Newport and the delicate doorway of the Colony Club in New York.

But it would be Augustus Saint-Gaudens, the son of a French father and an Irish mother who had been trained as a cameo cutter, who would have the most immediate impact on Stanford White's career. They had first met in 1875 in Saint-Gaudens's studio on the corner of Fourteenth Street and Fourth Avenue. In his *Reminiscences*, edited by his son, Homer Saint-Gaudens, the sculptor was graphically to recall that encounter:

> Here . . . in the German Savings Bank Building were brought to me, by I do not know whom, a couple of red-heads who have been thoroughly mixed up in my life ever since; I speak of Stanford White and Charles F. McKim. White . . . was drawn to me one day, as he ascended the German Savings Bank stairs, by hearing me bawl the "Andante" of Beethoven's Seventh Symphony. . . .

Their friendship had ripened when, in 1876, Saint-Gaudens was commissioned to paint the figure of St. Paul for the sanctuary of Trinity Church.

The last major commission White worked on for Richardson was the Senate Chamber of the New York State Capitol in Albany. Between 1876 and 1878 he attempted to create a room whose Romanesque opulence would express the power of the Empire State.

STANFORD WHITE'S NEW YORK

That same year the sculptor was asked to create a monument in New York's Madison Square to the Union admiral and popular clubman David Glasgow Farragut. Farragut, after one of his ships had been blown out of the water by Confederate mines in Mobile Bay and his flotilla brought to a dead halt, had become an American naval legend by shouting, "Damn the torpedoes!" and ordering his own ship to proceed full speed ahead. White was interested in the project from the first and wrote to Saint-Gaudens: "I hope you will let me help you on the Farragut pedestal. Then I shall go down to fame even if it was bad, reviled for making a poor base to a good statue." After receiving the letter, the sculptor quickly turned to his friend to design a pedestal that would be no sharp-edged block of glistening granite, no naturalistic boulder, but of a form that would conjoin statue and base into a seamless whole.

White's numerous letters to Saint-Gaudens, which, Homer Saint-Gaudens, the sculptor's son, observed, were "frequently written on tracing paper, more often on both sides of the sheet, jotted down in pencil and at the headlong speed with which the architect accomplished all things," reveal a special quality of intimacy. White often addressed Saint-Gaudens as "Beloved Snooks" and "Doubly Beloved," while the sculptor returned the compliments with salutations such as "Darling" and "Beauty." Out of both affection and admiration, White was at this time trying to obtain an important commission for Saint-Gaudens. In 1875 Richardson had become involved in the completion of the New York state capitol in Albany, a structure whose tortured architectural history can only be compared to that of New York's Cathedral of St. John the Divine, and White immediately began urging him to use his sculptor friend. In a letter of May 1877 to Saint-Gaudens, who was in Paris working on the Farragut, White wrote: "Oh, most illustrious of the illustrious. I scent a big job for *thee* . . ."

White's assignment at Albany was the decoration of the Senate Chamber and here he devised a sumptuous composition of gray and red granite, golden sienna marble, and milky Mexican onyx which would have echoes in the entrance hall of Henry Villard's house. White longed to have Saint-Gaudens work with him on the chamber:

> There are about one hundred and fifty feet by twenty feet of decorative arabesque, foliage and the like . . . There are two marble friezes in the fireplaces, and one damn big panel of figures, Washington crossing the Delaware or cutting down a cherry tree, about forty feet by eight feet, also in colored cement, and a lot of little bits beside . . . if you do get it, you will have a chance to immortalize yourself like Giotto or Michel Angelo.

Saint-Gaudens did not get the commission. White, at this point in his career, was not ready to push too hard. In a letter of the same period to the sculptor he tells of a contretemps with a client and his urge to walk out, but the precocious twenty-four-year-old notes that he did not, for "I remembered that I was poor and young . . ." But even if Saint-Gaudens had gotten the Albany commission, Stanford White would not have been there to collaborate with him. He was soon writing his friend that he had paid "a final visit to the abode of the Great Mogul of Brookline . . ." It was time to depart. He had completed his apprenticeship. He had saved and borrowed enough money to buy a season of freedom. Europe, and particularly Paris, beckoned.

CHAPTER 3

PARIS BOUND

White's artistic abilities are evident in this sketch of a seasick Charles McKim aboard the Periere on his way to Europe in July of 1878. White delighted in the fact that while he proved to be a good sailor and could eat almost anything without suffering ill effects, McKim, for most of their voyage, was "past a joke."

Stanford White sailed from New York on July 3, 1878, on the *Periere*. He expected to travel alone and had written to Saint-Gaudens:

> I will write you before I sail for Europe, and I may ask you to look me up a cheap room in the fifth story of some building. You must help me to avoid being fleeced when I first get there. Indeed, I mean to test your friendship by boring you a good deal in many ways.

But he was not to travel solo, for, at the last minute, Charles McKim, whose marriage had broken up, decided to accompany him. "I'm tickled to death," White wrote to Saint-Gaudens. "It's bully." "Bully" for White, as it was for his friend Theodore Roosevelt, was the supreme accolade. Ten days later, after a particularly rough crossing, during which White delighted in downing clams, mackerel, kidneys, pigeons, and Gruyère cheese, while McKim and most of the other passengers suffered recurring bouts of mal de mer, they were in Paris.

OPPOSITE:

On their first Sunday in Paris, White and McKim attended services at the eleventh-century church of St.-Germain-des-Prés, the oldest in the city. Standing where the Boulevard St. Germain, the rue de Rennes, and the rue Bonaparte meet, the powerful Romanesque structure is one of the major landmarks of the Left Bank.

The Luxembourg Gardens and Palace about the time White first went to Paris. The rooms that he and McKim shared at 1 rue de Fleurus were to the left of this photograph. "We overlook the Palace and Gardens of the Luxembourg," White wrote to his mother on July 18, 1878, "and most beautiful gardens they are—certainly the most beautiful I have ever seen." The two friends paid 30 francs a week for their lodgings.

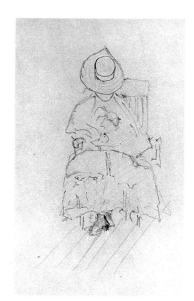

OPPOSITE:

It was Parisian monuments such as St.-Sulpice, with its imposing eighteenth-century façade by Servandoni, which made an indelible impression on White. The church was near where he and McKim had their rooms and on Christmas Eve of 1878 White and Saint-Gaudens attended a concert there.

Their destination was the Left Bank, that part of the city which Percy Lubbock described as "the heart of the civilized world." The pair was soon settled in rooms at 1 rue de Fleurus—curiously, the street where, after the turn of the century, Gertrude Stein would conduct her legendary salon. "I am at present domiciled in the sky parlor of a very pleasant 'tinniment' in the Latin Quarter," White notified his mother. "We overlook the Palace and the Gardens of the Luxembourg. . . ." The location had been chosen by McKim, who remembered it fondly from his Ecole days when his *atelier* had been in the nearby rue du Four. McKim had vividly described the neighborhood in his letter printed in the Auburn, New York, *Morning News*:

> Instead of running about the Tuileries and the Palais Royal, and wasting our time listening to English, . . . let us strike at once across the Seine, and get into the old town, as yet untouched by Napoleon III, still ancient in appearance and manners, and as foreign to the side we have just left as centuries could make it.
>
> Almost immediately we remark the change in things: the streets become narrower, the housetops higher and more projecting and even the people themselves seem to wear a different aspect, till at last you are compelled to admit that we are fairly abroad.

The site had also been chosen because it was near the apartment that Saint-Gaudens and his wife, Augusta—whom White felt was insufferably bossy—had taken in the rue Herschel and Saint-Gaudens's studio in the rue Notre-Dame-de-Champs. "We went to church like good boys in the afternoon, St.-Germain-des-Prés," White informed his mother in a letter recounting his first Sunday in Paris, "and the theatre like bad boys in the evening. The church, on the whole, was more interesting."

Number 1 rue de Fleurus was the ideal setting in which to savor the true essence of Paris. The tall cream-colored house is still there, almost unaltered, and at its feet, enclosed within its gilt-tipped palings, stretches the Luxembourg Gardens, a luxurious urban mix of gravel walks, of perfect beds of marigolds and gera-

niums and mignonettes, and of allées of chestnut, perpetually fashionable, changing seasonally from green to gold to black. The roofs of Salomon de Brosse's palace for Marie de Médicis could be glimpsed from the windows of 1 rue de Fleurus, as could the mismatched towers atop Servandoni's baroque Church of St.-Sulpice. At first White gave some small evidence of resisting the city's charms, but within a short time he would be writing whenever he was in the provinces: "Paris is like a snake. I feel a fascination a day or two before I get there . . ."

It was a spectacular moment in which to see the French capital, for barely eight years after the humiliating defeat of Napoleon III at Sedan by the Prussians, which had extinguished the Second Empire, and only seven after the burning of the Tuileries and other civic monuments by the Communards, Paris's recovery had been lightning-like. Philippe Julian captured the period brilliantly in his biography of Robert de Montesquiou:

> There was even greater luxury than during the Second Empire. After the defeat of the leading families . . . the business world assumed power and began to construct palaces for itself from the Plaine Monceau to the Champs-Elysées . . . Their carriages rolled down avenues bordered by houses heavy with caryatides and bank-like mansions in a style calculated to appeal to Ludwig of Bavaria. Driven by English coachmen, baronesses muffled in sables left their cards at the houses of Rumanian princesses, Spanish highnesses and American commoners . . .

This lesson in the connection between architecture and power was not lost on Stanford White. The Paris press was full of descriptions and the magazines filled with illustrations of the exuberant interiors of the *à la mode* palaces of the new masters of France: "The Renaissance dining-room gave on to an aviary full of cockatoos; vine branches in crystal hung from the pillars in the salon; and bear-skins covered the steps down to a marble pool." Pools and pillars and bear skins would make frequent appearances in the White ornamental repertory. Indeed, during his lifetime the architect con-

ducted a voluminous correspondence on the subject of the quest and care of animal skins for himself and his clients.

To celebrate its remarkable resurgence, France was staging in Paris one of those self-promoting nineteenth-century extravaganzas, an Exposition Universelle. (This may well have been a reason for the urgency of White and McKim's trip to Paris.) Their friend David Maitland Armstrong had been appointed director of American Fine Arts at the Exposition and had asked Saint-Gaudens to help him hang the American pictures. Indeed, Paris was alive with artists from the United States. One evening, for example, Armstrong gave a dinner in the restaurant of the Hotel Foyot, an

One of the chief reasons Stanford White wanted to be in Paris in 1878 was the International Exposition held there that year. His letters home are filled with the phrase "Paris in the morning, exposition in the afternoon." The Exposition's centerpiece was the Moorish-inspired Trocadéro Palace which, in 1937, was replaced by the Chaillot Palace.

establishment on the rue de Vaugirard favored by Americans, which, in addition to White and McKim, included Frederic Crowninshield, Alfred Greenough, Frank Millet, and Russell Sturgis. Both White and McKim were intrigued by the Moorish and Near Eastern decor in the Exposition's exotic Trocadéro Palace and by Millet's Montmartre apartment, which was an Aladdin's cave of hanging lamps, damascene implements of war, and brass- and ivory-inlaid furniture in the taste being popularized by French dandies such as Pierre Loti and Emile Gallé. These themes and devices would appear in the two rooms which White would help Louis Tiffany design in New York's Seventh Regiment Armory.

During his months in Paris, White's letters home are filled with names which form the nineteenth-century American Parisian Baedeker: Notre Dame, the Louvre, the Orangerie, the Opéra Comique. The city would be captured by White's discerning eye and cunning hand and placed within the covers of the six sketchbooks he filled during his fourteen months abroad. Over the years shards of it would rise in his memory to help form his New York masterpieces: the scale of the arch of the Carrousel reflected in the scale of the arch in Washington Square; the portico of the Panthéon before that of the New York University library; the plinths beneath the Place de la Concorde's Cheveaux de Marly reappearing with the "Horse Tamers" in Prospect Park.

White, though, had a dreamed-of destination other than Paris. Ever since he had lovingly studied the photographs of Romanesque churches pinned up in Richardson's office, the young architect had longed to see the monuments themselves in the South of France. It was not difficult to persuade McKim to join such an expedition, but Saint-Gaudens, who White hoped would come too, was a far more difficult proposition. The sculptor was under considerable pressure to finish the Farragut statue. As McKim's biographer, Charles Moore, reported, it was adverse criticism which propelled Saint-Gaudens into the adventure:

> One July day, when the call of the open country was urgent, McKim and White burst in on Saint-Gaudens at work in his studio, with the

While in Europe White filled
six large notebooks with drawings
and watercolors. They would
serve him as an aide-mémoire
upon his return to America. This
view of the interior of the
Cathedral of Notre Dame reveals
the young architect's sure eye for
spatial effects and composition.

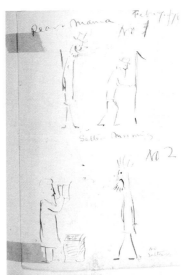

After Charles McKim returned
to the United States in September
of 1878, White moved into the
large apartment that Saint-
Gaudens and his wife occupied on
the rue Herschel. In this cartoon,
which he sent to his mother in
February of 1879, White
contrasts the large volume of
letters received by his host with
the meager mail coming to him.

Decorative ideas from Parisian
interiors, such as the Louvre's
magnificent Louis XIV Apollo
Gallery, would reappear in
White's New York work.

53

urgent suggestion of a walking-tour to the south of France. The sculptor demurred. The Farragut committee, he said, were coming to look at his sketch. . . . After the ordeal was over, they found Saint-Gaudens whistling. "Evidently," they said, "the ladies were pleased." "No; they weren't," was the answer; "if they had been I should have known it was bad!" Again the walking-tour was urged; but no, the "boys" (fellow students) were coming. So they waited for the verdict of the boys. It was concise: "Saint-Gaudens, you have given Farragut your legs!' . . . Then Saint-Gaudens, carefully lifting off the head, tipped the figure over on the floor, where it was shattered into a thousand pieces. "Come on," he exclaimed, "I'll go to Hades with you fellows now!"

By August 2, the trio was ready to explore the seedbed of the Romanesque and, traveling by train, by boat, and on foot, they covered an impressive amount of territory. They went as far south as Arles, as far west as Tours, and as far east as Dijon, a great swath, as White made evident in his letters home, of architectural richness, oenological delight, and feminine pulchritude:

The excitement White felt when he saw the photographs of Romanesque monuments in Richardson's studio, led him, in August of 1878, to convince McKim and Saint-Gaudens to join him on a tour of the South of France. The supreme moment architecturally of that journey was the discovery of the façade of the abbey in the village of St.-Gilles-du-Gard. St.-Gilles's majesty is evident in this etching by Joseph Pennell.

At Beaune, besides the beauty of the town itself, we came across two very attractive and inseparable things, viz. good wine and pretty women . . . The town is still encircled by its old walls, crowned with machicolations and guarded by round towers.

The day all through was of the most perfect description & we arrived safely at Avignon (which towered up from the river like a rock) in the evening, found a very good hotel, had a most excellent dinner & a fine old bottle of Hermitage.

    Avignon was the residence of the Popes for two hundred years & has the largest and most grandiose medieval castle in the world . . .

Everywhere, in this part of France which Prosper Mérimée said was a foreign country when compared with Paris, White's notebooks laid up stores for future use. Nowhere, though, were the consequences to be more clear-cut than in St. Gilles in the department of Gard:

> At St.-Gilles—a little out-of-the-way town (with the best piece of architecture in France in it, the triple marble porch of the church)— we were taken in charge by the abbé, who seemed delighted to come across some educated people . . .

The object of Stanford White's effusive praise was the lower half of the façade of St. Gilles's twelfth-century abbey. Finally he had found a Romanesque monument that lived up to every expectation. A quarter of a century later it would reappear on the façade of New York's St. Bartholomew's Church as a Vanderbilt memorial.

    "At Nîmes," White wrote, "we sighted the Mediterranean & turned our faces sorrowfully homeward." The travelers were back in Paris by August 13, and Saint-Gaudens struck a small bronze commemorative medal with humorous likenesses of White, McKim, and himself. The composition—which also included the façade of St. Gilles and a T square, not unlike a cross—was consciously reminiscent of the tokens given to medieval pilgrims after they had reached Jerusalem or Santiago de Compostela.

The death in 1899 of Cornelius Vanderbilt II, a grandson of the Commodore, provided White with the opportunity to place upon the façade of James Renwick's old St. Bartholomew's Church a version of St. Gille's portal. Originally, Vanderbilt's widow, Alice, had wanted the memorial to consist only of a set of bronze doors, but the architect, anxious to make use of St. Gilles, convinced her that what the church needed was an entirely new entranceway.

To celebrate their eleven-day walking tour of the South of France, Saint-Gaudens designed a bronze medal some six inches in diameter. It bore caricatures of the sculptor on the left, of McKim on the right, and of White sporting the beard that he had grown. To the right is the beloved portal of St. Gilles.

McKim returned to the United States in September, but White remained in Europe until the following August. He was helping Saint-Gaudens—in whose apartment he was now living—with the Farragut, and he made a short trip to Italy, visiting Rome, Verona, and Venice. But the majority of his time was spent touring the historic cathedral towns of France: Rheims, where the ancient houses clustered about the august church like ducks about their mother; Rouen, whose Tour de Beurre had helped inspire the tower of Trinity; and Beauvais, where the Gothic, in a flight of spiritual and physical hubris, soared to more than 150 feet. Everywhere he found sights which made him exclaim, "Holy Moses, Gin and Seltzer!"—a form of praise on a par with "bully." Traveling with-

OPPOSITE:

The Vanderbilt Memorial is seen here shortly after its completion in 1903 gracing the old St. Bartholomew's which stood at the southwest corner of Madison Avenue and Forty-Fourth Street. In 1917 White's portal was moved to the new St. Bartholomew's on Park Avenue, designed by Bertram Goodhue.

Beauvais was another stop on Stanford White's tour of the ancient cities of France. Its cathedral of St. Pierre, with its astonishing 150-foot-high vault, is one of the supreme monuments of Gothic architecture. Beauvais also possessed an important museum dedicated to the local tapestries the architect admired. Every structure in this photograph, except the cathedral, was obliterated by German bombing in 1940.

STANFORD WHITE'S NEW YORK

out his friends, White was often lonely, but Paris, happily, was always there. On November 21, 1878, he wrote to his mother:

> How fortunate that fate permits me to return to Paris for a day or two every three or four weeks. I should die, I think, if I did not . . .

He would return throughout his life and, more importantly, he would carry something of the Paris he had seen, its opulence, its style, its joie de vivre, to New York. On August 23, 1879, his cash reserves exhausted, Stanford White sailed out of Liverpool for home. "Turn down my bed spread," he wrote to his parents, "dust out my room . . ."

OPPOSITE:

White carried his brushes and pencils with him everywhere and sometimes complained, as he did at Lisieux, of "villainous boys, who plague the life out of me when I am sketching." This sketch of the thirteenth-century cathedral in the Norman town of Coutances shows the architect's fondness for picturesque towers.

CHAPTER 4

MCKIM, MEAD, & WHITE

The New York to which Stanford White returned on September 5, 1879, was a fallow field ripe for cultivation. It was the safe little world of the hereditarily secure which the mordant New York novelist, Edith Wharton, would portray so vividly in short stories such as "New Year's Day"; a world constructed of brownstone, which gave it, as she declared in her autobiography, *A Backward Glance*, a "universal chocolate-coloured coating of the most hideous stone ever quarried"; a world which Henry Adams had the heroine of his novel *Democracy* characterize as a "wilderness of men and women as monotonous as the brownstone houses they lived in"; a world which could hear at its back "Time's winged chariot." The venerable Dutch Knickerbockers—Stuyvesants and Schermerhorns—and the slightly more recent English grandees—Newbolds and Livingstons—still issued forth from their brownstone lairs furnished with red-hued Turkey carpets, dark walnut furniture, and self-satisfied family portraits in bright golden frames to perform ritualistic pavans which carried

Stanford White about 1880, sporting the rather fierce-looking mustache that was his trademark as a young man.

63

them to the countinghouses and law offices of Wall Street, to the Academy of Music on Fourteenth Street, to correct clubs such as the Union at Fifth Avenue and Twenty-first Street, and, on the Sabbath, to sober sanctuaries, Protestant Episcopal, Presbyterian, or Dutch Reformed. But if the "chocolate" had not yet exactly melted, it most certainly showed signs of an incipient thaw.

Whereas Charles Astor Bristed, writing in the 1850s, declared that smart New Yorkers had to live above Bleecker Street, by the late 1870s the social Maginot Line of Twenty-third Street had been breached. One of the chief causes was the inauguration in 1878 of the Third Avenue and Sixth Avenue elevated railways, which introduced true rapid transit into the city. The trains consisted of four cars, pale green on the outside and dark brown inside, and the price was ten cents. Though the coal-burning engines showered the streets with soot, cinders, and even occasional burning coals, New Yorkers were proud of their new transit system. The combination of the elevated and the Vanderbilts' New York Central Railroad, which thrust ever northward from its recently inaugurated red-brick terminal designed by John B. Snook at Forty-second Street, opened up the top of Manhattan Island and all of Westchester County to the possibility of commuting. For the fashionable it was now practicable to reside on upper Fifth Avenue and still be at one's office on Wall or Nassau or Broad streets during business hours. The population of New York, within the present city limits, barely topping 1,000,000 at the outbreak of the Civil War, had by 1879 reached 2,000,000.

This booming Gotham was mirrored in almost every aspect of the city's life, including that of the perennial reality of civic corruption, for in the spring of 1878 William Marcy Tweed died in the Ludlow Street Jail. Tweed was a man who, weighing more than 300 pounds, reflected in his very person the burgeoning of the city he ran and looted. Inordinately fond of women and, curiously, of flowers and canaries too, Tweed, through his hold on the powerful Tammany Society, controlled the Democratic Party, and thus New York. Through outright theft, bribes paid for lowering real estate taxes, plunder from rigged franchises, and the issuance of bonds at extravagant interest rates, it is estimated that the Tweed Ring filched more than $200,000,000. When he was first charged with malfeasance by the New York *Times*, Tweed's riposte was a sharp "Well, what are you going to do about it?" When he was indicted and sentenced, most New Yorkers were astonished, not that he had plundered the city, but that there had been so much to plunder. In fact, fabulous wealth, until recently limited to a few families such as the Astors, of whom the London *Spectator* said only the Czar of all the Russias had more money, was now spreading, and it would not be long before Mrs. Stuyvesant Fish, gazing at the mansions of the Vanderbilts, could jest with some seriousness, "We are only moderately well off; we have but a few million dollars."

The municipality was changing in other ways as well. On the evening of May 11, 1877, in the Hotel St. Denis at Broadway and Eleventh Street, Alexander Graham Bell demonstrated that he could speak to an assistant in Brooklyn two miles away. Six months before Stanford White returned to his native shore, the Bell Telephone Company had opened a commercial exchange, and soon Manhattan had its first telephone directory, a card bearing a grand total of 252 names. The first operators were boys, and the new subscribers were advised to open their conversations by shouting "Ahoy!" Almost immediately one of the most conspicuous elements of the metropolis's streetscape was the thick net of telephone and telegraph lines woven across the thoroughfares. "In the old or lower part of the city," a British visitor observed in 1878, "you look upon a perfect maze of telephone and telegraph wires crossing and recrossing each other from the tops of the houses. The sky, indeed, is blackened with them . . ."

The city to which White returned was still a municipality in which the picturesque lamplighter made his rounds at twilight, firing the gas lamps lining the cobblestone streets. But within three months of his landing, New York witnessed a new illuminating wonder. Along Broadway, from Fourteenth to Twenty-sixth streets, electric arc lights, the invention of Charles Francis Brush, were installed on tall poles. The location chosen was the heart of the "Ladies' Mile," that stretch of Broadway where, arrayed in a Second Empire panoply of cast-iron classical columns and high mansard roofs topped with delicate filigree crestings dreamed up by architects such as Griffith Thomas and James H. Giles, New York's leading shops—among them Arnold Constable and Lord & Taylor,—purveyed the necessities required for the elaborate toilettes of the time. Among the desiderata, according to the *Ladies' City Guide*, were "pongees and grenadines and feather fans and Japanese sunshades." Mr. Brush's arc lights, it was hoped, would attract females like so many moths around a flame, but the result was, to everyone's surprise, exactly the reverse. The lights proved to be so dazzlingly brilliant that they were unbearable, and the ladies promenading along the Mile complained that Mr. Brush's arcs gave to their carefully preserved peaches-and-cream complexions the ashen pallor of death.

Succor, though, was just around the corner, or at least just across the Hudson. The same month that the arc lights were raised along the Ladies' Mile, Thomas Alva Edison demonstrated in Menlo Park, New Jersey, his new incandescent lamp. Edison's bulb produced a warm, soft, pleasing glow, and he immediately petitioned New York's aldermen to use it to light the city's streets, but the town fathers replied that the Brush Electric Illuminating Company was already doing the job. It was left to the invariably astute J. Pierpont Morgan to perceive that Edison's incandescent lamp could accomplish something that Brush's dazzling arc lights could not, and that was illuminate private residences. Thus when, at the beginning of the 1880s, Morgan built his new house on Madison Avenue in Murray Hill, he had Edison install an electric lighting system, and though his next-door neighbor, Mrs. James M. Brown, complained about the vibration of the dynamo providing the power, the future and the profits belonged to Morgan and to Edison.

If Brush's arc lamp and Edison's incandescent bulb were casting a bright glow upon New York's thoroughfares, the architectural styles they illuminated were a murky mélange. The ardor for the

Second Empire had cooled somewhat following the ignominious defeat of Napoleon III by Bismarck in 1870 and the flight from Paris of the Empress Eugénie in her American dentist's cabriolet, but there were still plenty of flavors to choose from in the architectural bonbonnière. Certainly affection for the Second Empire lingered in some quarters, while the full riotous range of building fashion in America in the late 1870s is manifest in the edifices which three great New York institutions raised just as Stanford White came back to his hometown. It is not too much to say that at no other period was Montgomery Schuyler's trenchant remark that "American humor has never found full expression except in architecture" more to the point.

Just as 1877 ended and 1878 commenced, the new American Museum of Natural History—of which the omnipresent Morgan was a founder—opened its home on Central Park West. The structure, housing a taxidermist's paradise of stuffed birds and mammals, was designed by Calvert Vaux and J. Wrey Mould in a Venetian Gothic style which owed not a little to the English aesthetician John Ruskin. Venetian Gothic, though, was not for the Roman Catholics, and when, in May 1879, John Cardinal McCloskey fulfilled the twenty-year-old dream of New York's Catholics and dedicated James Renwick's St. Patrick's Cathedral on Fifth Avenue, the eleventh-largest church in the world was seen to be in a paper-thin, attenuated Gothic reminiscent of Paris's St. Clothilde or the new towers of Cologne. "Fearless and alone, it stands above all churches here, as the faith which inspired its erection is superior to all creeds," the preacher at the cathedral's dedication trumpeted with delightful certitude. A year after the consecration of St. Patrick's, the Metropolitan Museum of Art—with Mr. Morgan again one of the shakers and movers—inaugurated its new galleries in Central Park. Of bright red Victorian brick with limestone trim, the museum, also the work of Vaux and Mould, was sometimes labeled Venetian, sometimes Tuscan, but was notable chiefly for its dazzling, if not astounding, polychromy. Interestingly, the Metropolitan had been encouraged by the city fathers to settle in that stretch of the park along Fifth Avenue between Eightieth and Eighty-fifth streets because it was the site of Seneca Village, Gotham's largest, most noxious squatter camp.

Strangely, the year of Stanford White's homecoming also marked the first use of a name that would be forever associated with one of his supreme architectural achievements, with his lifestyle, and with his death. At the beginning of the 1870s, the renowned showman P. T. Barnum had leased the New York & Harlem Railroad's depot on the block bounded by Madison and Fourth avenues and Twenty-sixth and Twenty-seventh streets, which had been abandoned when the line moved its terminal northward to Forty-second Street. Barnum converted the utilitarian one-story structure into a drafty arena, named it the Great Roman Hippodrome, and offered the public something that was one part museum, one part menagerie, and one part circus. In 1873, Barnum relinquished the lease of the Hippodrome to Patrick S. Gilmore, "the bandmaster of the Union Army," who had gained fame by writing the lyrics to "When Johnny Comes Marching Home." For a time the new proprietor called the place Gilmore's Concert Garden, but in 1879 it was given the appellation that would make the site immortal, Madison Square Garden.

It is not unlikely that Richardson had had an understanding with White when he left his employment, some sort of first refusal, for as soon as his former draftsman returned from Europe, "the Great Mogul" offered him a job. But the energetic twenty-two-year-old, who had already tasted glory with the Trinity Church project, who had seen the opulence of Paris, who now dined with America's most promising artists, and who dreamed of magnificent projects with Saint-Gaudens, was not about to enter another's employ; nor did he wish to return to Boston. The same verdict opposing provinciality which had made McKim opt for New York against Philadelphia was now rendered by White against Boston. The architectural critic John Jay Chapman stated one reason why this decision was almost inevitable:

The moment of Stanford White's appearance was coincident with a change in our municipal life. New York was turning from a large provincial city into a world-center, a true metropolis. No doubt the shift in the world's banking interests was at the bottom of the matter; but banking interests, architecture and social life are closely related.

Another reason was that White wanted to work with Charles McKim, and, fortuitously, the opportunity now presented itself. The firm which McKim had established with Mead and William Bigelow had foundered in the aftermath of the unhappy dissolution of McKim's marriage to Bigelow's sister. White had already had feelers from McKim about joining the firm, and any lingering doubts regarding his technical training on the part of Mead were quelled by McKim's historic pronouncement: ". . . he can draw like a house a-fire!" The accolade was not a disinterested one, for the fact was that neither Mead nor McKim was a first-rate draftsman and Stanford White's well-honed skills were exactly what they were looking for. Thus scarcely two days after setting foot again on Manhattan Island, White began work in McKim and Mead's office on the top floor of 57 Broadway at the corner of Tin Pot Alley. From the window there was a view of New York's spacious harbor, while the nearest landmark was Richard Upjohn's crocket-encrusted Trinity Church constructed of the ubiquitous brownstone which, under the smoky pall of a thousand coal fires, grew daily more funereal. For all practical purposes McKim, Mead & White was born.

It was a curiously varied but faultlessly fitted triumvirate, resembling nothing so much as a tripod with each leg of a unique material and design but with the three working together to achieve a perfect balance. "They differed—McKim, Mead and White," Charles Baldwin reported in his 1931 biography of Stanford White, "yet Mrs. White tells me, a better natured trio never got together." John Jay Chapman, in a fine essay on the firm, astutely defines McKim's role in the office:

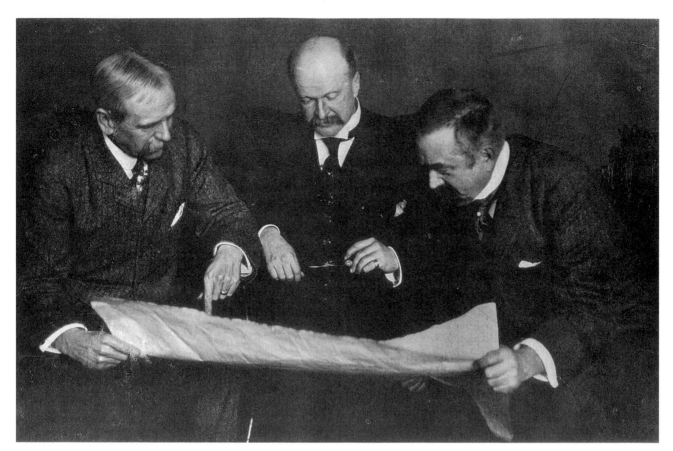

The great triumvirate, left to right, William Rutherford Mead, Charles Follen McKim, and Stanford White in a 1905 photograph by Arthur Hewitt. Mead would outlive his two partners and would be the "helmsman," as McKim dubbed him, of the firm until 1920. He would also carry on McKim's work at the American Academy in Rome, becoming president of the institution following McKim's death in 1909. William Rutherford Mead died in 1928.

By a strange freak of destiny Stanford White was professionally linked to another man of genius of the opposite artistic type. Charles F. McKim was an artist who pursued his course with indefatigable idealism. Nothing defeated him nor delayed him. He sought the bones, the structure, the intellect of his craft . . . To one whose eyes are filled with the ornamentation and facility of American architecture, McKim's work looks positively classic. It speaks from the brain.

White was, at times, baffled by his partner's relentless intellectualism. In a letter to McKim written on March 30, 1905, he reports that he was astonished by the audacious glass-and-steel train shed of Pennsylvania Station and much preferred the more traditional travertine waiting room. The shed, White declared, was "something alien."

White, in these early years, has been characterized by his son, Lawrence Grant White, as "exuberant, restless, a skyrocket of vitality. He worked at terrific pressure." He also worked at breakneck speed, sketching out his ideas with a rapidity which astonished onlookers. If McKim was the brain of the firm, it is not too much to say that White was the heart, willing, as he once said to a draftsman, to "bend the axis" when necessary to achieve a desired result. This may be the reason for the extraordinary protean quality of his buildings as distinguished from McKim's consistent high classicism. In *From Seven to Seventy*, the painter Edward Simmons, who worked with White on a number of important commissions, including the decoration of the Metropolitan Club's library ceiling, observed firsthand the architectural reality:

> Nothing could be more different in style than the buildings Stanford designed—the Madison Square Garden, the Metropolitan Club, Dr. Parkhurst's Church . . . or any of his business buildings . . . His personal tastes were absolutely under control of his artistic feelings, and his sensitiveness was so great that he could lose his own personality.

While McKim was likened to Bramante, White was thought of as the Benvenuto Cellini of 57 Broadway.

William Rutherford Mead, the other leg of the tripod, who was caricatured by Saint-Gaudens as flying two balky kites labeled "McKim" and "White," once defined himself as the water which makes the chemical reaction of acid and alkali lose its power to harm. Looking at the firm's logo, a caravel under sail with the legend "Vogue la Galère," "let the ship sail on," one wag said that while White was the sail of the ship and McKim the hull, Mead was the rudder. The other two partners always referred to the Vermonter, out of affection and respect, as "dummy." It was he who was in charge of the firm's day-to-day operations and it was he who fought valiantly to imbue it with at least a modicum of order.

Mead's correspondence is laced with Yankee good sense. On

The McKim, Mead & White logo as it appeared on a bookplate in Stanford White's library.

January 18, 1895, he wrote to White concerning a project of which Albert Randolph Ross, one of the architect's chief assistants, was in charge:

> Mr. C. E. Harrell 151 Fifth Avenue is coming in today and expects to find a sketch for the building which Ross is working on . . . I would take out the Caryatides, which Ross is so fond of getting in all his buildings, if they would represent any considerable expense, for I think this man is building with the idea of selling.

And in September of the same year, when Joseph Pulitzer, who was pressing White to come up to Bar Harbor, Maine, to suggest alterations for his house, asked what the consultation fee would be, Mead gave this canny advice: "If you go, I would suggest that you state you are a very busy man, and that this consultation fee shall be—for example, say—$100 a day from the time you leave New York." Mead was also adept at avoiding the web of social activities in which White was constantly attempting to entangle him. A telegram sent from Washington on March 30, 1895, states bluntly: "Don't count on me for La Farge dinner. Have rheumatism. W. R. Mead."

At 57 Broadway, this unexpectedly well-suited trinity presided over an office which, like Richardson's own, espoused the atmosphere of those Left Bank *ateliers* where, working together in contagious bonhomie, the architecture students of the Ecole des Beaux-Arts generously helped and encouraged one another. "It was esteemed a great privilege to be admitted to the offices of these architects," William A. Boring recalled. For him they seemed "to breathe the spirit of the fifteenth century." The art critic Royal Cortissoz, who also apprenticed with McKim, Mead & White, felt that "there probably never was an office with more effective teamwork, with fewer bosses, with more of the character of a studio." At 57 Broadway, one could meet an astonishing staff, including John M. Carrère and Thomas Hastings, the future architects of the New York Public Library; Francis Hoppin, whom Edith Wharton would ask to design her house, The Mount, in Lenox, Massachusetts;

Henry Bacon, the man responsible for the Lincoln Memorial; Cass Gilbert, the creator of the Woolworth Building; and Edward York and Philip Sawyer, whose Bowery Savings Bank on Forty-second Street is one of New York's preeminent interior spaces. Only Richard Morris Hunt in the previous generation and Frank Lloyd Wright ever engendered such a "school" of American architecture.

Stanford White's love of the beautiful, his passion for collecting, which, in time, would become almost a frenzy, revealed itself in the old American cherry-wood desk and Windsor chair which took up most of the space in his minuscule private office. Before long, White's incessant prowling through junkyards became so famous that an article in a local newspaper reported: "It is well known that some of the most beautiful 'colonial' and other mantelpieces which now adorn certain remodelled houses in New York were picked up by Mr. Stanford White in the yards of a housewrecker on the East Side near the river."

Although White had hit the ground running his first day at 57 Broadway, he remained deeply involved in the Farragut commission. He and Saint-Gaudens were also collaborating on a memorial for Richard Randall, the founder of Sailors' Snug Harbor, a retirement home for seamen on Staten Island. Writing to Saint-Gaudens, who was still in Paris, on May 8, 1880, White was explicit as to the type of base he envisioned for Saint-Gaudens's statue of Randall:

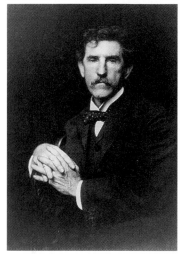

Augustus Saint-Gaudens photographed by James L. Breese. White's settings for Saint-Gaudens's statues such as the Farragut and the Adams Memorial in Washington set a new standard of aesthetics for American monuments.

> Sometime in January I received a letter from Thomas Greenleaf, controller of Sailors' Snug Harbor, asking me to call on him in reference to the pedestal, which I did. I then made a sketch of a pedestal with a big seat behind it.

White wanted a relief on the back of the big seat, "a yawl boat in a storm or something," and he hoped that the material would be bluestone. But the cost, estimated at $75,000, frightened the memorial committee, and the architect was forced to come up with a design which he described as "severe and simple as possible, one stone on top another." The price was a more congenial $4,600.

But his scheme for the Randall Memorial was not wasted, for it would come to a splendorous fruition in the Farragut. Here White once more proposed a horizontal base in the form of a classical seat to counter the dramatic verticality of the statue itself. And once more he asked that it be made of bluestone, so that there would be no sharp contrast with the bronze statue, and he also wanted it to be decorated. White showed his sketches for the project to Richardson and to Olmsted, to La Farge and to George Fletcher Babb, an architect in the firm to whom he often turned for aesthetic counsel. But it was his partner who gave him the wisest advice, as White wrote to Saint-Gaudens: "I began floundering around trying to improve matters, until McKim came along and said: 'You're a damn fool—you've got a good thing; why don't you stick to it?'" Slowly the monument took final form. Early in 1880 the bronze was cast in Paris and then Saint-Gaudens returned to New York to complete the decorative program of the base.

When on May 25, 1881, the cloth was stripped away and the Farragut Memorial was unveiled, the crowd of 10,000 was first silent and then broke into cheers. There, in uncompromising reality, stood the admiral, with his sea legs spread to balance him just as they had been that August day in 1864 when the *Hartford* cut through the rollers of Mobile Bay. The sense of his flagship's movement is heightened by Farragut's coat being blown open by the wind, while the set of his jaw personifies the defiance which cast a curse upon torpedoes. In Madison Square, David Glasgow Farragut's feet were planted upon Stanford White's magnificent base—an exedra—of bluestone. Just beneath the hero, the symbol of his office, an admiral's sword, is magically washed by waves as though it were Excalibur, while the ends of the bench are formed of sea-splashed dolphins of an almost Art Nouveau sensuousness. The noted lawyer Joseph Choate, who delivered the dedicatory address, praised the "creative genius of the young and brilliant artist, who produced this noble statue," but Richard Watson Gilder, who had followed the creation of the monument every step of the way, was to write that it was the work of two men of "genius." After the

The Farragut Memorial as it was originally placed after its completion in 1881 facing Fifth Avenue at the northwest corner of Madison Square. White's graceful base and Saint-Gaudens's realistic figure were the result of a close collaboration between the architect and the sculptor during White's stay with Saint-Gaudens in Paris in 1878–79.

Farragut, most of the memorials in New York's parks looked like Victorian bric-a-brac.

The structure which White and McKim were commissioned to build in late 1879 on Newport's most modish street, Bellevue Avenue, was a Wonderland looking glass through which the essentially simple society of the 1870s passed on its way to becoming the Byzantine establishment of the century's later decades. It presaged a demarcation as palpable as that which separated the mellow old New York Dancing Assembly from that 1872 creation of Ward McAllister, the "Patriarchs," twenty-five men who would "lead society" by giving its most exclusive balls. After that it would require but a few stately cotillions and a dozen years for the Georgian of good family and few prospects to blithely inform the New York *Tribune*:

> Why there are only 400 people in fashionable New York Society. If you go outside that number you strike people who are either not at ease in a ballroom or else make other people not at ease . . .

The Newport Casino, according to Maud Howe Elliott, the daughter of the redoubtable Julia Ward Howe, author of the words to "The Battle Hymn of the Republic," "was the first thing of its kind in the country, and its building marks an epoch in Newport life." The impetus behind the Casino was James Gordon Bennett, Jr., the brilliant, erratic editor-publisher of the New York *Herald*. Bennett's life was a series of outrages against the august proprieties. His nose had been broken one afternoon at Delmonico's in the 1860s after he slapped Ned Stokes, who would later gain notoriety for murdering the financier Jim Fisk. But Bennett's most notorious social contretemps had occurred at an 1876 New Year's Eve party given in New York by the parents of his fiancée, Caroline May. After a good deal of imbibing, Bennett announced that there was not a bathroom within half a block and then proceeded to urinate into the drawing-room fireplace. He was thrown out of the house and just as quickly the engagement broken off. A week later, Caroline May's brother Fred, spying him outside the Union Club,

An engraving of the eccentric publisher of the New York Herald, James Gordon Bennett, *who ran his New York, London, and Paris newspapers from his office on the Champs Élysées. His commissioning of McKim, Mead, and White in 1879 to build the Newport Casino gave the young firm a dazzling opportunity in the grandest of the Gilded Age resorts.*

attacked him with a horsewhip. The result was a ritual duel during which both Fred May and James Gordon Bennett fired into the air. Though the duel proved harmless, the social consequences of his action were fatal. Finding himself shunned, Bennett settled in Paris, returning to New York only for brief visits almost always relating to the business of the *Herald*.

The immediate raison d'être for the establishment of the Casino was another Bennett misadventure. On a bet, a guest of his, a British army officer named Candy rode his polo pony up the steps and into the hall of the Newport Reading Room, the town's most exclusive male retreat. Ultimately, as legend has it, the horse was noticed, and the offending rider's guest privileges were revoked. Bennett, in one of his notorious rages, immediately resigned his Reading Room membership and announced that he would build his own club across the avenue. Furthermore, he thundered, his club would have something Newport sadly lacked, courts upon which to play the newly fashionable game of lawn tennis.

The structure of the Newport Casino strikingly demonstrates White and McKim's particular gifts and their inevitably intelligent

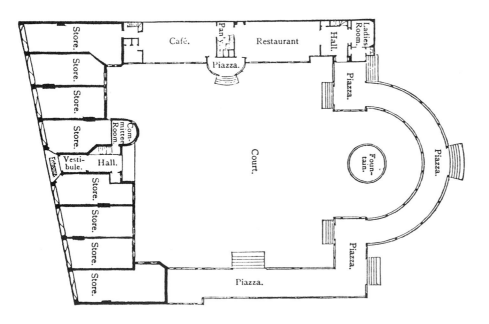

This plan of the Newport Casino clearly reveals how McKim's orderly row of shops screen the tennis courts from the bustle of Bellevue Avenue, while White's café, galleries, and horseshoe piazza surround the first court with an architecture at once utilitarian and festive.

In The Architectural Heritage of Newport, Rhode Island, *the distinguished architectural historian, Vincent Scully, expressed unreserved praise for the Casino's trellis-trimmed piazzas: "The piazzas themselves are excellent examples of White's real genius at this time. They are partially enclosed spatial volumes, where the skeleton construction creates airy voids . . ."*

division of labor. The Bellevue Avenue façade by McKim, with its row of shops with apartments above, conveys an air of wholesome, small-town, Main Street America. At first glance it appears to be in a romantic Norman Shaw shingle style, but a second glance shows that the equidistant triple pediments which complete the composition make the whole façade essentially classical. At the center of this tasteful carapace, a bold, red-brick arch draws the visitor into another world, that of Stanford White. Straight before one, the broad expanse of the grass tennis courts and the horseshoelike sweep of the great veranda—a stage for music and dancing—signals that this is the realm of play and of pleasure. This note is heightened by White's prodigal use of dark green treillage of a faintly Japanese design, which, like crepe paper decorating a high school gymnasium, is an irresistible invitation to gaiety. Turning around, the

viewer perceives that, on the inner façade, White has dissolved McKim's classicism into a romantic asymmetrical composition dominated by a strong, cloche-shaped tower lifted from one of his French sketchbooks, a tower sporting a Tiffany clock like a watch pinned upon a matron's bosom.

  White's work at the Casino, for the first time, fully revealed a gift which would be one of the most valuable in his teeming armory of talents, that of inevitably creating the correct stage set for his clients. At the Newport Casino, his use of treillage, his Japanesque touches, and his verandas, conjure up something of the spirit of the British Raj. It is absolutely the right setting for late Victorian and Edwardian golden afternoons when Vanderbilts and Astors, clothed in thin voile and starched white linen, were served cool drinks by silent servants with the only sound that of a ball against a racket or a

The interior façade of the Casino, with its picturesque arrangement of dormers upon a steeply pitched roof and its bold cloche-shaped tower, was inspired in part by White's French sketchbooks. The clock by Tiffany was placed so that it could be easily seen by the players on the courts. The center passage leads to Bellevue Avenue.

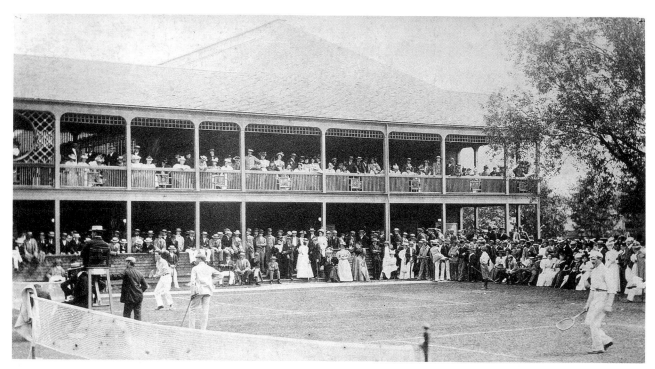

*F*rom *its opening on August 2, 1880, the Casino became the focus of tennis in this country and its annual invitational tournament marked the height of the Newport season. This photograph of about 1890 shows White's delightful viewing galleries.*

Gilbert and Sullivan medley played by a modulated band. "Rural but not rustic," was Marianna Van Rensselaer's judgment of the Casino. There could be no higher praise.

The unqualified success of the Casino just at the moment Newport was shedding the last vestiges of its informal summer colony atmosphere, characterized by people like White's friend John La Farge and the architect Richard Morris Hunt, for the *stylé* regime of White's patrons the Oelrichses and Fishes, made it an invaluable advertisement for its two young architects. A world whose chief concern, in the words of Henry James, was the "return of the *Revue des Deux Mondes*" to the literary Town and Country Club was about to be vanquished by one whose overriding question was whether Mrs. Stuyvesant Fish had described Alva Vanderbilt Belmont as resembling a frog or a toad?

In 1880, David King, Jr., whose family had made a comfortable fortune in the China trade and had important New York connections, commissioned Stanford White to design a three-story addition to Kingscote, his 1840 Gothic Revival villa by Richard Upjohn situated not far from the Casino. Though White's addition is much larger in scale than the original toy summer cottage—it contains bedrooms, bathrooms, and a dining room which could also serve as a ballroom—his work reveals a sensitive respect for the past and a profound sense of architectural appropriateness and scale. Indeed, the two parts of Kingscote blend surprisingly well. The dining room is one of America's supreme Arts and Crafts interiors. There is a wonderful aura of caring workmanship about this space evident in the handsome built-in Colonial Revival sideboard, in the daring herringbone-patterned cork acoustic tiles—perhaps the first ever used for decoration—which sheath the upper walls and ceiling, and in the carefully selected green, gray, and blue opalescent Tiffany glass which surrounds the fireplace. It is particularly notable in the refined spool-and-spindle mahogany screen that separates the dining room from the foyer and which can be removed for parties. Here

The dining room which White added to Kingscote, a Gothic Revival cottage not far from the Casino, in 1880, is a faultless blend of Colonial Revival and Arts and Crafts sensibilities. At Kingscote White daringly experimented with the use of cork on the upper walls and ceiling, with translucent Tiffany tiles on the fireplace wall, and designed the screen so that it could be removed to enlarge the space for dances.

are the consequences of lessons learned while working on the Sherman house; here are sweet memories of that tour through old New England.

Just as White was completing the additions to Kingscote, he was commissioned by Robert Goelet in March 1882 to design a vast cottage, Southside, on Newport's smart Narragansett Avenue. The Goelets, New Yorkers of Huguenot ancestry, possessed one of Gotham's greatest real estate fortunes and their property, stretching from Union Square to Forty-seventh Street, was estimated in 1870 to have a book value approaching $100,000,000. The family had long maintained a French Protestant parsimony, mending their own clothes, saving used envelopes for stationery, and keeping a cow, which one of Robert Goelet's uncles, Peter, milked himself. By the 1880s, the Goelets, had managed to shed some of their relentless frugality. They would become friends and consistent patrons of White, employing him to design the family real estate office on West Seventeenth Street, a commercial building on Broadway, the Judge Building at the northwest corner of Fifth Avenue and Sixteenth Street, and finally, to assure a fitting farewell, commissioning him to plan their Greek temple mausoleum in Woodlawn Cemetery.

The Goelet house, with its commanding chimneys, its stacked gables, and its extremely deep verandas, was about as far as one could go in the picturesque shingle style. The two-story living hall, a set for the parade of vassals before their liege lord in some irredeemably rural English county, is a giant version of the one White had created for William Watts Sherman. But the day was fast approaching when more opulent settings for more opulent fantasies would be required. One glimmer of the gilded future can be found in the Robert Goelet house. The veranda, which sweeps across its façade, ends in twin pavilions, pavilions which might be described without exaggeration as hayseed cousins of classical temples.

But before he embraced the high classical manner, White would participate in the creation of two masterpieces in an almost barbaric style far closer to the towers of Trebizond than to the Doric columns of Athens. Both would be the results of collaboration with Louis Comfort Tiffany, son of Charles L. Tiffany, founder of New York's renowned jewel emporium. White had met Tiffany in the mid-1870s through Richard Watson Gilder and his wife, the painter Helena de Kay. The two young men quickly found that they shared a passion for exotic, beautiful objects and materials: Roman glass, antique damask, Near Eastern metalwork, and semiprecious stones. They had almost certainly seen each other in Paris, where Tiffany had gone to study the colorful contents of the Trocadéro Palace, and their friendship had grown when White had asked the creator of Favrile Glass to supply decorative elements for the dining room of Kingscote.

American taste for the exotic had been fed by the international pavilions—especially the Japanese—at the Centennial Exposition held in Philadelphia in 1876. "The specimens from abroad of furniture, carpets, hangings, and broderies," wrote Hudson Holly in *The Home Magazine*, "formed an opportunity for the art students such as may not occur again in many years." The aesthetic which sprang from the Exposition displayed Levantine armor against heavily embroidered Chinese silks, blue and white porcelain against painted peacocks. The result in New York would be two interiors that can only be described as fabulous.

In 1876, the very year of the Centennial, New York's elite Seventh Regiment—whose origins reached back to 1806—decided to move its headquarters and drill hall away from the increasingly unsavory purlieu of Tompkins Square to an Upper East Side location at Park Avenue between Sixty-sixth and Sixty-seventh streets. One of the chief incentives for the move was the fear by New York's upper classes of riots of the kind that had rocked the metropolis during the Civil War. A nearby armory was reassuring. Thus, while the land for the Seventh Regiment Armory was provided by the city, the $600,000 needed to build the Italianate rock-faced granite-and-red-brick structure was raised by private subscription. The building was virtually complete in 1879 when a fair—opened by President Rutherford B. Hayes and vigorously supported by

The exterior of the Seventh Regiment Armory, designed by Charles W. Clinton, on what is now Park Avenue, as it appeared shortly after its completion in 1880.

William B. Astor and William K. Vanderbilt—was held to raise funds for furnishing and decorating the interior. The handsome sum of $140,000 quickly flowed into the regiment's coffers, and a number of New York's leading decorators were commissioned to brighten various rooms. Louis Tiffany and his Associated Artists—painters Samuel Coleman and Lockwood de Forest and textile designer Candace Wheeler, with Stanford White as consulting architect—were placed in charge of the decor of the important Veterans' Room and its adjoining library. After the Associated Artists completed their task, the Veterans' Room emerged as an extravagant fusion of chain-coiled columns, wrought-iron chandeliers set with rows of electric bulbs, windows made of vivid chunks of stained glass, a fireplace of turquoise-colored Tiffany blocks, all beneath an oak-beamed ceiling daringly decorated with vigorous aluminum-paint stenciling. "The preponderate styles appear to be the Greek, Moresque and Celtic, with a dash of the Egyptian, the Persian and the Japanese in the appropriate places," *The Decorator and Furnisher* magazine of May 1885 observed with understandable astonishment.

Though jeweler Charles L. Tiffany was proud of his son's

work at the Seventh Regiment Armory and elsewhere, he was disturbed about Louis's lifestyle, which he considered to be, in a word, "fast." He wisely kept him away from the lordly family firm, whose customers were more interested in an oriental pearl dog collar than in one of Louis's dragonfly pins with Favrile Glass wings and a peridot body. In order to keep a parental eye on his son and other children, Charles Tiffany now asked Stanford White to design a structure which would house him and his family in separate apartments under one roof. The money available for the project was almost limitless, for in their Union Square location the firm was annually selling some $6,000,000 of diamonds in their revolutionary

The Armory's Veterans' Room, which White worked on with Louis Tiffany and his Associated Artists, cemented the close relationship between the two men. The room is a chamber of exotic opulence.

One of the most astonishing houses ever to rise in New York was the one that Stanford White designed for the Tiffany family at the northwest corner of Madison Avenue and Seventy-second Street in 1882. Divided into apartments for Charles Tiffany, the founder of the great jewelry emporium, and two of his children, the bluestone and yellowish brick behemoth was demolished in 1936.

new six-prong setting. It was a good thing that Tiffany's was doing so well, for their mansion, located on the northwest corner of Madison Avenue and Seventy-second Street, was eventually to cost the impressive sum of $500,000. Portions of the top three floors and the great expanse under the roof were reserved for Louis Tiffany, and while Tiffany was in charge of the interior decoration, White also brought in John La Farge and Augustus Saint-Gaudens to lend a hand. In these vast spaces—with their gargantuan fireplaces, their constellation of hanging lamps, their sumptuous multicolored materials—White and Tiffany surpassed even the fantasies of the armory. Here was made visible Louis Tiffany's dictum that "God has given us our talents, not to copy the talents of others, but rather

to use our brains and our imagination in order to obtain the revelation of True Beauty." The "True Beauty" revealed within the chambers of the Tiffany mansion most certainly came from no copybook.

Though Louis Tiffany made some rough preliminary sketches to show what he thought the exterior should look like, in reality the mansion was the climax of everything that Stanford White had learned during his Richardsonian apprenticeship, all the Queen Anne curiosities, all the Romanesque recollections. Indeed, the composition was an urban brick-and-stone translation of the shingle villas White had run up in Newport. Standing upon a basement and ground-level podium of North River bluestone, the house rose

The Tiffany house's arched entranceway with its portcullis reflected White's immersion in the Romanesque during his apprenticeship to H. H. Richardson.

STANFORD WHITE'S NEW YORK

through three stories of light brown and ochre Roman brick—a material that would become a leitmotiv in White's work—with decorative terra-cotta elements to an immense roof of silvery black tiles. The fortresslike quality of the dwelling, which Charles Tiffany wanted emphasized, was proclaimed by the elaborate iron portcullis within the Richardsonian arched entranceway, while the broad expanse of glass on the top floor announced the presence of the artistic son, whose studio lay behind it. "The Tiffany House gave me the same impression that some of the grand 17th century chalets in Switzerland give, a sort of vastness as if it had grown like a mountain," the English aesthetician Sir Edmund Gosse wrote in the *Critic*. "It is the house that pleased me most in America." The Tiffany house might please Sir Edmund, but by the time of its completion in 1885, its style was falling out of favor with fashionable Americans. The rigors of the Swiss Alps were about to be abandoned for the delights of the Roman *campagna* and the charms of the Ile-de-France.

At the heart of Louis Tiffany's vast top-floor studio was a central four-sided fireplace designed to resemble the bole of a tree. In his monograph, The Art Work of Louis C. Tiffany, *Charles de Kay reported that the room was filled with "suspended lamps of many shades of red, rose, yellow and creamy white. . . ."*

CHAPTER 5

BESSIE SMITH OF SMITHTOWN

During these first successes, Stanford White, following the pattern of unmarried sons and daughters in the nineteenth century, continued to live with his parents. His father, now retired and in failing health, adored his younger son and often complained that he rarely saw him. Richard Grant White's attachment is not surprising, for in Stanford he saw the flowering of his own creativity. In contrast, his elder son, Dick, who was living in New Mexico, had made a career of financially disastrous gold-, silver-, and lead-mining ventures. Almost the only time that the family heard from him was when he appealed to Stanford for help.

The architect tried from time to time to find positions for his brother, as he did in 1896 when he had him appointed an assistant to the superintendent of works at the University of Virginia, but these attempts almost always ended in disaster. In 1902, already in his fifties, Richard was still writing to his younger brother begging him to stake him to yet another chase after golden rainbows:

Elizabeth Springs Smith, always called Bessie, whom Stanford White married in 1884, was a Smith of the Smiths of Smithtown, Long Island. Until her death at the age of ninety she reverently spoke of her husband as "Stanford White."

Dear Stan,

I wrote you a little while ago asking you if you could send me $1200 to prospect with for the year. Please answer me? Let me know by telegram if you can send me anything.

White's taste and gift for society, elements of his personality which had been first revealed in Boston, now came into full bloom. Edward Simmons remembered the architect's overwhelming gregariousness and generosity: "Stanny was the great driving force of all our entertainments," he wrote in *From Seven to Seventy*, "and as he was the type of man who always paid for everything and shoved anyone aside who tried to get in first, my lack of money did not make much difference." White was already well on his way to becoming one of New York's preeminent clubmen.

But in the middle 1880s much of White's social life centered on the apartment building for bachelors, the Benedict, which McKim, Mead & Bigelow had designed in 1879 on the east side of Washington Square. Modeled on the English concept of gentlemen's chambers, the structure attracted tenants as varied as the reserved Yankee William Rutherford Mead and the flamboyant romantic novelist F. Marion Crawford. It even achieved literary immortality when, in *The House of Mirth*, Edith Wharton gave a similar name to Lawrence Selden's apartment house and has Lily Bart exclaim: "Ah, yes—to be sure: The Benedick." The person who most frequently drew White to the Benedict was Joseph Wells, a sensitive, neurotic, talented draftsman in the office. Wells's manner of conversation was vivid and startling. He once announced that if he had not had to work for a living he would have made a superb Communist, and when, after he had vehemently declared that the American West held nothing worth visiting, a dubious listener asked if the young draftsman had been there, Wells shot back: "I've been to Hoboken and that's far enough!" Joseph Wells also possessed a profound knowledge of decorative design and the partners adored him. Mead was to write:

Too much cannot be said of his unswerving devotion to the Italian Renaissance. He was a direct descendant of Samuel Adams, and I think no one ever got further from New England ideas than Wells did.

Most certainly no one other than McKim at 57 Broadway had as profound an effect on Stanford White's taste. After "Wellzey's"—White's pet name for him—death of pneumonia in 1890 at the age of thirty-seven, Stanford White was to say that his "hand was seen all through our work."

Accompanying Stanford White's sociability was a sure eye for talent, something akin to the possession of perfect pitch by a musician. It surfaces again and again in the memoirs of the period, stretching from, early in White's career, the recognition of painters like J. Alden Weir to the championship of the interior decorator Elsie de Wolfe, at the very end of his life. Typical is the way White in 1887 in Newport took over and promoted the relatively unknown John Singer Sargent, who was in America to paint the portrait of the wife of the New York banker and philanthropist Henry G. Marquand. White had heard of Sargent from Frank Millet, and he quickly invited the artist to New York, where he organized a dinner with a glittering guest list and shamelessly badgered those present to give Sargent commissions. Among those who agreed was a granddaughter of Commodore Cornelius Vanderbilt, Mrs. Elliott Shepard, for whom McKim, Mead & White was designing a house in Scarborough, New York. Sargent always felt that this American visit had been the turning point of his career. Eventually White would arrange for Sargent to paint one of his most telling male portraits, that of Edwin Booth in the Players Club.

At 57 Broadway, White was already famous for the rapidity of his problem solving and the sureness of his pencil. With his blazing red hair and his stagy handlebar mustache, the tall, long-limbed architect seemed to radiate energy and enthusiasm. "To White architecture meant color first, then form, texture, proportion and plan last of all," one colleague observed. "Mr. White," William A. Boring wrote, ". . . dazzled us by his flashes of genius."

Augustus Saint-Gaudens's marriage in 1877 to what the architect had dubbed a "cross-grained . . . frau" had profoundly disturbed White. Time would prove that his assessment of Augusta Homer was on the mark, but it is also undoubtedly true that White felt betrayed by the wedding of his best friend, for throughout his life the architect revealed a happy faculty for male bonding.

In 1880 Charles McKim was to play the part of the go-between who introduced White to the woman who would make him the ideal wife, a woman who was no "cross-grained . . . frau" and who, either from nature or from intention, could turn a blind eye to White's male bonding as well as to his other peccadillos. McKim had been asked to design a house at St. James, on the North Shore of Long Island, for Prescott Hall Butler, a distinguished lawyer who had been a Harvard classmate. Butler had married Cornelia Smith, one of the five daughters of Judge J. Lawrence Smith of Smithtown, Long Island. The Smiths of Smithtown—the title is a decent republican one akin to the Scrantons of Scranton, Pennsylvania—were authentic New York gentry, allied to such eminent families as the Floyds, the Nicollses, and the Van Cortlandts. According to a family legend, when McKim brought his young partner to visit the Smiths, Bessie, the youngest of Judge Smith's daughters, spied on White— who was once described as having an "all-over cowlick"—through

A photograph of Bessie and her four sisters taken about the time she met White in 1880. Bessie is first on the left. White always had a good relationship with his sisters-in-law and designed houses for two of them near the Whites' own country house at St. James, Long Island.

a keyhole and exclaimed, "Oh, I'd give anything to touch the hair on the top of his head!" The eighteen-year-old Bessie Springs Smith, tall, with an ample figure which over the years expanded to Rubensian and beyond, immediately attracted White, but it would take three years of what Prescott Hall Butler characterized as "a protracted siege" before she agreed to marry him.

White was undoubtedly physically drawn to Bessie, but it is also certain that the position of the Smith family, well off, stable, with impeccable social credentials, was also a factor in his decision to wed. There was another factor as well. The meeting with Bessie Smith came at the right moment in White's career. Earning more than $12,000 a year from the firm—a considerable sum—he was now ready to set up his own establishment. White, it must also be said, had also grown weary of competing with his father for the attention of the dates he brought home, for Richard Grant White, the collector of erotica, remained a ladies' man until the end.

Bessie is not to be underestimated. A good example of her shrewdness was her unshakable decision to have a separate bank account and to rebuff the blandishments of the Knickerbocker Trust—where White had his accounts—to move her money there from the Second National Bank. Bessie's notes to her husband—invariably dashed off in pencil—reveal a woman running her houses with a sure hand:

> Dear Stanny—
>   Please remember about the servants bath-room at St. James & the leaks in the roof. Also please begin to think about the work around the barn yard. . . .
>   The Drapers dinner is at 7:30 tonight!

White always treated his wife with great respect, and his letters are filled with affection and concern. Typical is one written in February 1905—scarcely a year before his death—to Bessie, who was in Italy. The four-page missive opens with "My darling Bess" and closes "With many kisses and hugs" and "lovingly," hardly the words of an uncaring or estranged husband. It is also significant that

This photograph, made shortly after White's wedding, captures something of the architect's energy which dazzled Bessie. "His voice would rise with his enthusiasm . . . like a bagpipe," she once recalled. The solar topee would indicate that the photograph was taken during one of White's many extended journeys abroad.

Bessie was liked by White's colleagues. When she became engaged, McKim wrote to her: "But how can I say it—*it* that I wish to say— that I wish you both all that is good and best and happiest—and to you that you are very welcome among us whose office is now yours." Bessie always called McKim "Kimmie," and it would be in a cottage near the Whites' country home in St. James, that, in September 1909, Charles McKim would die.

The list of those who organized Stanford White's bachelor's party at Martinelli's at the corner of Fifth Avenue and Sixteenth Street the night of February 2, 1884, and the names of those who attended, discloses just how wide the thirty-year-old architect had cast his net. Already "There goes Stanford White!" could be heard on Fifth Avenue when he passed, and heads turned when he attended an opera at the Academy of Music or dined on lobster and champagne at Delmonico's Twenty-sixth Street establishment, where he was known as a "regular." "Stanny always looked to me like Vercingetorix," Edward Simmons observed. "I used to say that his proper clothing was a wolfskin and battle-ax, and that he should let his hair grow long . . . Unlike most big men, he was always in a hurry, dashing about here and there and with his body always slightly bent forward . . ."

The organizers of the soiree included Saint-Gaudens, who decorated the menu card; Loyall Farragut, son of the admiral; J. Alden Weir; Robert Goelet; Richard Watson Gilder; and Prescott Hall Butler. Among the guests that evening were McKim, Mead, and Wells; the painters Thomas Dewing, Frank Millet, Albert Pinkham Ryder, and William Merritt Chase; Frederick Law Olmsted; and David Maitland Armstrong. Gilder stood and recited these verses:

> *I'm a young man*
> *From Man-hat-tan!*
> *I'm the tail of the kite*
> *Of McKim, Mead, and White,*
> *My hair stands up straight,*
> *I am five minutes late,*
> *And, as usual with me,*
> *In a terrible hurree!*

Saint-Gaudens's wedding present to the Whites was a glorious marble bas-relief of Bessie arranging her wedding veil before a mirror. The handsome Italian Renaissance—style frame is by White. Bessie always kept the sculpture with her. It was photographed here in the apartment she took at 24 East 84th Street after her husband's murder.

The wedding took place on February 7, at the old Protestant Episcopal Church of the Heavenly Rest on Fifth Avenue between Forty-fifth and Forty-sixth streets. Saint-Gaudens presented the couple with a white marble bas-relief of Bessie, Dewing did an oil

White's good friend, Thomas Dewing, painted Bessie about the time of her marriage. The architect was particularly fond of the portrait and designed an elaborately carved frame for it. His sure eye for the correct frame for a work of art made him the designer of choice for many artists, including William Merritt Chase, Augustus Saint-Gaudens, and Abbott Thayer.

Stanford White's protean talents are wonderfully illustrated by the necklace with two golden crabs clasping an oriental pearl, which he designed as a wedding present for his bride. The crab had a special significance for the architect. The inscription on Saint-Gaudens's medallion commemorating the famous 1878 walking trip in France notes that it was done "in the month of the crab" and White set a bronze crab with his name inscribed on it before the Farragut Memorial.

ELEVATION OF FRAME

PLAN

SCALE ¾" = 1'-0"

portrait of the bride, while one of White's gifts was a necklace he himself designed: golden chains terminating in two gold crabs clasping an iridescent oriental pearl. The crabs resembled the one with his initials on it which he had embedded before the Farragut Memorial.

The couple's six-month European honeymoon was to be the prototype of many of Stanford White's journeys abroad, a dazzling combination of social calls, artistic sightseeing, intensive scouting for furniture, objects, and architectural elements for clients and hoped-for clients, and, always, staggering spending. (Among the items purchased were all the tiles from a demolished Turkish mosque.) There were the prescribed Grand Tour visits to Munich, Vienna, Rome, Naples, and Paris, where he acquired a particularly fine set of tapestries, but the ancient monuments of Athens came as a revelation. "Modern Athens is an extremely uninteresting city," White wrote to his father, "bright, new and horribly dusty—and, shades of Phidias, there is a steam tramway running around the base of the Acropolis." But the ruined temples of the Acropolis— the Parthenon and the Erectheum—lured him into hours of solitary sketching. The architect did not want these sacred precincts touched. Only the 1862 revolt against King Otho, he informed the elder White, had "saved the Parthenon and Erectheum from complete restoration at the hands of the Bavarians."

Near the end of his long engagement-party tribute to White, Richard Watson Gilder had recited these lines:

> *If you built on the plan*
> *Of the unfortunate Queen Anne,*
> *Which was good till it began*
> *To be copied by young apes*
> *From the lakes to the capes—*
> *If you ran this into the ground*
> *You're a duffer and a hound,*
> *And I'll bid you farewell*
> *And start you for hell.*

OPPOSITE:

For Thayer's life-sized painting of an angel, White created a heavenly classical frame.

The Whites' second and only surviving child, Lawrence Grant White, called "Larry" by family and friends, was born in 1887.

In 1885, the Whites rented a characterless frame farmhouse at St. James on Long Island's North Shore. They bought the place in 1892, and over the years the architect transformed what became known as Box Hill into a graceful country seat.

STANFORD WHITE'S NEW YORK

The focus of the dining room at Box Hill was its wall of glass and the great window seat which stretched the full length of the room.

Though he was about to banish to stylistic never-never land both the Queen Anne of the Goelet house and the Romanesque of the Tiffany mansion, the architect would, in 1885, design one last masterpiece in the style of "the Great Mogul." The structure was a six-story yellow Roman brick commercial building commissioned by the Goelets. Gracefully rounding the southeast corner of Broadway and Twentieth Street, the Goelet Building expresses a restrained lyricism which is emphasized by the rhythmic Romanesque arches of its high base. In *The Brown Decades*, Lewis Mumford, a devout believer in the theory that American architectural apostolic succession moves from Richardson to Louis Sullivan to Frank Lloyd Wright toward a blessed modernism, singled out this build-

STANFORD WHITE'S NEW YORK

By a curious coincidence, two buildings designed by *White* which illustrate his farewell flourish of Richardsonian Romanesque and his hearty embrace of the Renaissance manner stand cater-cornered from each other at Broadway and Twentieth Street. The Goelet Building, completed in 1887, on the southeast corner of Broadway and Twentieth Street, was a robust tripartite composition of base, shaft, and crown cornice whose dominating design element is the rhythmical Romanesque arches of the base. At the northwest corner of the intersection, the Warren Building, designed in 1890, is sheathed in a surface encrusted with swags, rosettes, and palmettes from the decorative vocabulary of the Italian Renaissance. Both buildings survive, though the Goelet has had four stories added to it.

ing for high praise: "Here again was a building above fashion. That nothing so fresh was done in New York for a whole generation is a manifold cause for astonishment. Did the architects themselves fail to realize how far they had gone?" Mumford's question is purely rhetorical, for the Goelet Building is honored only at the price of dismissing all that White and McKim accomplished later on: ". . . it far outweighs the learned eclecticism for which the architects became popular and famous." The "learned eclecticism" is evident in the Warren Building, which White designed at the northwest corner of Broadway and Twentieth Street at the beginning of the 1890s. Here the façade is a veritable feast of terra-cotta ornament carried out in a jocund prodigality of Renaissance design. Like a resplendent butterfly emerging from its chrysalis, McKim, Mead & White was casting aside bargeboards and bottle glass, shaped shingles and somber shades, for McKim, Mead & White was about to become McKim, Mead, White & Gold.

CHAPTER 6

A DOOR THROWN OPEN

There are structures that speak a new language, record and foretell a change as profound as when Galileo, by observing that the earth moved around the sun, re-created the astronomical universe. One thinks of Jefferson's porticoed Virginia capitol in Richmond, the father of a thousand Taras, or William Le Baron Jenney's 1884 Home Insurance Company Building in Chicago, whose iron-and-steel frame transformed edifices from shell-enclosed crustaceans into structural mammals with their skeletons hidden behind their skinlike curtain walls. The building which marked this sea change in Stanford White's architectural life brought together three essential realities: White and McKim's readiness to strike out into a new style, a draftsman in the office with the necessary knowledge to execute that style, and a patron prepared to accept the style.

Henry Villard, born Ferdinand Heinrich Hilgard in 1835 in Bavaria, emigrated to the United States in his late teens and became

Stanford White's first opportunity to design a complete house of worship came in 1888 with the commission for the Judson Memorial Church on the south side of Washington Square. The architect's devotion to the Renaissance is proclaimed by the church's hooded entrance, which evokes those of a number of Italian structures, including that of the Scuola di San Marco in Venice.

a part of what Richard Grant White had characterized as the "Teutonic alluvium" spreading over the center of the country. He settled in Illinois, assumed the more mellifluous name of Henry Villard, and became a journalist working on various German-language abolitionist Midwestern newspapers. By 1866 Villard was the Washington correspondent for the prestigious Chicago *Tribune*. But he was an ambitious man and a newspaperman's life offered only limited prospects. At the beginning of the 1870s, Villard met the financier Jay Cooke, who was rushing to complete his Northern Pacific Railroad to its western terminus in Oregon. In order to achieve that goal Cooke needed cash—some $1,000,000 in bonds each month—and hordes of people to settle along the right-of-way and thus generate business for the line. Henry Villard was intrigued by the prospect of reaping a quick fortune, and when in 1873 he made a journey back to Germany, he went as an agent for Jay Cooke & Company. Villard began recruiting Germans for the Northern Pacific's lands and also began encouraging them to invest—through him—in Northern Pacific bonds. He was so successful that by 1880 Henry Villard controlled more than $30,000,000 worth of the railroad's stock and had become the line's president.

Like A. T. Stewart, the new multimillionaire wanted a residence that would proclaim his spectacular rise in the American capitalist hierarchy, and in 1881 he took the first step, purchasing a plot of land on Madison Avenue across from St. Patrick's Cathedral. When it came time to select an architect, it was natural for him to turn to McKim, Mead & White, for Villard was married to Helen Garrison, daughter of the celebrated abolitionist William Lloyd Garrison, a close friend of McKim's father. To solidify matters further, Helen Villard's brother was married to McKim's sister, Lucy. In fact, McKim, Mead & White were already designing stations and a hotel in Portland, Oregon, for the Northern Pacific. A letter from Stanford White to Bessie Smith from the West at this time reveals the architect's rather jaundiced view of his client:

My darling Bess,

I have been awfully busy since I arrived here last Monday. Tuesday I saw his royal highness Mr. Villard. I do not know whether the papers have been full of him and his party in New York; but here you think of nothing else. The whole air is full of it: if he was a King there could not be more of a row.

I came here on business, and have kept clear of the whole affair as much as possible; but I had to go up to Tacoma with him and his collection of English and Yarmen Dukes, Countesses, and high Cockalorums generally. I cannot say I was much impressed, and I think myself just as good as any ———— old Lord in his party—don't you?

The type of residence Henry Villard desired—a house for himself and five attached ones for others, all behind a unifying common façade—was very different from the general run of assertive, individualistic palazzi being constructed on New York's avenues. White and McKim quickly developed a plan for the Villard Houses—as the block came to be called—a deep U-shaped form with Henry Villard's own residence occupying the southern wing of the letter. But with McKim taken up with projects in Boston and

Henry Villard, the German-born promoter and journalist who in 1882 commissioned McKim, Mead & White to design the complex of houses named for him. Villard lived in his house only from December of 1883 until the spring of 1884.

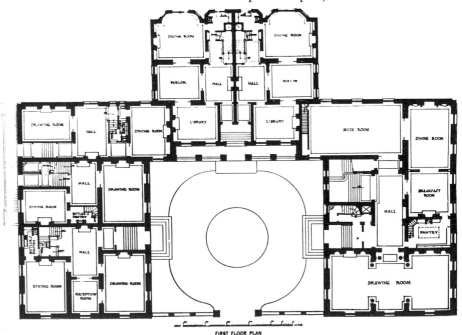

FIRST FLOOR PLAN

The entire south wing of the Villard houses—now part of the Helmsley Palace Hotel—was originally occupied by Henry Villard. The north wing—which now houses the Municipal Art Society—contained separate residences for, among others, Harris C. Fahnestock, a banker who had been involved in the financing of Villard's Northern Pacific Railroad, and for his son, the stockbroker William Fahnestock.

Newport and White often in the West, the responsibility for completing a design for the exterior was turned over to Joseph Wells. A first visit to Europe in 1880 had reinforced Wells's passion for the Italian Renaissance, and now, discarding any suggestions of French châteaux or English castles, the erudite designer turned for inspiration to Rome's fifteenth-century Cancelleria, attributed to Bramante. The choice was not surprising, for, as Royal Cortissoz noted, "the works of Bramante constituted his Bible." It also reveals the soundness of Wells's taste, since the qualities, in the words of the English critic John Addington Symonds, which made Bramante the foremost architect of the Italian Renaissance, "the proper subordination of beauty in details to the grandeur of simplicity and to unity of effect," were also the qualities called for in the design of the Villard project. The exteriors of the Villard Houses, with their subtle double-scaled rustication, their crisp string courses, their reserved but clearly articulated window moldings, and their quietly assertive cornices, set a new standard for New York residential design. Curiously, though, while the exterior details of the Villard Houses are Italian, the form which White and McKim gave to the structures is French and relates to the private residences of eighteenth-century Paris such as Germain Boffrand's Hôtel de Montmorency. The center of the complex is nothing less than a *cour d'honneur*.

The Villard Houses have one irredeemable flaw and that is the material used to construct them, brownstone. In preliminary sketches Stanford White had indicated that a rough gray granite or limestone should be used, but Villard hesitated. J. P. Morgan and August Belmont dwelt behind brownstone façades and the immigrant promoter did not have the self-assuredness of Alva Vanderbilt, who had broken with tradition and opted for glistening sandstone for the Francis I château that Richard Morris Hunt was completing for her at Fifth Avenue and Fifty-third Street.

Thus, while the Villard Houses, in their design, look to the future, their somber, gummy walls make it difficult to fully appreciate just how good that design is. This would be the last time that

McKim, Mead & White would be forced to go to the chocolate quarries of Connecticut and New Jersey for building material. After the Villard Houses the firm would shift to the sparkling, light palette advocated by the Ecole des Beaux-Arts and thus help transform Gotham's streets and avenues into sun-splashed thoroughfares of luminary limestone and creamy marble. The importance of this tonal revolution, led by White, is given an interesting interpretation by Edward Simmons:

> I believe Stanford set the fashion here of building to our latitude. We had formerly copied the British in our homes, using red brick and brownstone, with small windows, rep curtains, and nailed-down carpets of warm dark brown or scarlet—the stuff of the north for New York City, which is the latitude of Madrid.

The original interiors of Henry Villard's house expressed an aesthetic as schizophrenic as that of its exterior. Once again Alva Vanderbilt had conjured up the future in the luminous white-and-gold Louis XV salon that Hunt and the French decorator Gilbert Cuel had devised for her, and once again Villard equivocated. The dreary triple drawing room facing Madison Avenue came not from Stanford White—whose extraordinary gifts as a decorator had not yet been fully recognized by McKim—but from others in the firm who had engaged the noted woodworker Joseph Cabus to carry out the scheme. The rooms are choked with dark, overly elaborate marquetry in designs lifted from the English Renaissance. It is all retardate Queen Anne Revival, and as the architecture critic Montgomery Schuyler wrote in 1883, the Queen Anne revivalists "sucked the dregs of the whole English Renaissance. Unhappily, nowhere in Europe was the Renaissance so unproductive as in the British islands."

Where Stanford White was permitted to work his will, sweetness and light are the order of the day. Passing through the entrance doorway, whose fanlight and side lights are of jewel-like Louis Tiffany glass, one steps into an entrance hall which is as golden honey compared to the murky molasses of the triple drawing room.

The *Villard Houses, on Madison Avenue between Fiftieth and Fifty-first streets, as they appeared in 1918. They were, in fact, six separate houses behind a common brownstone façade. Based upon Rome's Cancelleria, the edifice introduced the Italian Renaissance style to New York.*

W*hite employed glittering mosaics by David Maitland Armstrong to provide a note of Renaissance opulence for the Villard entrance hall. The noble fireplace on the right is by Saint-Gaudens.*

This fireplace, which was originally located in the Villard dining room, was embellished by Saint-Gaudens with overmantel figures and with fountains on either side of the fireplace holding dolphins which recall those on the base of the Farragut Memorial.

White has used cheerful Siena and Galena marbles for the walls, which rise to vaults of sparkling glass mosaic of an antique Roman pattern by David Maitland Armstrong. The hall's magnificent fireplace, designed by Augustus Saint-Gaudens, has for its overmantel a carved image of a woman in classical garb, the Lar or household spirit of the place, flanked by putti holding flaming cornucopias. The single word beside her is "Pax," a part of the prayer ancient Romans recited each morning before their hearths. The stairs to the second floor rise on Eschallon marble treads with a balustrade enriched by panels of lovely *brèche violette* marble, past a wall clock whose bronze face is surrounded by incised signs of the zodiac designed by White, and executed by Saint-Gaudens. The whole is lit by John La Farge's elegant leaded windows.

At its eastern end, the entrance hall opens into a two-story music room, a marked contrast to Cabus's rabbit warren at the western end. In order to signal the room's function, White set above a musicians' gallery five plaster casts of Luca della Robbia's "Can-

One of the most beautiful objects in the Villard House is the zodiac clock which Stanford White and Saint-Gaudens designed for the grand stairway's first landing.

toria" from the Duomo in Florence, a monument of the Italian Renaissance. Nevertheless, the tall room with its barrel vault, its wood wainscoting in French Renaissance design, and its floor of white mahogany and English oak laid in a Fontainebleau pattern has about it the air of some antique chamber of the time of Francis I. The atmosphere here is decidedly French.

By the time Villard moved into his still incomplete house in December 1883, it was because, in his words, "I have nowhere else to go." Through miscalculation the cost of the Northern Pacific had exceeded the original estimates by $14,000,000. Villard, it turned out, was a shrewd promoter who knew nothing about railroads. With the line's debts approaching $30,000,000, both Villard and the Northern Pacific were bankrupt. One month after he settled into his dream house Villard resigned, not only as president of the Northern Pacific but from all the directorships of the numerous other companies in which he had invested. His downfall ruined thousands of Northern Pacific bondholders, and angry crowds gathered nightly outside his residence, incensed by the rumor that he was building the luxurious block-long palace for himself alone. In the spring of 1884, with matters becoming threatening, Villard and his family fled to Dobbs Ferry. In 1886 his house was purchased by Mrs. Whitelaw Reid.

Elisabeth Mills Reid, daughter of copper baron, financier, and philanthropist Darius Ogden Mills, was burdened by none of the diffidence that dogged Henry Villard. After all, her sister-in-law Ruth Livingston Mills would summon Stanford White to fashion one of the Hudson Valley's stellar country houses and would challenge *the* Mrs. Astor for New York Society's Papal Tiara. Mrs. Reid, who would cut a wide swath as an international hostess in Paris and London, wanted rooms equal to anything in Mayfair or on the Avenue du Bois. With a patron of this ilk White finally had a chance to prove himself. The plain vault of Villard's music room was elaborately decorated and gold-leafed, while La Farge was commissioned to paint the lunettes at either end. In the northern one, Mrs. Reid herself, looking every bit as composed as Paulina Borghese reclining upon Canova's marble couch, is depicted enjoying a concert. With perhaps vengeful gusto White swept away the fusty marquetry of the rooms on Madison Avenue, and, in place of three constrictive boxes, created one capacious, dazzling French-style salon with polished marble columns and pilasters topped by gilded Corinthian capitals. The walls of this shimmering salon were animated by Boucher-like paintings by the French artist P. V. Galland, who had decorated grand drawing rooms from Paris to Petersburg. The appointment in 1888 of the inexhaustibly ambitious and pomp-

In 1886, the editor/publisher of the New York Tribune, *Whitelaw Reid, and his wife, Elisabeth, purchased the Villard House for $350,000. It was the Reids who commissioned Stanford White to redecorate the Music Room and the Drawing Room.*

STANFORD WHITE'S NEW YORK

ous Whitelaw Reid as United States Minister to France facilitated the selection by Stanford White and Mrs. Reid of furniture appropriate to this marvelous chamber.

The December 1883 issue of the magazine *Building* announced that "Aladdin's lamp never revealed a hall more magnificent" than the one Stanford White had created for Henry Villard. But the Villard house was a private residence. What White needed to properly publicize his possession of that most rare of combinations, flair and taste, was a public commission. It came to him in 1885 and in a perfect place to proclaim the American Renaissance in triumphal splendor. The Protestant Episcopal Church of the Ascension on Fifth Avenue at Ninth Street was a typical Richard Upjohn brownstone preaching barn, too broad for its length with balconies that marked it as more evangelical theatre than church. Indeed, when it was constructed in the early 1840s its low church, anti-ritual congregation asked Upjohn to omit a chancel so that there would be no chance of some future rector performing "masses" within its Reformed precincts. The result was a flat wall, embellished by three thin lancet windows filled with mediocre stained glass. By the 1880s the parish had relaxed to the point that it had ceased looking for Jesuits under its beds and the new rector, E. Winchester Donald, was permitted to become an aesthetic miracle worker. In his engaging memoir, *Day Before Yesterday*, David Maitland Armstrong succinctly sums up the genesis of the project:

> When Doctor E. Winchester Donald became rector of the Ascension, it was one of the ugliest churches inside that were to be found in New York, which is saying a good deal, but Doctor Donald had a great love of beauty, and he raised the money and chose the artists who made it what it is today.

Dr. Donald selected Stanford White as his architect impresario. White instantly demolished the Ascension's balconies and, with Dr. Donald's approval, brought in a company of artists—John La Farge, Frederic Crowninshield, David Maitland Armstrong, J. Alden Weir, Joseph Lauber, and Frederick Wilson—who would

THIS
DO·IN
REMEMBRANCE
OF·ME

At the Church of the Ascension on lower Fifth Avenue, a pair of angels by Louis Saint-Gaudens, Augustus's talented brother, float against a mosaicked background by David Maitland Armstrong.

make Ascension's windows collectively one of the supreme achievements in American stained-glass art. Dr. Donald originally had also hoped to extend the church westward and thus build a true chancel, but once again the recusant vestry balked. Stanford White was thus forced to devise a brilliant plan which would accomplish by artifice what had been forbidden to architecture. As the re-decorating scheme evolved, it had been decided that a painting by John La Farge would be its centerpiece. It is not surprising that La Farge was given this commission, for through his wife, Margaret, a granddaughter of Commodore Matthew C. Perry, he was allied by marriage to August Belmont, Ascension's most illustrious parish-ioner. In order to give the church's flat western wall a trompe l'oeil vista, White designed an immense gilded perspective frame—whose pilasters and other details recall Bramante—to enclose La Farge's spectacular painting of the Ascension of Christ. While the painting's composition is generally based on that of Raphael's "Transfiguration" in the Vatican, La Farge sought to give an added sense of depth by using as background mountains painted in the manner he so admired in Japanese screens and prints. In fact, La Farge became so obsessed with the background that, in the midst of the project, he set off with Henry Adams on a journey to Japan where, at Nikko, he found the perfect peaks for his picture. This extended journey, as Charles Baldwin reported, had immediate ramifications:

> The reredos and the architectural setting are by White—who worked at top speed. Yet the scaffolding remained in place for years. La Farge, it seems, needed time. White vainly, and profanely, urged him to hurry. The rector, too, objected, and quite rightly, to the delay. "It's perfectly hellish," said White. To which Donald replied: "Thank you; I'm a clergyman, White, but you express my sentiments admirably."

To complete the desired sumptuous effect of the chancel, which he had lined with amber Siena marble, White asked Louis Saint-Gaudens, Augustus's brother, to execute two high-relief angels, after Donatello, and commissioned David Maitland Armstrong to create two golden mosaic angels, after Giotto.

At the Church of the Ascension—building on his experience at Trinity Church Boston—Stanford White made real the dream of the artists of the American Renaissance that, like the artists of the Italian Renaissance, they could work together to raise monuments of surpassing beauty. Later, to complete the furnishing of the chancel, Charles McKim would design a superb French walnut pulpit inspired by a medieval panel he had found in Paris. It was of work such as the ensemble at Ascension that McKim was thinking when he wrote to Edith Wharton: "By conscientious study of the best examples of classic periods, it is possible to conceive a perfect result . . ."

During his last visit to his hometown in the spring of 1905, Henry James was stunned by the unexpected perfection he found in

the chancel of the Ascension. Speaking of his affection for the old churches of lower Fifth Avenue, James, in *The American Scene*, informed his readers:

> It reached its maximum for me, I hasten to add, on my penetrating into the Ascension . . . and standing for the first time in presence of that noble work of John La Farge, the representation, on the west wall, in the grand manner, of the theological event from which the church takes its title. Wonderful enough in New York, to find one's self, in a charming and considerably dim "old" church, hushed to

admiration before a great religious picture, the sensation, for the moment, upset so all the facts. The hot light outside might have been that of an Italian *piazzetta . . .*

A collaboration similar to that at Ascension was carried out at the barnlike Roman Catholic Church of St. Paul the Apostle on Columbus Avenue at Fifty-ninth Street. The seat of the New York parish of the recently founded Paulist Fathers, the curious structure was designed in 1876 by Jeremiah O'Rourke and its somewhat macabre appearance is due to the fact that the body of the church was constructed of old stone from the Croton Aqueduct while its towers are of material salvaged from the reservoir which occupied the Fifth Avenue site where the New York Public Library now stands. St. Paul's architectural distinction comes from the transformation of the interior begun by White in 1887. At St. Paul's, Stanford White did not have to rely on trompe l'oeil effects to produce the illusion of a chancel, for here, where Rome reigned, there was a real one of enormous size. In this vast sanctuary White could express that feeling for religion which had surfaced briefly, intensely, in his late teens and which, if one considers the care lavished upon the chancel of the Church of the Ascension, the amazing portal of St. Bartholomew's, and the elegant Madison Square Presbyterian Church, surely never totally deserted him. The main altar, constructed of marble that White had found in an ancient Sienese monastery, is sheltered by a noble baldachino inspired by that of Santa Maria Maggiore in Rome. Dominating the chancel's hemicycle, the baldachino unabashedly revels in its luxurious materials—porphyry, onyx, alabaster, and gold—proclaiming at once the Church triumphant and the Church magnificent. Near it glitter windows by John La Farge, above it are murals by Robert Reid, while atop it angels, the first important commission by Frederick MacMonnies, complete the magnificent composition.

MacMonnies was typical of the talented artists whose careers owed everything to Stanford White. Having met him in 1881 when MacMonnies was a sixteen-year-old assistant to Saint-Gaudens, the

As a setting for John La Farge's great painting of the Ascension of Christ in the Church of the Ascension, Stanford White audaciously designed a golden proscenium arch. The effect is to dissolve the sanctuary's western wall and present the sacred event as dramatic theatre. Both the painting and the church have recently been sensitively restored.

STANFORD WHITE'S NEW YORK

architect saw at once the makings of a great sculptor and he and McKim paid to send him in 1884 to the Ecole des Beaux-Arts. "My dear White . . . I received the $1,000 by cable . . . today," MacMonnies would later write from Italy, "and I once more have to thank you for saving my life." While he was directing the decoration of St. Paul the Apostle, White designed the graceful columnar base for MacMonnies's elegant statue of Nathan Hale in City Hall Park.

The architect's concern about the financial plight of artists, a concern which stemmed in part from his firsthand knowledge of his father's precarious existence, was a continuing interest throughout his life. Typically, Child Hassam, when he was having pecuniary problems in the 1890s, knew where to turn for help:

> Dear Stanford:
>
> Do you want that picture of mine? I am just back from the country and am hard up as hell and it would help me very much just now.

In 1888 Stanford White was given the opportunity to design a complete church, though construction was not to begin until 1893. The site, a magnificent one on the south side of Washington Square, provided the rare opportunity in Manhattan to position a building so that it could be seen from the middle and far distance, not just from close up, the view generally enforced by the unimaginative "grid plan" imposed upon the city in 1811. The church, commissioned by a Baptist congregation which had been in existence for half a century, commemorated Adoniram Judson, much of whose life had been spent in the worthy but jejune task of translating the Christian scriptures into Burmese. Judson Memorial would be the first New York structure to benefit from the philanthropy of the Rockefellers, for the founder of the family fortune, John D. Sr., had just moved from Cleveland to New York to be near his recently hatched Standard Oil Company of New Jersey. Sincere Baptist that he was, John D. found time to teach Sunday school on the one day when he was not swallowing up competitors.

The collaborative artistic efforts which marked the Villard Houses and the Church of the Ascension continued with White's redecoration of the vast Roman Catholic Church of St. Paul the Apostle on Columbus Avenue at Sixtieth Street. The project lasted from 1887 until 1890 and included the high altar by White, with its angels by Frederick MacMonnies, stained glass windows by John La Farge, and a magnificent hanging sanctuary lamp by Philip Martiny.

The architecture of the church is the embodiment of a notion which swept through Protestant denominations in the 1880s that the Gothic was the province of the Roman Catholics and the Episcopalians, while the earlier Romanesque and classical styles more accurately expressed the Reformation's intent to return to the theology and the manner of primitive Christianity. The architectural historian Leland Roth has accurately analyzed the sources of the design:

> The arcades of the sanctuary, the campanile, the flat golden Roman brick and the details of the entire building are based on the eleventh and twelfth century Italian churches, most specifically Santa Maria in Cosmedin, Rome, c. 1120–1200.

The sanctuary, constructed of brick similar to that used in the Tiffany house, stands upon a high podium that is deeply channeled and decorated in a guilloche pattern. The façade is further embellished with terra-cotta elements and by bits of marble used in a way to suggest that they are the fragments of some venerable shrine where Peter or Paul might have prayed.

The essential brilliance of the design of the Judson Memorial Church, though, lies in the way White has solved the problem of transporting what is fundamentally an open arcade and campanile from sunny Italy to the less clement clime of New York. The arcades which form the body of the church are sometimes blind, sometimes filled with glass, while all of the arcades of the ten-story tower, except the top one, are similarly enclosed. Yet the overall effect is one of openness, of airiness. The secret lies in the fact that Stanford White has set the glazing of the windows and the brickwork of the blind arcades well back from the plane of the wall. This, together with the use of boldly profiled cornices, causes them to partially dematerialize. With the Judson Memorial Church one witnesses the artifice of an architect grown to greatness.

The Italianate character of the Judson church, of the high altar of St. Paul the Apostle, and of the chancel of the Church of the Ascension reflected the flowering in America of a seed planted early

in the nineteenth century. It was a tradition composed of elements as diverse as Thomas Cole's painting "The Colosseum, Rome" of 1832; Thomas Crawford's bas-relief "Venus as Shepherdess" of 1840; Margaret Fuller's cry "Those have not lived who have not seen Rome"; Nathaniel Hawthorne's *The Marble Faun* of 1860; and Henry James's *Daisy Miller* of 1878. For White and for Charles McKim—both of whom were to become in 1904 incorporators of the American Academy in Rome—it was a tradition encapsulated in Saint-Gaudens's remark that Italy was a "door thrown open to the eternal beauty of the classical." Stanford White's personal love for Italy vied with his love for France and revealed itself not only in his architecture but also in the heavy Genoese velvets and variegated columns and extravagant baroque furnishings with which, throughout his life, he garnished his and his clients' houses.

The four upper stages of the conspicuous campanile of the Judson Memorial Church—seen here in 1905—recall the twelfth-century campanile of the Roman church of San Giorgio in Velabro. Judson Memorial's fine stained-glass windows are by John La Farge.

CHAPTER 7

THE GARDEN

By the 1880s Stanford White's life and career were settling into the course they would keep until his death. Shortly after their marriage the Whites had moved into a brownstone at 56 West Twentieth Street. Their son, Lawrence Grant White, described the house in his unpublished journal *Before the War: Memories of the Years 1887 to 1914*:

> It was the usual small brown-stone house of the period, with a high stoop and a dark, narrow hall; but my father, who was already making a name for himself as an architect, had disposed, in the interior, antiques which he had brought back from his European travels, so that the rooms were far different from the current Victorian horrors. I can just remember the walls of the Dining Room; they were covered with blue-and-white mattress ticking, serving as a background for a collection of Italian Renaissance majolica plates.

When, in December 1884, a first child, a son, was born to the young couple, they named him Richard Grant after Stanford

Madison Square Garden, completed in 1891, was incontrovertible proof that Stanford White was a force to be reckoned with in Gotham. The Garden's high terra-cotta-embellished arcades, built to shelter the throngs waiting to attend events such as the Horse Show, were added only after a prolonged fight with New York City officials who argued that they encroached upon the public sidewalks. Their inspiration came from such Renaissance precedents as Brunelleschi's beautiful Loggia degli Innocenti in Florence.

White's father. Eighteen eighty-four had been a good year for the elder White. With the publication of his highly readable and witty novel *The Fate of Mansfield Humphreys*, Richard Grant White had finally received the literary recognition he had sought for so long. This tale of an American, Mansfield Humphreys, who marries an English woman of gentle birth, Margaret Duffield, and brings her to America, allowed Richard White to enumerate at length the faults of his native land. Here is Margaret's impression of the Fifth Avenue Hotel on Madison Square:

> Everything seemed painfully big, brilliant, and obtrusive. The great white building that glared in the sun; the high-colored carpets that glowed equally in the light of the day or in the blaze of gas; the throng of people who seemed to have no time for anything but motion, not even to talk, but who rushed about in silence with sad faces, out of which sharp eyes looked doubtfully . . .

While Richard Grant White, in his reactionary Anglophilia, viewed Gotham's growth in wealth, population, and vitality as a deluge about to drown what remained of the city's grace and gentility, his son saw it as a force to be channeled and used to build a metropolis which would show, as Stanford White often announced, that "America was taking a leading place among nations."

The 1880s were indeed one of New York's exuberant decades. The number of inhabitants passed 2,000,000 and in the cyclopean mansions rising along Fifth Avenue gold was rapidly replacing silver as the metal of choice for flatware while the exotic hothouse orchid was pushing aside the native American Beauty rose as the prime posy for table decor. The English journalist George Augustus Sala, who spent four months in New York at the beginning of the 1880s, found the city more expensive than Paris. A room—without meals—at the Brevoort was an astounding $7.00 a day, while the daily rate for a suite—with meals—at the Fifth Avenue Hotel was a phenomenal $30. Sala also reported that it was virtually impossible to buy a decent cigar for less than a staggering 18 cents.

This was, it should be noted, at a time when a bricklayer earned between $12 and $15 a week and stone masons and plumbers received between $12 and $18. In his definitive study, *The Saga of American Society*, Dixon Wecter reports that the necessities for nobs had also skyrocketed. In the decade of the 1880s, a butler's wage rose from $40 a month to $75, while that *sine qua non* of fashionable feasts, the canvasback, shot up from $2.50 to $8.00 a brace. But then this was the era when high society's procedural theologian, Ward McAllister, announced in his fatuous magnum opus, *Society as I Have Found It*, that "a fortune of only a million is respectable poverty." As more and more Gothamites climbed above the "respectable poverty" line, not a few members of *le beau monde* were following McAllister's advice and constructing ballrooms "to be used for one night, and made large enough to comfortably hold . . . one thousand or twelve hundred people." While this might be costly, it allowed one to decide who would be frolicking nearby. Stanford White would transform this extravagance into magnificence.

The year 1885 was to mark the death of both Richard Grant Whites. Stanford White's father, though suffering for some time from heart disease and having at least one serious seizure, continued to write and to find pleasure in playing Brahms with his string quartet. But in the spring he grew weaker, and on April 8, died. His funeral was in the venerable Church of St. Mark's in-the-Bowery, which the family had attended because its pews were less expensive than those at the other nearby Episcopal church, fashionable Grace. Stanford White felt his father's death deeply, but with the estate not large enough to cover even Richard Grant White's debts, his immediate concern was for his mother. Shortly after his wedding, White had written reassuring her that she could always count on him:

> My darling Mama,
>   I hardly had any time to speak to you before I went off—but we will have plenty of time before we sail. I do not wish you to think

that you are in the least bit less to me now than before I was married. If you have any troubles, you must always tell them to me, and you may be sure I will do everything in my power to help you.

During his honeymoon White's frequent letters home reveal an extremely close bond between mother and son. Typical is this one written on July 14, 1884, from St. Moritz, Switzerland:

My darling Mommie,
Here we are safe and sound, seven thousand feet in the air in the heart of the Alps. It is not cold!—Oh, no!—and if in an inadvertent moment you take a drink, you have to be taken in and thawed out in front of the kitchen range. The swell rig is fur-lined caps and overcoats; and Bess and I deliberate every morning whether we shall put on three or four undershirts.

After another paragraph, the letter concludes: "Bess sends all kinds of love—lots to Papa and Dick and to thyself, my darling mother, from thy loving son." Whatever kind of love Bess did in fact send, she understood her husband's filial feelings and gave her approval when he asked to bring his mother to live with them. Bess and Alexina White would have an uneasy relationship until the old lady's death in 1913 at the age of ninety-two.

Late in the summer Stanford White was to suffer another and this time totally unexpected bereavement, for on August 9 his son suddenly died of cholera. The seven-month-old infant was buried in the churchyard of St. James Episcopal Church, which had given its name to the Long Island village where that summer, for the first time, the Whites had rented a simple frame farmhouse. St. James, only a few miles from Smithtown, was the home of three of Bessie White's sisters: Kate, the wife of the Reverend James B. Wetherill, who had assisted at the Whites' wedding; Ella, Mrs. Devereux Emmet; and Cornelia, Mrs. Prescott Hall Butler. After the birth in 1887 of their second son and only surviving child, Lawrence Grant White, St. James became the center of Bessie's life. She spent entire summers there while her husband, as was typical of the time for people of their social position, came out for weekends. Lawrence Grant White describes the setting in his journal:

> Not far from the church there is the crest of a hill commanding an extensive view of the harbor and Sound. This place, which my mother loved since her childhood, she bought soon after she was married; and there we have spent our summers ever since. On the property, there stood a totally undistinguished wooden house which was three times enlarged by my father to its present proportions, and altered beyond recognition.

The farmhouse, together with some fifty acres, was not in actuality purchased until 1892. Christened Box Hill after its boxwood garden, the property would become White's country seat, permitting him to attempt to fulfill his maxim: "Always live better than your clients."

When, in 1904, Barr Ferree published his sumptuous volume *American Estates and Gardens*, "devoted to the architectural and gardening features of some of the more notable of recent American country houses," included among the stately homes the architect had designed for others was "The House of Stanford White, Esq. St. James, New York." Box Hill was also a place where he could line walls and ceilings with split bamboo, build a staircase of apple-green tiles, run a stretched window seat along one entire side of the dining room, and, in a kind of proto-high-tech act, leave unadorned a steel beam spanning the drawing room. It was also a house where he could bring together furniture and bibelots for no reason other than that they pleased him: an English Sheraton sideboard, antique American chairs, French tapestries, Venetian mirrors, gilded baroque putti. "The bamboos form the background for a rich collection of objects," Ferree reported, "which this indefatigable collector has gathered from all parts of Europe."

White was as involved in the design of the gardens at Box Hill as he was in that of the house itself. He was constantly searching for new and better shrubs, for handsomer urns and statues, and in 1899 he began negotiations with Eugene Lentilhon, the contractor in charge of the demolition of the old reservoir on Fifth Avenue between Fortieth and Forty-second streets, for cornice stone for garden seats. The cornice, it turned out, had already been spoken for, but White did manage to get some of the reservoir's granite, which he used for walks and walls. The quality of Stanford White's garden design is evident from a letter written to him on September 24, 1903, by W. L. Partridge, who was working with Frederick Law Olmsted, Jr.'s firm at Harvard: "Mr. Olmsted has asked me to prepare some drawings of landscape work for Harvard University. The plan of your garden at St. James, L.I., is exactly the kind of thing he wants."

If one were looking for the essential Stanford White of the late 1880s and early 1890s, a structure designed by him which would reveal the progressive flowering of his creativity the way that Trinity's central tower did in the 1870s and the Casino's inner façade did in the early 1880s, the choice would have to fall on Madison Square Garden. This edifice was truly, as Grace Mayer observed in *Once Upon a City*, "a multiplication table of elegant adaptabilities and gaieties." "The Garden" lingers in the consciousness of New Yorkers the way that the demolished Pennsylvania Station does, the architectural equivalent of the *Normandie* or the *Hindenburg*, a luminous achievement of man which, in its too brief life, lit the landscape like a sheet of lightning. Madison Square Garden was the quintessential exposition of the Beaux Arts conception that while a structure should be well planned and practical it should also, in its materials and design, bring joy and beauty to the urban scene and thus help socialize the populace into civility. Architecture, for the practitioners of the Beaux Arts tradition, was engineering with a human face.

The original motivation for constructing the Garden was the need for an elegant, spacious setting for New York's annual National Horse Show. The social importance of this November spectacle cannot be overestimated. E. Berry Wall, "The King of the Dudes," placed it perfectly in his breezy memoir, *Neither Pest nor Puritan*: ". . . held in Madison Square Garden, the New York Horse

Show was timed to open about a week before the Opera. Indeed, the Horse Show Ball was the first big event of the season."

Writing in *The New Metropolitan* for April 1903, John Corbin emphasized the radiating glamour of the event:

Not only the Garden, but the neighboring stretch of Fifth Avenue swarms with fresh and characteristic life during the week of the horse show. The hotels are jammed, the shops crowded, the theatres filled. For weeks beforehand the most fashionable dressmakers are so over-busy that they refuse to take orders, unless, indeed, one is able to play upon their sympathies by the plea that the gown is wanted for the horse show.

New Yorkers who compared the purlieu of their show—P. T. Barnum's utilitarian Hippodrome—with that of the English equivalent, London's commodious Agricultural Hall, were frankly embarrassed. In the late 1880s the property between Twenty-sixth and Twenty-seventh streets on the east side of Madison Square was purchased by the National Horse Show Association, and a new body, the Madison Square Garden Corporation, was organized to erect an appropriate building on the site. Among the devotees of equine flesh purchasing shares in the corporation were some of the city's most glittering names: James Stillman, Adrian Iselin, Herman Oelrichs, James T. Hyde, and, naturally, J. P. Morgan, who was president. White was not only the project's architect; he was also an investor, eventually owning more than 1,000 shares. Indeed, beginning in the 1890s Stanford White was regularly receiving telegrams from brokers reporting that they had bought him hundreds of shares in this or that company. By the end of the decade, he was the recipient of letters such as the one from H. B. Hollins & Co. at the corner of Wall and Broad streets, asking for a check for $78,000 "In accordance with the terms of your subscription to the Preferred and Common Stock of the above-named company . . ."

Stanford White's growing interest in investing, particularly in the stock market, was fueled not only by the increasing income from his architectural practice but also by Bessie's inheritance from Mrs. A. T. Stewart, the widow of the man who had built the astonishing marble palace at Fifth Avenue and Thirty-fourth Street. The connection is spelled out in Lawrence White's journal:

> My maternal grandmother lived at 537 Fifth Avenue, and I can just remember being taken there to lunch with her. . . . Her aunt, Mrs. A. T. Stewart, the widow of the man who had invented department stores, had been the richest woman of her time . . .

Bess had been left $100,000 by Cornelia Clinch Stewart, but her mother had received $5,000,000. Upon the deaths in 1889 and 1890 of Bessie White's parents, a portion of this very considerable fortune came to her. Construction of the Garden began in the summer

As this view down Madison Avenue in the 1890s makes clear, Madison Square Garden, with its cheerful combination of yellow brick and buff terra cotta, was a striking contrast to the omnipresent brownstone that had for decades been the favorite building material of New York.

STANFORD WHITE'S NEW YORK

The heart of Madison Square Garden was the vast amphitheatre, whose steel truss roof spanned 277 feet. At the center of the roof was a 55-by-135-foot skylight that could be opened to provide ventilation. This photograph shows the amphitheatre during the 1906 New York State Democratic Convention which nominated William Randolph Hearst for governor.

of 1889 and was essentially complete by June 1890. One of the first noteworthy happenings was the fatal chill caught there in November by August Belmont while judging a coaching event.

"There is something tremendously imposing in its vast dimensions and . . . something exceedingly agreeable in the excellence of its proportions and the impression of combined strength and gracefulness in its constructive details," announced the New York *Daily Tribune* when the centerpiece of the complex, the amphitheatre, opened on June 16. With permanent seating for 10,000 and room for 4,000 more when chairs were placed on the floor, the amphitheatre would be the site not only of the horse show but of P. T. Barnum's and John Ringling's circuses, of the Westminster Kennel Club Show, of New York's annual flower show, and, in 1900, of America's first automobile show. In the amphitheatre Jack Dempsey would become a pugilist hero, and there, in 1924, after a record-breaking 103 ballots, the Democratic Party would deny the presidential nomination to New York's favorite son, Alfred E. Smith.

The buff-brick structure with its flamboyant decoration in terra cotta—a material championed and perfected by White—held other wonders in addition to the amphitheatre. There was a resplendent 1,500-seat concert hall designed in a Louis XVI manner which could be converted into a shimmering white-and-gold ballroom; a restaurant; a roof garden with a stage and tables for 300; and the 1,200-seat Garden Theatre. When the theatre opened in September with the English comedy *Doctor Bill*, the New York *Times* panned the play but praised the playhouse, saying that "no fault can be rationally found" with it.

In addition to its superb planning and incomparable facilities, Madison Square Garden had two matchless assets going for it. The first was its location. In the last two decades of the nineteenth

This layout of the Garden's third story shows Stanford White's genius for planning as well as for design. He has brilliantly fitted together the Garden Theatre, dressing rooms, and the ballroom.

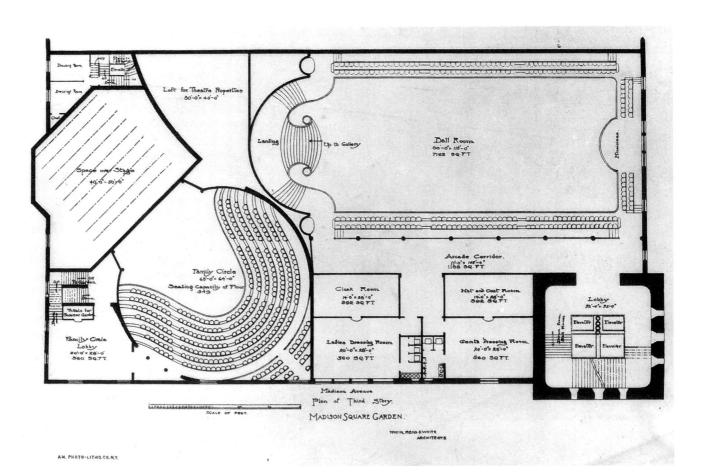

century Madison Square was the crossroads of New York. Its coming of age had been marked by Lorenzo Delmonico's decision in 1876 to move his dining establishment up Fifth Avenue from Fourteenth to Twenty-sixth Street. The editors of the New York *Herald* had immediately grasped the importance of this northward migration: "When the Nestors of the restaurant business in New York open a new house, it is as much an event as the opening of a royal bottle of Johannisberg or of Château d'Yquem . . ."

Madison Square was where august Fifth, the address of the city's rich "avenoodles," crossed bold Broadway, the thoroughfare which even the procrustean gridiron plan could not make straight. At Madison Square the alluring shops of the Ladies' Mile came to a collective halt as Broadway, from Twenty-third Street to Long Acre Square at Forty-second Street, became show business's original Great White Way. This was the Broadway where, in the words of Richard Harding Davis, "the theatres blaze out on the sidewalk like open fireplaces." This was the legendary Broadway where, at the Abbey Theatre in 1896, the no-longer-young Sarah Bernhardt could still bring an audience to its feet with the mere magic of her voice; the street where, in 1905, after a quarter of a century, Lillian Russell deserted Tony Pastor's Theatre for Proctor's and created a sensation with the tune which became her theme song: "Come Down Ma Evenin' Star." It was this Great White Way which so enthralled Theodore Dreiser's Sister Carrie:

> The walk down Broadway, then as now, was one of the remarkable features of the city. There gathered, before the matinee and afterwards, not only all the pretty women who love a showy parade, but the men who love to gaze and admire them.

Around Madison Square too were the city's fashionable hotels: the St. Germaine; the Fifth Avenue, whose lobby was the headquarters of New York's Republican Party; the Brunswick, at which the colorful spring coaching parades began; the Victoria; the Holland House; and the 400-room Hoffman House, whose bar boasted Bouguereau's faintly scandalous "Nymphs and Satyr."

The Madison Square Garden tower—seen here in 1895—dominated New York's midtown skyline. Below the open loggias of the upper stages of the tower were seven floors of apartments. The complex's roof garden, where Stanford White was murdered, lay behind the colonnades surrounding the top of the building.

THE GARDEN

The Garden's second great asset was its Tower, which at 341 feet vied with Joseph Pulitzer's World Building for the title of New York's tallest structure. Inspired by the part-Moorish, part-Renaissance campanile or "Giralda" of the cathedral in Seville, the Tower was completed only because of Stanford White's persistence. With costs for the Garden skyrocketing past $4,000,000, the Building Committee, loath to spend another half million on a grandiose belvedere, began lofting trial balloons regarding an abbreviated tower or no tower at all. But White, who knew that Madison Square Garden without an attention-getting spire was like a theatre without a marquee, began frantically lobbying the committee members. Finally, the contractor, David H. King, Jr., driven almost to distraction, announced: "White is raising such a row about this thing that he is simply hounding me into my grave. . . . We've got to shut him up somehow. I'll put up half the amount necessary if you will raise the other half." In a sensational aesthetic move, White crowned the Tower with Augustus Saint-Gaudens's 19-foot, 2,000-pound sheet-copper figure of Diana, Roman goddess of the hunt and, naturally, of horses. "Well, you've designed quite a pedestal for Saint-Gaudens this time," George Fletcher Babb quipped.

When at 10 P.M. on November 2, 1891, the Tower was, as it were, unveiled, White saw to it that the event did not go unnoticed. For an hour spectacular fireworks—one of his passions—showered the structure and its gorgeous finial with rainbows of color. The architect himself, with the unrelenting attention to detail which was already his trademark, was seen, hot and grimy, moving from installation to installation making certain that the flares and skyrockets and Roman candles were fired in proper sequence. White's instinct concerning the indispensability of the Tower was correct, for it made Madison Square Garden, like Richard Upjohn's Trinity Church before it and William Van Alen's Chrysler Building after it, one of those structures which cut into the skyline of New York with an unmistakable silhouette. "There is probably not in the whole world a handsomer building," cooed the New York *Herald.*

"The tower is surmounted with a statue, in whose outlines I recognized the Diana of the great sculptor, Saint-Gaudens," observed the novelist Paul Bourget on arriving in New York in August 1893. "It is the first evidence of beauty that I have seen since I set foot outside of the ship." It is not surprising that Bourget, a Frenchman, would approve of this Diana, for Saint-Gaudens's inspiration was a Diana by the eighteenth-century French sculptor Jean Antoine Houdon, and followed the French tradition of showing her unclad. As William Vance points out in his two-volume study, *America's Rome*: ". . . when Augustus Saint-Gaudens conceived his only nude in the French image of Diana, he went Houdon one better by having her actually drawing her bow to let fly an arrow. The absurd pose made her a beautiful figure atop Stanford White's new Madison Square Garden, besides making her useful as a windvane. It also made her instantly recognizable as a virgin rather than the French Venus she certainly might have been mistaken for."

The guise of virgin goddess failed to fool the eagle-eyed Anthony Comstock of New York's beguilingly named New York Society for the Suppression of Vice. Comstock had recently given Herman Knoedler quite a surprise by raiding his dignified Fifth Avenue gallery and departing with, among other things, a photograph of a Bouguereau nude. The voice of Comstockery was soon being heard concerning the very large female in the buff in full public view atop Madison Square Garden. As the New York *Mercury* reported:

> During the past two weeks there has been a marked change in the character of the frequenters of Madison Square. Formerly this beautiful little park was the gathering place of children. Now all this is changed. Occasionally a stray child may still be seen, but more generally what children come there are rushed through at breakneck speed in the tow of a nurse or some older person. In their place the Square is now thronged with clubmen armed with field glasses.

The *Mercury* went on to make clear that the gentlemen's binoculars were trained on the 19-foot Diana, which one newspaper said

Augustus Saint-Gaudens's lovely 13-foot second Diana atop the Garden tower replaced the awkward 19-foot first version of the goddess. By the time this photograph was taken in 1905, a storm had ripped away the drapery attached to her left shoulder. After the demolition of Madison Square Garden in 1925, Saint-Gaudens's only nude statue was given shelter by the Philadelphia Museum of Art.

"resembled a lady stepping from her bath." The controversy continued when, because of White and Saint-Gaudens's dissatisfaction with the scale and modeling of the original figure, they replaced her with a new, 13-foot version. Saint-Gaudens had also been upset because the metal workers had incorrectly poised his goddess on her heel rather than on her toe. The original—despite the protests of some Windy City moralists—was dispatched to Chicago to crown McKim, Mead & White's Agricultural Building at the 1893 Columbian Exposition.

It is not unlikely that the clubmen's field glasses were also employed to scrutinize the seven stories of apartments beginning at the second floor in the Madison Square Garden Tower, where White had moved in 1892. It was of one of White's Tower apartments that a stagestruck Pittsburgh girl with a bit part as a Spanish dancer in *Florodora* would write:

The room was lined with gorgeous divans and exquisitely carved antique chairs from Italy and Spain. An entire corner was taken up by one particularly lovely couch, while on the opposite side stood a large round table at which supper parties were served.

All the divans were covered with bear, tiger and leopard skins, and rich rugs of the same skins covered the floor. . . . Scattered here and there were artificial orange trees from which nestling electric bulbs, resembling oranges, shed a roseate glow over the room.

Evelyn Nesbit, that Pittsburgh girl, was sixteen when Stanford White met her in 1901.

Though White's Madison Square Garden Tower apartments—he first rented one on the sixth floor, but eventually leased one two flights higher on the top floor—became enveloped in a legend concocted of a combination of the *Arabian Nights* and the *Memoirs* of Casanova, the rather mundane reality was that the architect moved into the Tower because his West Twentieth Street house was being torn down and the new house that he had rented on East Twenty-first Street was not ready for occupancy. Among the highly respectable inhabitants of the other Tower apartments were Daniel Chester French, the architect Whitney Warren, the inventor Peter Cooper Hewitt, and Mrs. Robert Goelet, who used her flat as a painting studio. In *A Musician and His Wife*, Anna de Koven, the spouse of the composer of "O Promise Me," recalled:

Mr. White . . . often gave parties in his rooms in the tower of the Madison Square Garden. To one of these we were invited. A crescent table was covered with old golden damask and spread with orchids, lights twinkled in surrounding bay trees, a mandolin band shed music like a sprinkling fountain, and about the table were women as lovely and varied in type as he ever assembled.

And Margaret Chanler, the quite proper niece of Julia Ward Howe, expressed in her memoirs, *Roman Spring*, her frank delight in White's Tower parties: ". . . he also gave gay parties in his studio rooms, in the Madison Square Tower over which Saint-Gaudens's graceful Diana stood with lifted foot in virginal nakedness." Thus the tower and its splendorous image became all things to all men and to all women. In his short story "The Lady Higher Up," O. Henry writes: "The golden statue veered in the changing breeze, menacing many points on the horizon with its aureate arrow."

Madison Square Garden was at once a colossal achievement, a concrete image of hubris, an urban ornament, a lightning rod for animosities. It was, also, in the years immediately following its completion, the heartbeat of the city. John Corbin expressed this reality as well as anyone:

> What thronging Piccadilly is to London, what the brilliant, chattering Boulevards are to Paris, what the waltz-laden air of the garden of the Ring Strasse is to Vienna, this the Square and the Garden are to the metropolis of the new world.

It was also a momentous moment in its architect's career, for as Henry Collins Brown remarked, in his delightful *Brownstone Fronts and Saratoga Trunks*, after Madison Square Garden, "New York had readily risen to its feet in appreciation of the genius of White."

CHAPTER 8

ARCHITECT TO CLUBLAND

There was always one place where Stanford White could escape the scrutiny of the clubmen's binoculars and that was in their clubs. In his perceptive essay on McKim, Mead & White, John Jay Chapman made this judgment of White: "He was a great man in his love for everyone. Friendship was to him a form of religion." One of the manifestations of this "religion" was his penchant for male coteries, ranging from the demimondain "Sewer Club," which he, Saint-Gaudens, and others formed in rented quarters in the Benedict, to the gilt-edged social clubs which were proliferating in New York in self-conscious imitation of London's exalted male bastions. Some of these, such as the Union and the Knickerbocker, were formed to erect a silk-link fence between the possessors of "new money" who were flooding into the city and those who, if they had not actually been born with a silver spoon in their mouths, at least knew which silver fork to use. Cleveland Amory in his wickedly incisive *Who Killed Society?* quotes these apt

The Players at number 16 on the south side of Gramercy Park was Stanford White's favorite club. In 1888 Edwin Booth had purchased the structure and that same year the architect gave the brownstone a classical 2-story entrance and loggia of a type that was to be repeated on many of his private dwellings.

lines of "Chat from the Clubman," which appeared in an 1887 number of the New York social scandal sheet *Town Topics*:

> I sympathize deeply with my friend Ten Broek Van Rotterdam, who says Society is going to the dogs—that is the Knickerbocker side of it, and "Good Gawd! dear boy, what other side is there?" Look at the list. How many of the swellest of the swell today were anything at all twenty years ago—fifteen years ago even?

Some of the clubs, like the Tile, were organized by men who shared a mutual interest in the arts or in a profession, and a few, a very few in this land of puritanical diligence—the Brook, for example—were organized for sheer pleasure. Between 1893 and 1901, the number of clubs in New York jumped from 119 to 157, while membership climbed from 24,000 to 38,000, excluding some 32,000 repetitions. The proof of the accuracy of Margaret Chanler's observation that Stanford White was the "lively link between 'Philistia *felix*' and high Bohemia" may be found in the catholicity of his memberships: which included, among others, the New York Yacht Club, the Manhattan, the Metropolitan, the Racquet, the Union, the Grolier, the Riders, the Strollers, the Players, the University, the City, the Meadow Brook, and the Century. It is also supported by the fact that his firm designed more than fifty clubhouses in the United States, while in New York City and vicinity alone White cast his architectural net wide enough to snare the German Freundschaft Society at Park Avenue and Seventy-second Street, the exclusive Shinnecock Hills Golf Club, and the theatrical Lambs Club on West Forty-fourth Street.

No club, though, meant more to Stanford White than the Players. Not only did its formation in 1888 come just as his beloved Tile disbanded, but its location, on the south side of Gramercy Park, was in the heart of the quarter where White had chosen to live. There was yet another consideration. His father, with his long career as a drama critic and his interest in the English playwrights, had known the club's founder, Edwin Booth, and Richard Grant White's edition of William Shakespeare had been praised by the man who had made the role of Hamlet his own. Now the great tragedian wanted to create a club "where actors and men of education and refinement might meet on equal terms." Edwin Booth, whose father, Junius Brutus, had been the archetypal alcoholic-actor-genius, and whose brother, John Wilkes, had assassinated Abraham Lincoln, knew better than any man alive the difficulties those on the stage had in being accepted into good society. On January 7, 1888, the Players was incorporated by, among others, Mark Twain, General William Tecumseh Sherman, and the actors Joseph Jefferson and John Drew, and in May, Booth purchased from the widow of New York congressman Clarkson Potter number 16 Gramercy Park. The actor deeded the property to the club, while reserving the third floor for himself. It was natural for him to ask Stanford White, a founding member, to convert the rather dour brownstone into a clubhouse.

The architect once again revealed his sure touch in producing the correct mise-en-scène. The exterior of the 1845 Gothic Revival dwelling was vivified by having its tenuous cast-iron verandas swept away and replaced by a gracious Italianate loggia, while the club's new street-level entrance was dramatically proclaimed by a pair of projecting gas lanterns reminiscent of those on the façade of Florence's Palazzo Strozzi. Inside, White hewed to a tasteful line, carefully avoiding any sign of the flash which the hypercritical might expect to find in a theatrical society. The Great Hall, with its handsome marble mantel carved with the masks of Comedy and Tragedy, the Reading Room furnished with deep chairs and tables piled high with books and periodicals, and the Grill Room with its long members' table all combined to project an aura of a house long inhabited by a patrician family, "a beacon to incite emulation in the 'poor player,'" as Booth phrased it. Edward Simmons noted the subtle perfection of the architect's arrangement:

> It is a very beautiful club. Stanford White is responsible for the architecture and gave his services gratis, as he did at The Lambs. Men coming from the Old World say that it is the only place in

America that reminds them of home. The tonality of the rooms is like that of the very old houses of Europe.

When the clubhouse was officially opened on New Year's Eve 1888, the donor was ecstatic. He wrote to his daughter Edwina of "last night's delightful success, the culmination of my professional hopes," while White, equally pleased, exclaimed, "Even the log burned without smoking!"

Already, by the late 1880s the architect's interest in the theatre extended a good deal beyond the orderly precincts of the Players. With Bessie spending more and more time in St. James, White was often seen having late-night suppers with pretty actresses in fashionable establishments such as Louis Sherry's at Sixth Avenue and Thirty-eighth Street, convenient to the Metropolitan Opera, where he had a box, and to the theatres of Broadway. Among Sherry's specialties which drew White, as well as the men who ran the Patriarchs' balls, were oyster patties, lobster salad, aspic galantine, and mille-feuille.

Unlike the Players, the Century Association was not a new organization. Indeed its founding date of 1847 made it a veritable aboriginal in New York's clubland, while its intent to be "an association to be composed of artists and men of letters, and of others interested in promotion of a taste for the fine arts," made it both a glittering prize and an object of ridicule. A typical example of the latter is a conversation overheard by a Centurian at the New York Athletic Club: "Did you know there was a club down on Forty-third Street that chose its members for intellectual eminence? Isn't that a hell of a way to run a club?" The Century had been happily ensconced for more than thirty years in a delightful old house on East Fifteenth Street, but with its roster eight times the original limit of 100—which had given the organization its name—and with its members rapidly moving uptown, the club decided in 1889 to make the daring leap to Forty-third Street, just west of Fifth Avenue.

As with the Players, both Stanford White and his father had an intimate connection with the Century. Years before, in the days when members such as the poet William Cullen Bryant and the historian George Bancroft had made induction his heart's desire, Richard Grant White had been blackballed by the club, but in 1886, with friends such as John La Farge and Augustus Saint-Gaudens already members, Stanford White had easily been elected a Centurian. It is not surprising that the club turned to him to design its new home.

At the Century, White took for his model Sanmicheli's sixteenth-century Palazzo Canossa in Verona, another monument of the Italian Renaissance. But the architect skillfully reshaped the original to his own ends. For a club with a large number of writers

The reading room of the Players, with its comfortable English furniture and rows of periodicals and racks of newspapers, was a conscious evocation of a London gentlemen's club. Dominating the room in this 1907 photograph is the full-length portrait of Booth which White persuaded John Singer Sargent to paint. It was in place for the club's opening on January 1, 1889.

The façade of the Century
Association at 7 West Forty-third
Street drew its inspiration from
the Renaissance palaces of
northern Italy. The charming
Palladian loggia on the second
floor, where members could enjoy
the air and a cigar, is now
glazed. The Century, which had
been located on East Fifteenth
Street for more than thirty years,
moved into its new clubhouse on
January 10, 1891. McKim,
Mead, and White were all
Centurians.

among its members, White has appropriately opened up the façade to the type of literary-symbolic interpretation developed by Victor Hugo and John Ruskin. Whereas Sanmicheli's façade is a single unit whose transition from base to piano nobile is marked only by a molding, White has employed his façade to express the reality of the club behind it. The lower half of the Century, with its deeply channeled granite, its heavily barred windows, its withdrawn, almost hidden doorway, announces that these are exclusive precincts, difficult to enter. In electrifying contrast, the upper half of the façade uses smooth Roman brick, elaborate Corinthian pilasters, and profuse terra-cotta ornament around the windows to proclaim the joys of membership. This cerebral and architectural dichotomy is further emphasized by the welcoming loggia—originally open—formed by a Palladian window in the center of the upper façade set significantly just above the somewhat elusive street-level entrance. The entire composition is brought to a delightful conclusion by a roof balustrade which manifests the promise of mid-summer-night fetes.

In completing the Century, White received some help from Joseph Wells, but by now he needed no New England cicerone to guide him through the delicious labyrinths of Renaissance design. Charles Baldwin makes it clear that, by the time of the Century, Stanford White's mind and eye encompassed the entire architectural universe:

> . . . he knew that there is in architecture a natural beauty, the beauty of function, of an athlete, of a bridge or a yacht. There is also an aesthetic . . . beauty, the beauty of music, a matter of tones and shadows resulting from the clear expression of an idea . . . as in . . . the architecture of Rouen Cathedral or the Century Club.

The tones and shadows of the façade of the Century immediately placed it in the rarefied ranks of the chancel of the Church of the Ascension and the bluestone base of the Farragut.

Though the budget for the Century grew from the original modest $150,000 to something in the neighborhood of $200,000, the stipulation that there be a large library and a day-lit art gallery stretched thin the funds available for the interiors. In these interiors—where White received valuable critical advice from McKim—the architect relied on the paintings by the club's members to give color and panache to the Century's handsome and spacious but economically designed rooms. An exception was the library, where he was assisted by Francis Hoppin. According to Walker Cain, a partner in the firm of McKim, Mead & White from 1940 until 1951, Lawrence White reported that the library's high, coved ceiling had originally been covered with gold leaf.

The next club for which Stanford White fabricated a home most certainly could not be twitted for selecting its members because of their "intellectual eminence," nor did the architect have to work within the confines of a stringent budget. As James Gordon Bennett's pique was the driving force behind the establishment of the Newport Casino, so J. Pierpont Morgan's perturbation was the driving force in creating the Metropolitan Club. John K. Winkler in *Morgan the Magnificent* gives this astute summation of the city in which this financier *sans pareil* lived:

> Morgan was operating in those days in a metropolis of susceptibility. New York was the ruddy, uncouth harlot of the continent's cities, drunk on Pittsburgh steel, Ohio oil, California gold—the capital of the Gilded Age, of Canfield's, of Anna Held, of Anthony Comstock, and Koster & Bial's; of Olga Nethersole's "Sapho" and Eleonora Duse's "Camille"; of Bradley Martin's Monkey Ball and Ward McAllister's Four Hundred.

Morgan was a member of that most aristocratic club, that "mother" of New York clubs, the Union. But some of the business associates of the man who with one hand could create the United States Steel Corporation and with the other save the United States Treasury from bankruptcy fell a bit short of measuring up to the standard later enunciated by Emily Post in the first edition of *Etiquette*: "The perfect clubman is another word for the perfect gentlemen." By no stretch of the imagination could John King, president of the Erie Railroad, whom Morgan proposed for Union

J. *Pierpont Morgan, whose contretemps with the Union Club led to the founding of the Metropolitan Club, at the age of forty-five. Morgan had been involved with White in the construction of Madison Square Garden and knew that the architect could produce the sensational setting for the club that he desired.*

Undoubtedly the most luxurious clubhouse Stanford White designed was that for the Metropolitan Club at the northeast corner of Fifth Avenue and Sixtieth Street. The white marble edifice is still under construction in this June 3, 1893, photograph. The occasion is the visit of the Infanta Eulalia of Spain. The marching men are members of the fashionable Seventh Regiment and the building behind the reviewing stand is the New Netherland Hotel.

membership in 1890, be considered a gentleman. Not only was King blackballed by the Union, but club members spread demeaning stories about him, saying, among other things, that he ate with his knife. Morgan, whose credo was "Don't get mad, get even," determined to found a club so dazzling that the social princelings of the Union would melt in the heat given off by its incandescence. It was in this spirit that, according to E. A. L. Bennett, a librarian of the Metropolitan, he summoned Stanford White and ordered him: "Build a club fit for gentlemen. Damn the expense."

With Cornelius and William K. Vanderbilt—who had had an in-law blackballed by the Union—as well as a passel of Goelets, Iselins, and Roosevelts in tow, Morgan had the artillery to carry out his campaign. When, in the spring of 1891, nearly half a million dollars was spent on a spectacular site at the northeast corner of Fifth Avenue and Sixtieth Street and a building budget of $700,000, which soon grew to a million dollars, was announced, it was clear that the new club was prepared for grandeur and for war. The clubhouse of what was quickly dubbed "the Millionaire's Club" would overlook Grand Army Plaza, whose southern border was occupied by Cornelius Vanderbilt's awesome 100-room French château while to the east and west posh new hotels—the Plaza, the Savoy, and the New Netherland—were rising. Yet the Union did not quail before this costly panoply. Shortly after Morgan announced that the Metropolitan would have 650 members, the New York *Times* asked a former Union governor if it were possible for a club to take in that many members at a jump and still be considered exclusive? The answer that shot back was an unqualified "Of course it isn't!"

The inspiration for the general form of the Metropolitan club is the Palazzo Pandolfini in Florence, attributed to the painter Raphael. Like the Metropolitan, the Pandolfini consists of a massive main block with its principal entrance on the side. Because of the lavish budget, White did not have to create an opulent effect out of brick and terra cotta as he had done so skillfully at Madison Square Garden and the Judson Memorial Church and at the Century. Here

he could fulfill the Beaux Arts dream of seeing his designs carried out in the supreme building material, marble. The Metropolitan Club's base—begun in 1891—is of white Tuckahoe marble which rises in deeply channeled courses to a superb molding of acanthus clusters and rosettes. Above this line, the material is fine white Vermont marble matched in quality only by that used in the construction of the New York Public Library. The fenestration of the clubhouse is admirable, as the simply framed windows of the ground floor give way to the richly framed windows of the second level embellished with medallions carrying the letter "M," while the third-floor windows have above them plain panels framed by con-

In this view taken shortly after it opened in 1894, the photographer has inscribed the Metropolitan's popular nickname on the print. The house just to the north is that of Elbridge T. Gerry designed by Richard Morris Hunt. The Gerry chateau has given way to the Pierre Hotel, but the Metropolitan Club remains a Gotham glory.

soles. The square windows of the top floor are linked by festoons of fruit to the cornice, which is one of the handsomest in the city. Projecting six feet beyond the façade, it is of marble and copper with a design that relates to that of the Erechtheum in Athens, which had so enthralled White on his honeymoon. By August 1893, as *Town Topics* noted, the club's façade was already something of a local sensation: "The exterior of the new Metropolitan Club at 60th Street and Fifth Avenue is now practically completed and is being generally pronounced the neatest and most imposing club structure in town."

The exterior is, in fact, but a chaste foil for the lavish magnificence of the interior. Typical is the West Lounging Room on the first floor, which sweeps 85 feet along the club's Fifth Avenue side and whose windows were positioned so that members could discreetly view the St. Patrick's Day parade. White had wanted the Parisian firm of Allard et Fils, whose work for Richard Morris Hunt at Marble House in Newport he had greatly admired, to carry out the decoration of this and the club's other major interior spaces, but Alva Vanderbilt, who owned Marble House, objected. She coveted the prestigious commission for her protégé, Gilbert Cuel. The architect had already opened negotiations with Allard in 1892, but when the Building Committee reported that William K. Vanderbilt—Alva's husband—and his brother Cornelius had each contributed $50,000 toward completion of the clubhouse, White gave in. Upbraided by another architect, who told him that he should have stuck to his guns, White gave a blunt reply: "It's a damn lot of money."

The West Lounge is in the Louis XIV style, considered the most safely masculine of the Bourbon modes. The chief decorations of the room's oak walls are octagonal panels depicting the twelve labors of Hercules based on those of Louis Le Vau's Galerie d'Hercule in Paris's seventeenth-century Hôtel Lambert. Had they been noticed, they might have elicited a responsive chord from the tired bankers, brokers, and industrialists who frequented the chamber. One can but wonder, though, what their reactions might have been had they divined that the ceiling's northerly panel, painted in a Boucher-like manner by Pereli, glorifies Fortuna, goddess of chance, while the southerly one celebrates Mercury, god of commerce, trade, cheats, and thieves. The mottled-gray-and-red marble fireplaces at either end of the lounge are particularly fine, but these fireplaces and the fact that Cuel used imported French craftsmen for much of the work in the building led to serious threats from New York's Ornamental Plasterers and Shop Hands Society. The resulting brouhaha almost prevented White from keeping to his promised deadline of the end of February 1894. Edward Simmons remembered:

> Stanny had bet a large amount with Ogden Goelet that he would have the club finished on the specified date. Just at the last moment the workmen struck. The mantelpieces, of which there were a large number, had not been polished in the state of New York and the unions demanded that they be done over again. There was no time the night before the limit expired, but I knew Stanny had a plan, so I went up to see the fun.
>
> Stanny and the contractor had a line of boats filled with the necessary materials waiting at the North River, and another line of carts and workmen to bring them up. A thousand men and women were waiting in the street—masons, handy men, scrub women, and what not. At six o'clock sharp every trades-union workman had left; then in came the army.

Stanford White, needless to say, won his bet.

The supreme interior of the Metropolitan Club is the Great Marble Hall, one of the city's most dazzling spaces. Here White's hand is everywhere. Entered through a Palladian archway similar to that which forms the loggia of the Century, the two-story hall is almost a cube—53 by 54 feet and 45 feet high—and the architect's use of black-mottled white Vermont marble in thinly sliced decorative panels reflects his devotion to yet another Renaissance masterwork, Pietro Lombardo's fifteenth-century church of Santa Maria dei Miracoli in Venice. On three sides of the hall these marble-paneled walls rise to galleries supported by 12-foot-high columns

STANFORD WHITE'S NEW YORK

topped by gilt Ionic capitals that reach up to a splendid white and wine-red coffered ceiling. On the fourth side is the hall's glory, Stanford White's majestic X-shaped grand stairway with its beautiful balustrade after designs by the seventeenth-century Huguenot ironworker Jean Tijou. Here is a sublime example of those two beauties of which Baldwin spoke: the "beauty of function" in the economy of space required for the staircase, which is pressed hard against the hall's north wall, thus allowing ample opportunity for its use as a ballroom, and the "beauty of music" expressed in the masterful line and proportion of the X, which breaks at last at the stairway's foot like a fountain of liquid marble.

The final cost of the Metropolitan Club approached the astounding sum of $2,000,000. Ironically, Morgan eventually came to the conclusion that the business associate who had been the first cause of the club's founding had not been worthy of the effort. But the dazzling monument to pique has survived, and when he was making notes for *The American Scene*, Henry James judged Stanford White's clubhouse as the only structure worthy of being in proximity to the Grand Army Plaza's Sherman monument:

> The best thing in the picture, obviously, is Saint-Gaudens's great group, splendid in its golden elegance. . . . The refinement prevails and, as it were, succeeds; holds its own in the medley of accidents, where nothing else is refined unless it be the amplitude of the "quiet" note in the front of the Metropolitan Club.

The "quiet" note that so pleased Henry James was the presence of the Italian Renaissance in the design of the club, the manifestation of Saint-Gaudens's "door thrown open to the eternal beauty of the classical." The view through that door was a familiar one to an author who had time and again used the Quattrocento churches and palaces of Italy as backdrops for his fictions and who would praise them in his *Italian Hours*. By the time of the completion of the Metropolitan Club, the manner of the Italian Renaissance, together with that of the French Renaissance, was the style of choice for most American structures with yearnings toward

Alva Vanderbilt, née Alva Erskine Smith of Mobile, Alabama, wished to have Gilbert Cuel, a décorateur whom she had discovered in Paris, do up the Metropolitan Club's rooms. Her relentless determination and the persuasiveness of the more than $60,000,000 that her husband, William K. Vanderbilt, had inherited from his father made her wishes reality.

One of New York's most brilliant spaces is the Metropolitan Club's 45-foot-high Great Hall. The X-shaped staircase has a forged iron balustrade embellished with plaques carrying a gilded letter "M" which some wits said stood for "Morgan." During parties, the landing serves as a musicians gallery.

Among Stanford White's numerous club memberships was one in the extremely exclusive Brook. It was formed in 1903 by William Jay; William K. Vanderbilt, Jr.; Oliver Belmont; White; and others who wanted a club which provided continuous twenty-four-hour service. The name was derived from Tennyson's poem "The Brook": "For men may come and men may go, / But I go on forever." The Brook briefly occupied a town house White did over for it on East Thirty-fifth Street, but in May of 1905 the club moved into another town house White had renovated at 7 East Fortieth Street. To that structure, shown here, the architect added a 2-story entrance and colonnade similar to but more restrained than the one he placed on the façade of the Players. In the 1920s the Brook moved to 111 East Fifty-fourth Street.

The origins of the Harmonie Club go back to 1852 when it was founded as an exclusive German-Jewish organization under the name "Gesellschaft Harmonie." Over the years its membership has included Seligmans, Sulzbergers, and Auerbachs. The club's present home at 4 East Sixtieth Street—the low white marble building in this 1910 photograph—was designed by Stanford White in 1904. Though still occupied by the club, the structure's height was raised and other changes were carried out in 1935 by Benjamin Wistar Morris.

magnificence. The exception was the ecclesiastical where many patrons still clung to Gothic pieties. The honor of this achievement belonged primarily to Richard Morris Hunt and to McKim, Mead & White, and the achievement has not gone unnoticed or uncensured. In the mid-1890s the American critic Russell Sturgis came down strongly on the side of the firm's Queen Anne-style houses because

For the clubhouse of another organization of actors and those interested in the stage, the Lambs, Stanford White turned to an Adamesque Federal style. This was appropriate since the group took its name from the English essayist and critic, Charles Lamb, and his sister, Mary. Located at 130 West Forty-fourth Street in the Theatre District, the handsomely restrained red brick and white marble clubhouse opened in 1904. It is still there but the Lambs have strayed.

"the picturesque side is the best side, after all, of the work of McKim, Mead & White." Sturgis preferred their "irregular symmetry, the gables and turrets" to the "level cornice and the balanced uniformity" of the partners' classical work "because they were the most independent of the past."

This prejudice against traditional architecture in general and against the Renaissance in particular was given a kind of canonical verity by Louis Sullivan's jeremiad against the Beaux Arts style of Chicago's 1893 Columbian Exposition. Sullivan lumped together Hunt's Administration Building, McKim, Mead & White's Agricultural Building, and all of the other structures of the Fair—except his own Transportation Building—under the heading of a "contagion," a pestilential "white cloud" which would spread across the land, killing in its cradle the nascent "American" architecture. Such has been the influence of Louis Sullivan and his disciples that in *The American Mind*, published in 1950, a historian as distinguished as Henry Steele Commager readily accepted their premise that the architecture of the Fair failed to reflect the reality of America: "For what had it all to do with Chicago—the Chicago of the stockyards and steel mills and railroads, young, lusty, brawling, looking to the future rather than to the past, conscious of power, conscious of almost everything but dignity and serenity."

The logic of Commager's simple equation had been demolished long before it appeared by the critic Gurdon S. Parker writing in the periodical *The World's Work* in October, 1906: "Messrs. McKim, Mead and White have worked almost entirely in the style of the Italian Renaissance. Too much emphasis cannot be laid on the fact that this is not entirely another architectural fashion. It is not only a return to the old classical tradition of the country, it is a return to the original inspiration of the colonial period." Wiser than Mr. Commager, wiser than all the critics of the Beaux Arts, Thomas Jefferson had raised the columns of the portico of the capitol of Virginia because he knew that the Republic, in its architecture, had to reach beyond the hurly-burly of the marketplace to that so blithely dismissed "dignity" and "serenity." Interestingly, one of

White once again employed the Federal style for the Colony Club designed in 1904, the year that the Lambs opened. Located on the west side of Madison Avenue between Thirtieth and Thirty-first streets, the elegant brick building was the first large-scale private clubhouse for women in America. The graceful cast-iron balcony, which provided the architectural logic for the parlor floor's tall French windows, was lost to the widening of Madison Avenue. In 1915 the Colony moved to new quarters on Park Avenue and the old clubhouse is now occupied by the American Academy of Dramatic Arts.

Stanford White's rare writings on architecture came about after he was asked to rebuild Jefferson's Rotunda at the University of Virginia following a disastrous fire in the autumn of 1895. Though some have questioned the manner of White's reconstruction, which has now been destroyed, the architect approached the Rotunda and its creator with reverence: "He was a shining example of intelligence and culture, and it is owing to these qualities that the University of Virginia has such an exquisite group of collegiate buildings, which in their singleness are unique in the world." Thomas Jefferson's Rotunda, set amid the foothills of the Blue Ridge Mountains, would be the image behind Stanford White's New York University library set upon a Bronx hill overlooking the Harlem River.

The ideological reason for the choice of the Renaissance style is wonderfully elucidated by the political philosopher Herbert Croly in his review of the work of McKim, Mead & White which appeared in the *Architectural Record* the year of Stanford White's death:

The Renaissance as a philosophical and moral ideal is receiving its most sincere and thoroughgoing expression in the United States. A democratic nation must necessarily be humanistic and must seek the traditional sanction for its humanism in those historical periods in which the humanistic ideal prevailed. Just as the first children of the Renaissance sought to enrich and strengthen their own faith in mankind by assimilating the culture and the art of classical antiquity, so must we keep in touch with the traditional source of our intellectual, moral and political ideals by assimilating what we can of the culture and art both of the Renaissance and of Greece and Rome.

The driving force behind the Colony's founding and its first president was Mrs. J. Borden Harriman, seen here speaking at a First World War liberty bond rally. Many found the very idea of a club where women could exercise, drink, and stay overnight without their husbands shocking.

Among the Colony's founding members was Anne Morgan, who persuaded her father, J. Pierpont Morgan, to serve on the club's Men's Advisory Committee. Other early members included Amy Lowell, Emily Post, and Jane Addams.

It is no accident that the most profound, the most moving, the most successful monument in Washington is the Lincoln Memorial, a classical temple designed by a graduate of the McKim, Mead & White atelier, Henry Bacon, to house a classically inspired statue of the martyred President by Daniel Chester French. Here one is raised above the mills and stockyards and railroads which formed such an integral part of Abraham Lincoln's life, raised to dignity and, hopefully, to serenity. Here is the Beaux Arts and the Renaissance and Greece and Rome working their manifest magic.

CHAPTER 9

FROM SQUARE
TO SQUARE

Throughout the 1890s Stanford White graced New York with Beaux Arts structures which drew heavily upon the decorative vocabulary of the Renaissance. They range in manner from the buff-brick dormitory of 1896 at New York University's Bronx campus, whose economical restraint is akin to that of McKim's buildings at Columbia College, to the Bedford limestone Bowery Savings Bank at the corner of the Bowery and Grand Street, whose marvelous pediment, with its figures by MacMonnies and its richly gilded banking room, carry the extravagant habiliments of the 1893 Chicago Fair, which opened the year the bank was designed, to a modest neighborhood. Two buildings of the decade reveal White using Renaissance embellishment on structures where he employed to the fullest iron-and-steel-skeleton construction. With the 12-story Broadway addition to the New York Life Insurance Company of 1893, Lawrence Wodehouse noted in his thesis, *White of McKim, Mead and White,* that the architect resorted to the latest building techniques: "concrete piles and

One of Stanford White's less well-known masterpieces is the Gould Library—a memorial to financier Jay Gould—on Fordham Heights in the Bronx. The library's circular reading room is a breathtaking exercise in Beaux Arts panache. Its sixteen rare green Connemara marble columns with gilded Corinthian capitals support an elaborate entablature which carries a balcony studded with classical statues. The sumptuous space is enclosed by a splendidly coffered dome.

Begun in 1896, the Gould Library became the focal point of what was the undergraduate campus of New York University. The buff-colored brick, limestone, and terra-cotta structure bears a striking resemblance to the Pantheon in Rome. The colonnade, which formerly housed the Hall of Fame, was constructed between 1900 and 1901. New York University has abandoned its Fordham Heights campus, and the buildings that Stanford White designed there are now occupied by Bronx Community College.

grillage foundations supported steel columns on cast iron bases, rolled steel beams and fireproof arches." The design of the exterior, though, was true to the Renaissance, beginning with a colossal screen of Ionic columns and terminating in a clock tower adorned with sculpture by Philip Martiny. The 10-story Sherry's Hotel of 1896 at Fifth Avenue and Forty-fourth Street was completely iron-and-steel-framed and could be classified as a "skyscraper," but here White has carefully made use of the Renaissance vocabulary of

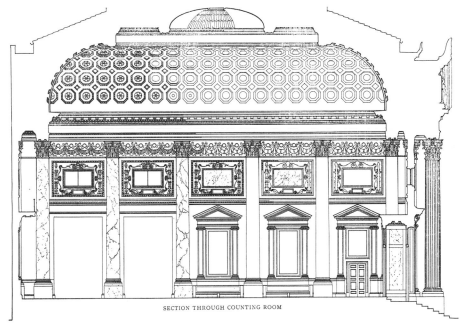

SECTION THROUGH COUNTING ROOM

Tall Corinthian columns, a beautifully decorated coved ceiling, and an art glass skylight make the Bowery's banking room one of New York's great commercial spaces. The Bowery is now part of Home Savings of America.

THE·BOWERY·SAVINGS·BANK

AD
MDCCCXXXIV

AD
MDCCCXCIV

SCALE   FEET
GRAND STREET ELEVATION
THE BOWERY SAVINGS BANK, NEW YORK CITY.
1895

The full impact of the Beaux Arts architecture of Chicago's Columbian Exposition is evident in the Bowery Savings Bank, Bowery and Grand Street, begun in 1893, the year the fair opened. The bank's limestone exterior was enriched with Corinthian pilasters, columns, and a pediment bedecked with sculpture by Frederick MacMonnies.

rustication, emphatic string courses, and a massive cornice to counter the structure's height and to bring it into intimacy with the street.

One of White's buildings of the 1890s is of particular interest, for it reveals how appropriately the architect used the decorative vocabulary of the Renaissance and how sensitive he was to making the program fit the purpose of the structure and the ethos of the site. Just as clubs had done, so newspapers were following the movement of the city's population uptown. It was a cause of general astonishment that by 1890 nearly 100,000 people were living in the newly "Annexed District" beyond the Harlem River and there was widespread speculation about the creation of a "Greater City" which would include Brooklyn, Queens, and Staten Island. James Gordon Bennett, the owner of the New York *Herald*, who was particularly anxious to move his newspaper's office from Park Row, the old "Newspaper Row," across from City Hall to a more central location, had purchased a trapezoid site between Broadway and Sixth Avenue at Thirty-fifth Street. Bennett wanted a building which would reflect the prestige of his paper and that prestige was indeed glittering. As the journalist Poultney Bigelow, who worked for him, wrote in *Seventy Summers*:

> The *Herald* had three features that gave it a prestige independent of political or theological affiliation. It spared no money in having the very best shipping and meteorological news from every part of the world. It had the fullest news of the fashionable world in both continents. . . . Moreover, the advertising columns of the *Herald* reflected the purses of its readers, for they became the medium dear to all dealers in things costly and superfluous—fancy dogs, yachts, horses, country places, and above all high-grade servants.

In addition, Bennett had given his paper an imperishable international reputation when, in 1869, he had sent Henry Morton Stanley to Central Africa to find Dr. David Livingstone, the Scots missionary, who had not been heard from in years. Their meeting at Ujiji in

Though in 1903 Stanford White uncharacteristically proposed a 60-story tower for the Grand Central Terminal site on Forty-second Street, the 11-story Sherry's Hotel, completed in 1898, was one of the tallest buildings designed by the architect. Its multi-corniced façade at Forty-fourth Street is readily identifiable on the left in this turn-of-the-century view up Fifth Avenue. The moresque edifice on the right is the old Temple Emmanu-El. Both the temple and Sherry's have disappeared.

November 1871 became one of the most famous events in the history of journalism.

Bennett had been pleased with White's work at the Newport Casino, and he had been delighted with the architect's decor for his 227-foot yacht, *Namouna*. In one of his typically flamboyant gestures, the publisher wanted White to re-create, on the somewhat seedy West Side of Manhattan, Venice's Palace of the Doges and was only persuaded to settle for Verona's fifteenth-century Loggia

Sherry's extravagant Louis XV–style ballroom was a center of New York social high life. Among the more bizarre events it witnessed was the dinner C. K. G. Billings gave there in 1903 for thirty-six guests on horseback.

del Consiglio (frequently referred to as the Palazzo del Consiglio) when the architect pointed out that the National Academy of Design at Fourth Avenue and Twenty-third Street already occupied such a structure and that to build another would make Bennett look like a copycat. All of the brilliant capacity for planning which Stanford White had displayed at Madison Square Garden was again called upon, for Bennett, in a conscious challenge to the tall tower Richard Morris Hunt had designed for the New York *Tribune*, insisted that the *Herald* be no more than two stories high. The architect managed to shoehorn the editorial offices and production facilities required to produce a great metropolitan daily into the

restricted site and, in a stroke of genius, made, on the Broadway side, the basement-level pressroom visible, thus creating a perpetual show for passing pedestrians.

Above the *Herald* Building's street-level arcades, White enlivened the exterior with yellow and buff terra cotta and, at the center of the principal façade, placed that favorite urban ornament of the Beaux Arts school, a public clock. The one atop the *Herald*

STANFORD WHITE'S NEW YORK

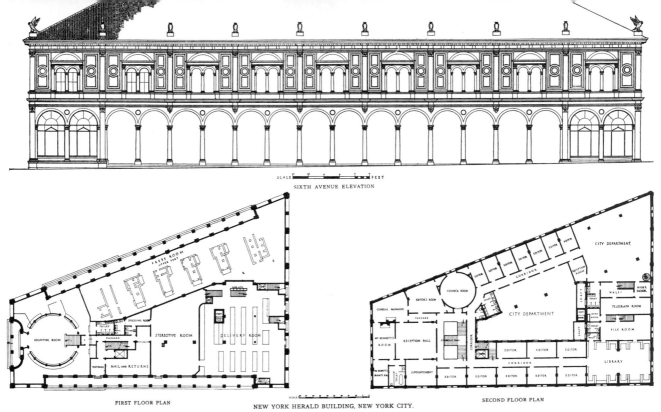

SIXTH AVENUE ELEVATION

FIRST FLOOR PLAN

NEW YORK HERALD BUILDING, NEW YORK CITY.

SECOND FLOOR PLAN

was an undulating bronze ensemble by Antonin Jean Carles, consisting of a vigilant Minerva, the Roman goddess of cities, flanked by two brawny bell ringers. On the roofline White—at Bennett's orders—set twenty-six bronze owls whose electrically lit eyes eerily blinked on and off throughout the night. The nocturnal bird, which Bennett's yacht sported as a figurehead, was the publisher's chosen totem, symbolizing his desire to be all-knowing, an urge that was a good deal enhanced by the spies he paid to follow his editors. Though Bennett, after a few initial complaints, appeared to be satisfied with his newspaper's headquarters when it was completed in 1895 and later asked White to design a mausoleum (which was never built) in the form of a 25-foot-tall owl to be placed at the family homestead on Washington Heights, the capricious publisher did not really like the building. That is a possible explanation for the fact that when, in Paris, Bennett heard of the architect's murder he set his reporters to work digging up every speck of dirt they could find on Stanford White.

White's monumental planning skills were put to the test when in 1890 James Gordon Bennett asked him to fit all of the editorial and production functions of his Herald *into a trapezoidal lot on West Thirty-fifth Street.*

OPPOSITE:

Another comparatively tall Renaissance-style building designed by White was the 9-story Hotel Imperial at the southeast corner of Broadway and Thirty-second Street, seen at center left in this 1909 photograph. From the moment it opened in September of 1890, the Imperial's public spaces were greatly admired for their murals by Robert Reid, Thomas Dewing, and Edwin Austin Abbey. The high-rise portion to the rear was not part of White's original scheme. The Imperial has been demolished.

*T*he Herald *Building, modeled on a Renaissance loggia in Verona, was an unforgettable advertisement for Bennett's newspaper. Though only 2 stories high, the structure, by the sheer perfection of its design, dominated the lively crossroads of Broadway and Sixth Avenue.*

Whatever Bennett's quibbles might have been, Leland M. Roth in his indispensable study, *McKim, Mead & White Architects*, noted the essential correctness of the structure's exterior design:

> The *Herald* Building was set down in the midst of the teeming theater district in what was then New York's tenderloin. Here flourished all manner of dance halls and cafes, and any building which hoped to secure its own place in this environment had to be as brazen as its surroundings. The *Herald* Building was a success, for it combined a modicum of order and balance with panache and audacity; it met the tenderloin on its own terms.

Just as Stanford White's Madison Square Garden became the generic name for a place designed for delight and joy, so his *Herald* Building gave its name to a square whose very mention in George M. Cohan's Broadway anthem summons up images of a glamorous Babylon.

Much of Stanford White's work of the 1890s was done in the commodious new offices occupying the entire fifth floor of R. H. Robertson's recently completed Mohawk Building at 160 Fifth Avenue, into which the firm moved in 1894. The Mohawk, between Twentieth and Twenty-first streets, was, as it were, in the heart of "Stanford White country," just south of his monuments at Madison Square, scarcely three blocks from his residence at 119 East Twenty-first Street, and eventually very near what would be White's most famous "hideaway," the two upper floors he rented at 22 West Twenty-fourth Street. One of the furnishings of that apartment would achieve immortality: "After lunch we . . . entered a marvelous studio where I saw, for the first time, the famous Red Velvet Swing!" That, at least, was how, long after the fact, Evelyn Nesbit was to remember it. The Mohawk Building was also in the center of the new vertical alabaster city which the combination of the iron-and-steel skeleton and the Beaux Arts propensity for ivory terra cotta, limestone, and pale marble was creating. The architectural historian Christabel Gough, writing about the quarter in the journal *Village Views*, sums up this development nicely when she speaks of:

. . . this intact enclave of early skyscrapers and palaces of commerce, so painstakingly imagined and built by a legendary group of American architects. The group was led, arguably, by McKim, Mead & White, but included many other equally great names: D. H. Burnham (and his followers), Henry Hardenbergh, R. H. Robertson,

Detlef Lienau, Napoleon Le Brun, Edward Kendall, Ernest Flagg, and George B. Post. All of these architects built in the district around Madison Square.

When McKim, Mead & White moved into the Mohawk, the partnership was near its apogee, for, with no fewer than eighty junior draftsmen, it could claim title to being the world's largest architectural firm. Its major projects being completed in the year 1894 alone included the Cable Building on Broadway, the Rockefeller Building at Brown University, the Puck Building in Chicago, the Naugatuck, Connecticut, Public Library, and the plans for Columbia College's new Morningside Heights campus. Julius Chambers, who was, in turn, managing editor of both the New York *Herald* and the New York *World*, said that the offices of McKim, Mead & White were the training ground for "the race of superior architects" responsible for the "splendid architectural development of the new metropolis, which began about 1885 . . ." "An immensely stimulating place," one draftsman wrote. "It was the center of the world." White, now approaching forty, continued to play the role of brilliant *enfant terrible*, shouting, running from desk to desk to make a suggestion, to examine work in progress, to encourage or condemn. His international telex code was "Giddydoll."

The office's kinetic energy occasionally became too much for the methodical McKim. After one of White's periodic bouts of rearranging everyone's office, the senior partner protested:

September 18th, 1902

Dear Stanford:

I had hoped that this matter had been settled for good and all, and supposed that you were happy in being just where you wanted to be. So far as I am concerned, my one thought was to be in a place where I could be quiet, and thereby get ahead better with my work, and I am perfectly satisfied with your old quarters. However, it is entirely immaterial to me, and if you would rather exchange back to them, by all means do so. Only, for Heaven's sake, make up your mind what you want to do, so that I can get settled!

Charley

"Everything was bully for White now," Charles Baldwin observed, "Holbein paintings, the towers of the cathedral of Laon, Sharkey's muscles, Blanche Ring's voice, Martin's wine, Delmonico's turtle soup . . ." The architect's persona, though, was becoming a curious mixture of fame and notoriety, of domesticity and debauchery. It was well known that he carried $20 gold pieces in a little chamois pouch to give to pretty chorus girls. Significantly, his personal stationery from Tiffany & Co. was ornamented with the figure of Aphrodite, the Greek goddess of love and beauty, of life and death.

This intriguing fusion of sunlight and shadow was evident at the dedication of the Washington Memorial Arch in Washington Square. As the centennial of George Washington's inauguration in New York in 1789 as the first President of the United States approached, William Rhinelander Stewart, a wealthy lawyer who lived on the north side of the square, proposed that the event be commemorated by the erection of a temporary arch at the foot of Fifth Avenue. Some $3,000 was quickly raised, and Stanford White was chosen as the designer. The rather spindly, cream-colored confection of wood and plaster topped by a folk art statue of the first President which rose 150 feet north of Washington Square proved to be a great success. Soon a committee consisting of such prominent New Yorkers as Henry G. Marquand, Richard Watson Gilder, Richard Morris Hunt, and Mr. Stewart was formed to raise funds for the architect to build a permanent arch. Stanford White now had the opportunity to design a nonutilitarian structure, an ornament which would further the Beaux Arts ideal of the city beautiful, of the city as a work of art. The cornerstone for the permanent arch was laid in 1890, but due to difficulties in raising the $80,000 required for its construction, the monument would not be completed for five years. White, because of the significance of the individual and the event honored, was led to write a rare commentary on the design he had chosen: "In style this monument is distinctly classic, and by this term is meant Roman in contradistinction to the less robust, more fanciful and more 'personal' style of the Renaissance. Although

For the 1889 centennial of George Washington's inauguration in New York, White was asked to design a temporary arch to commemorate the event. It stood on Fifth Avenue some 150 feet north of Washington Square and was topped by a primitive statue of the first President that White had found while rummaging through a New York junk shop.

The popularity of the temporary arch led to the commissioning of White to design a permanent one in marble. For the faces of the angels in the spandrels, Frederick MacMonnies copied that of Mrs. William Rhinelander Stewart— whose husband was the project's treasurer—for the one on the right, and that of Bessie White for the one on the left.

A *view of the dedication*
ceremonies of the Washington
Memorial Arch, May 4, 1895,
with Stanford White in the right
foreground.

having a discreet flavor of its own, this quality has been kept in
abeyance to the conservatism which seems proper in the designs of
a structure intended to stand for all time and to outlast any local or
passing fashions."

At the dedication on May 4, 1895, of the 70-foot marble arch
with its comely decoration by Frederick MacMonnies, Stanford
White's submersion of his preferences and personality in the design
of a monument honoring the Roman republican character of Washington did not save him from the sort of snide criticism which was
slowly rising around him. One of the principal speakers at the
dedication was General Horace Porter, a Civil War hero and a
friend of General Ulysses S. Grant, who was also a noted orator.

Rising and glaring at White, General Porter announced that "the true purpose of this work is not the display of architectural skill, but the perpetuation of the memory of the exalted patriot who founded this republic." Then, with his eyes still fiercely fixed upon the architect, toward whom everyone had now turned, the general went on to analyze Washington, who seemed, as one newspaper observed, to resemble General Porter more than anyone had suspected.

Yet that May day in 1895 was a moment of golden sunshine for White. ". . . when his beautiful Washington Arch reared its loveliness on lower Fifth Avenue," Henry Collins Brown, a collector of New York City tidbits, reported, "we began to think there was such a thing as beauty in buildings, after all, and the name of Stanford White was on every tongue."

CHAPTER 10

SUMMER PALACES AND COUNTRY COTTAGES

Agraphic glimpse of the scale of luxury prevalent in the great houses New Yorkers built outside of the city and elsewhere in the Gilded Decades is provided by Shirley Burden in his poignant memoir, *The Vanderbilts in My Life*:

> After Dad died my mother often took us to visit Grandma Twombly at Florham, her country house in New Jersey. The name is a combination of my grandmother's and grandfather's first names, Florence and Hamilton. I'll never forget my first trip to Florham. I must have been seven or eight. We drove through a wonderful tunnel with trains on top, and down a driveway to the biggest house I had ever seen. There were lions guarding the door, and a hall that had no end; thirty-six bedrooms, and living rooms for everything. A thousand acres to play in.

Burden's grandmother was a granddaughter of Commodore Vanderbilt, and the mansion that he remembered during the First World War had been built in the 1890s by McKim, Mead & White,

From 1898 until his death, Stanford White resided at 121 East Twenty-first Street in a house which was, in fact, an experimental laboratory for the residences he designed both in New York and in the country. The second-floor lobby was lined with rare tiles and boasted fine Renaissance bas-reliefs. The steps led to the picture gallery situated at the rear of the dwelling.

with White in charge of much of the interior decoration and furnishing. Coincidentally, he had also been an adviser on the decoration and furnishing of the magisterial mansion overlooking the Hudson at Hyde Park, New York, that McKim, Mead & White designed in 1895 for Mrs. Twombly's brother, Frederick W. Vanderbilt.

Stanford White's extraordinary gift for domestic architecture, a gift which had first revealed itself when he was a teenaged draftsman for H. H. Richardson, undoubtedly played an important part in the phenomenal expansion of the firm in the years after the turn of the century. Leland Roth has estimated just how well McKim, Mead & White was faring: "They received more than 210 commissions amounting to construction contracts worth $36,397,798. The office staff was increased gradually, to 92 people in 1902..." White's houses of the last years of the nineteenth century and of the six years he lived in the twentieth form an enchanting oeuvre which exemplifies all that the French imply, when speaking of the decades just before the battles of the Somme and Verdun, by the phrase *la vie douce*, and the period which the English call the "Edwardian Afternoon."

It is not too much to say that, along with Box Hill, the two town houses occupied by the architect on the north side of Gramercy Park were transient warehouses for his protean collection and laboratories for domestic decorative experimentation. In 1892 the Whites moved into 119 East Twenty-first Street, a brownstone owned by Henry A. C. Taylor, a financier and corporation director, who was a leading member of both the Newport Casino and the Metropolitan Club, which White was then at work upon. (Taylor's sister, Alberta, married Percy Pyne, for whom McKim designed one of his most attractive New York houses.) Paul R. Baker in his finely detailed biography, *Stanny*, explains why, surprisingly, the Whites remained renters: "Sometime later he tried to purchase the house, valued at about $60,000, but Taylor did not wish to sell; nonetheless Stan did make repairs and minor alterations. In 1894 he had the property wired for electricity, but two years passed before the

lighting system was in full operation. For six years this was the Whites' townhouse."

Desiring more space for his collections of paintings, furniture, and multifarious bric-a-brac, the architect, in the spring of 1898, moved into 121 East Twenty-first Street, a larger, adjacent corner house owned and until recently lived in by Taylor. Throughout the balance of the year White completely redecorated the interior. The consequential scale of this endeavor may be gathered from the fact that it was put into the hands of Allard et Fils, who had recently

White's large brownstone—which he only leased—occupied the northwest corner of Lexington Avenue and Twenty-first Street. It was replaced by the Gramercy Park Hotel in the 1920s.

The picture gallery, where White often entertained guests after dinner, presented a precious mix of paintings by old masters such as Tintoretto and canvases by friends such as Dewing and Sargent.

completed their work on Cornelius Vanderbilt's $7,000,000 Newport "cottage," The Breakers, and several ceilings were painted by no less an artist than Everett Shinn. The work was still in progress when, on January 14 of the new year, Allard wrote to White regarding the decor of the first-floor hall. The letter attests to both the architect's recondite knowledge of the techniques of decoration and the nearly limitless bounds of his collections, which were stored in art galleries and decorators' workrooms across the city:

> We beg to give you below the cost of treating the wall of your Hall—1st floor, as per design made by you.
> All the ornamentation to be in Carton Pierre—gilt with Aluminum leaf, and glazed to an old gold finish.
> You are to furnish the mirrors, which we think can be very easily found among the stock of mirrors which we have belonging to you.

Number 121 was soon overflowing with the artistic detritus Stanford White cherished—antique marble columns, ancient Roman sarcophagi, gilded Venetian canapés—as well as paintings covering the spectrum from old masters to works by friends. The value of 121's contents was estimated for insurance purposes at an impressive $300,000.

Lawrence Grant White in his journal precisely recalled this Xanadu on Gramercy Park:

> It was about that time that we moved next door to 121 East 21st. Street, a large sunny house on the corner of Lexington Avenue, again with a dreary brown-stone exterior that gave no hint of the splendor within; for my father had given rein to his lavish exuberance, and had made a series of magnificent rooms built up with antique fragments. In the Reception Room downstairs hung the Gothic tapestry with a falconer and his lady on a pink ground, that is now in Mr. Mellon's collection; and from the Drawing Room on the floor above, where Holbein's portraits of Henry VIII and Edward VI hung on the walls of ruby red velvet, one could look for a hundred and fifty feet through the hall and dining room with its pink Renais-

sance tapestries and its marble fountain filled with live trout, to the Music Room hung in yellow damask. At the end of this room hung … Robert Chanler's huge painting in gold and silver, of giraffes eating oranges off birch trees. There was a stage, with what someone described as a flight of thirteen antique harps; and other highly decorative musical instruments, some from my grandfather's collection, were hung on the walls.

Over the Music Room, my father had built on a picture gallery. In its curved oak ceiling was a skylight, operated by an electric motor that was the delight of myself and my friends. The room was approached through a vestibule whose walls were faced with Rhodian tiles set in white marble borders. The pictures in my father's collection were not of the first water, but they were effectively hung, and made a splendid decoration. The finest were the two Holbeins that I have mentioned; there was also a Zucchero of Mary Tudor, a good portrait of a woman by Quintin Matsys; a Reynolds now in the Van Horne collection, and a Hoppner and a Romney that my mother still owns; a beautiful little Ingres, that I wish we had kept; a Courbet, two Doges by Tintoretto, and, among the Americans, two Ryders, an Innes, as well as several examples of the works of his friends Brush, Metcalfe, Curran, Coleman, Alexander Harrison, and Simmons.

This glittering *folie de grandeur* was being devised just as Stanford White's financial situation became parlous. There was no logical reason for him to have been in financial straits. During the years 1896–97, for example, his share as a partner in McKim, Mead & White was a more than comfortable $60,000, and, in addition, there was Bessie's ample personal fortune. White, it would seem, had little "money sense." It is impossible to justify the more than $75,000 that he spent redecorating a rental property like 121 East Twenty-first Street, when, shortly after the project was finished, the real estate firm of Pease & Elliman offered to sell him 7 Gramercy Park, a fine house nearby, for less than $100,000.

But at the root of White's financial debacle was speculation. Perhaps, traveling in the company of very rich men, he was overwhelmed by the desire to be very rich. In addition to speculation in the stock market—almost always on margin—he moved at the

There is no evidence that the architect was neglectful of his wife and son. Indeed, he delighted in traveling with them as he did in Egypt where this photograph of him with Bessie, Lawrence, and a monkey was taken. The Whites had no difficulty getting Lawrence into New York's fashionable cadet military organization, the Knickerbocker Greys. Lawrence is second from left in this 1897 view of the battalion ready to parade in the Seventh Regiment Armory.

beginning of the 1890s into the far more perilous arena of grain futures. At first the architect had an unbroken streak of good luck and made thousands of dollars, but in the late 1890s he suffered devastating losses and began borrowing large sums of money from his brother-in-law Prescott Hall Butler and, through his friend Charles T. Barney, from the Knickerbocker Trust Company and the New York Loan and Improvement Company. Some of the loans, such as the one for $190,000 he began negotiating for in March 1899 with Lewis M. Norwood, who specialized in real estate mortgages, were gargantuan.

From this point on Stanford White's life was burdened by the consequences of his unsuccessful financial gambles. His mail became laden with demands for satisfaction for unpaid bills from, among others, Shreve, Crump & Low, the Boston jewelers; Hyde Brothers, designers and manufacturers of Venetian mosaics; Hulbert Brothers, makers of bicycles; and A. A. Vantine & Co., who notified White that his rugs and draperies would remain in the store until he settled his account.

The lessons of these first warnings of the financial disaster that would strike in 1901 were never taken to heart. White soon was once more spending enormous sums for paintings, oriental rugs, tapestries, Chinese vases. The value of some of these purchases startled his friends. On October 14, 1898, the constitutionally cautious John Singer Sargent wrote to the architect:

33, Tite Street
Chelsea, S.W.

My dear Stanford

A box has arrived from Allard who writes me that it is sent to my care at your command, and that I must unpack it to see if it is all right. It is—a Velásquez head of an Infanta, in perfect condition, delicious in color. Meanwhile I have screwed it up again in its case, renewed my fire insurance and hired a policeman to watch my house—until I hear from you what is to be done with it.

Edward Simmons, describing the architect's retreat in the Gramercy Park house, has come as close as anyone to explaining what these trophies meant to White:

A flight or two up was his own room. Vercingetorix in his cave with all his spoils piled around him! Everything he cared about (and he wanted it at once) and a heterogeneous mass of priceless books, paintings, draperies, all in a careless disorder, was happiness to him in his own den.

Stanford White's country houses of this period fall into two categories, as distinct one from another as Andrea Palladio's villas, which are sometimes ambitious porticoed palaces and at other times simple geometric masses adorned by nothing more than an elegant recessed arcade. The American vernacular classical style, which he had lovingly studied on his New England pilgrimage with McKim and Mead, always retained a corner of Stanford White's affection. He used it in his remodeling of Box Hill, and it is the style of the delightful gambrel-roofed house that he designed in 1892 at Shinnecock on Long Island's South Shore for his longtime friend the painter William Merritt Chase. White consciously made this summer residence a complete contrast to Chase's vast Tenth Street studio, which was celebrated for its intoxicating mix of carved high-

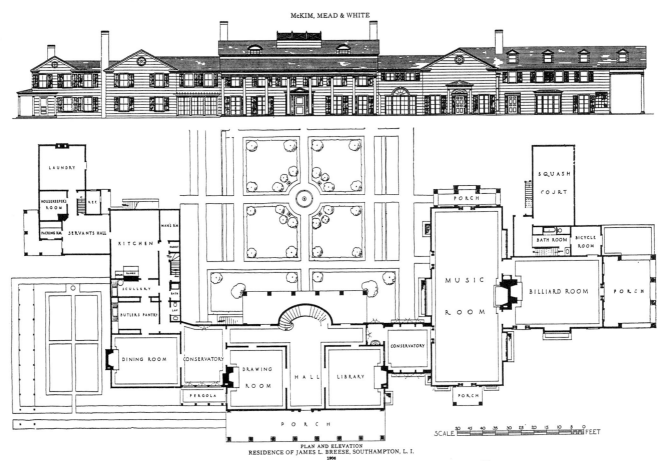

PLAN AND ELEVATION
RESIDENCE OF JAMES L. BREESE, SOUTHAMPTON, L. I.
1906

backed Spanish chairs, Turkish brass lamps, Japanese prints, painted silk fans, and heavy, bright-colored stuffs. The house, on property between Shinnecock and Peconic bays, given to him by a group of Southampton residents who hoped Chase would establish an art school on Long Island, is uncompromisingly American, a tightly controlled combination of Richardson's shingle style and the classical elements embraced by his brilliant draftsman. Like the firm's daring William G. Low house in Bristol, Rhode Island, of 1886, where the ruggedly boisterous shingles are summoned to order by an almost Athenian 140-foot-long pediment, the Chase house's slender, fluted Ionic columns, its pedimented dormers, and snowy cornices give classical form to this shingled dwelling. Chase, his wife, and his innumerable daughters loved the Shinnecock house. With its sensitive relationship to the sun-splashed hill it sits upon and to the sparkling coves below, it is easy to believe the anecdote that one summer day a daughter of the painter cried out, "Papa, come quickly! Here is a cloud posing for you!"

In 1898 White began designing a large country house, The Orchard, for James L. Breese in Southampton, New York. The façade, based on that of Washington's Mount Vernon, is similar to that of Hill-Stead, a house that the architect was designing at the same time in Farmington, Connecticut, for the Clevelander, Alfred Atmore Pope.

SUMMER PALACES AND COUNTRY COTTAGES

The Orchard's garden façade featured a Palladian window, a form which appears often in the architect's work. The statue in the center of the boxwood garden is by Janet Scudder. In the 1980s The Orchard was divided into condominiums.

A similar aesthetic informs The Orchard, the clapboard house which White, with some assistance from McKim, began working on in 1899 in Southampton, Long Island, for another longtime friend, the talented amateur photographer James Lawrence Breese. It had been in Breese's Carbon Photography Studio at 5 West Sixteenth Street in May 1895 that the famous Pie Girl Dinner had taken place. The unjustified notoriety that surrounded the event is further evidence of the cloud of suspicion that was beginning to envelop Stanford White's life. Planned as an anniversary celebration for one of White's friends, the dinner was attended by some fifty men. At the end of the banquet waiters carried out a huge six-foot pastry and placed it in the center of the horseshoe-shaped dining table. The waiters then began chanting the old nursery rhyme:

> *Sing a song of sixpence,*
> *A pocket full of rye,*

Four and twenty blackbirds
Baked in a pie—

As the words "When the pie was opened" were reached, the crust was broken and out flew a flock of canaries accompanied by sixteen-year-old Susie Johnson swathed in black veiling and wearing on her head a stuffed blackbird. Although the dinner guests included such reputable personages as Charles McKim, Cooper Hewitt, Charles Dana Gibson, and Edward Simmons, who wrote that the whole affair was "very moral and dignified," the press, led by Joseph Pulitzer's *World*, immediately attacked White and his crowd for their "bacchanalian revels." Soon the studio and its "Carbonites" came under fire as a secret place of lascivious intrigue, though it was used by a number of well-known photographers and Breese listed it openly in the *Social Register* as his place of business and regularly gave dinners there attended by Bessie White, the Goelets, and other highly respectable friends.

Though most of the rooms in The Orchard were decorated in an American Colonial style, the 72-foot-long Music Room was designed in a sumptuous European manner. Beneath its handsome Italian ceiling, the Music Room presented a rich mélange of French furniture, superb tapestries, and antique oriental rugs.

While the core of The Orchard was a small Greek Revival dwelling already on the thirty-acre site, the social requirements of Breese and his wife, Frances, a niece of Episcopal Bishop Henry Codman Potter, and their four children, demanded a bit more amplitude than that. Behind a portico suggestive of Mount Vernon, The Orchard quickly grew to thirty-two rooms. The project brought out the knowledgeable scavenger in White, who found antique doors and mantels to blend the new rooms with the old. "The house is a frank adaption of the old Southern colonial house to modern requirements," was how Barr Ferree described it.

White's mother's South Carolina roots must certainly have been in the architect's thoughts as he worked on The Orchard, for the residence was filled with Breese's important collection of Southern furniture, reflecting his Maryland connections, and for some rooms White had his plasterers carefully copy the designs of ceilings which he had found in Southern colonial homes.

While it is clear that for friends who were artists or who had an artistic bent White favored country houses in an American vernacular style, for the imperious rich he employed a very different vocabulary. By the late 1890s Stanford White had had a considerable relationship with the Mills family. In his sumptuous redecoration of the Villard Houses he had worked closely and harmoniously with Elisabeth Reid, whose father, Darius Ogden Mills, had, during the California gold rush, skillfully advanced from selling picks and shovels to those who worked in the mines to selling the mines themselves. The $400,000 that Darius Mills had given Elisabeth to purchase the Villard mansion apparently had not dented his fortune, for in 1887 he presented his daughter with an eighty-four-room Normanesque castle, Ophire Hall, near Purchase, New York. While alterations were underway to ready the castle for the Reids, a workman's blowtorch ignited a conflagration which consumed everything but Ophire Hall's thick walls. White was summoned to rebuild the rocky pile along its original lines and to redecorate the interior. At the Reids' request he installed within the reconstructed shell the busy Queen Anne-style paneling which he had happily

ripped out of the Villard house's triple reception rooms. Since the design of Ophire Hall fell somewhere between that of an armory and a brewery, the elaborately inlaid woodwork finally found a suitably hideous home.

Soon he was called upon to work for Mrs. Reid's brother, Ogden, and his determined wife, Ruth Livingston Mills. Clare Brandt in her invaluable study, *An American Aristocracy: The Livingstons*, tellingly dissects Ruth Mills's character:

> What Ruth Livingston Mills lacked in charm and subtlety she made up for in determination and audacity. Disdaining her cousin Caroline Astor's Four Hundred . . . she announced that society consisted of exactly twenty families. The Four Hundred naturally demurred; and their queen, Mrs. Astor, was to beat off the challenge of her younger kinswoman. Ruth Mills, "defeated . . . by her own exclusiveness," retreated, Livingston-like, into the Hudson Valley to lick her wounds and plan her next campaign.

Just as Alva had needed a Château du Bois on Fifth Avenue to launch the upstart Vanderbilts into New York society, Ruth Mills required a Dutchess County palace to carry out her own ferocious

While the Breese house resembled Mount Vernon, the Mills mansion on the Hudson River at Staatsburg, New York, echoed the façade of the White House. Commissioned by Ogden Mills and his wife Ruth Livingston, the residence began as a rather modest Greek Revival dwelling, but by the time White had finished his work in 1897 the Mills mansion had expanded to sixty-five rooms.

The Mills mansion's majestic entrance hall effortlessly combined gilded Louis XV furniture and Livingston family portraits. Used by the Millses for only a few weeks each autumn, the mansion became a state museum in 1938.

social skirmishes. Once more, the core of the mansion was a Greek Revival house, this one a sixty-year-old Livingston family property in Staatsburg, New York, which Mrs. Mills had inherited at the beginning of the 1890s from her father. Ruth Mills was determined that this ancestral dwelling should be preserved like some Shinto shrine at the heart of her new palace. Here would hang a stunning array of family portraits, visible proof that the Livingstons were most certainly one of the "twenty families" qualified to govern American society. At Staatsburg there would be no whiff of the vernacular. The sixty-five-room mansion, completed in 1897 on a spectacular site overlooking the Hudson, was essentially English Palladian, a princely sweep of sparkling stucco with, at its center, a soaring six-columned portico reminiscent of that of the White House. The Mills mansion's splendid spaces included a library, short on books but long on pilasters and paneling; a gilded boudoir; and a vast dining room of varicolored marbles which could vie in awe-power with those at Alva's Marble House or Alice Vanderbilt's The Breakers.

Having lost the battle to succeed her cousin Caroline, *the* Mrs.

Astor, as Queen of New York Society, Ruth Mills had to content herself with queening it over various Livingston relatives and over her Reid in-laws. But with Whitelaw Reid successively American Ambassador to the Republic of France and to the Court of St. James's, she was hard pressed to match the seemingly endless stream of exalted titles—Princess Patricia, the Duke and Duchess of Connaught, and the Prince of Wales—which coursed through Stanford White's gala rooms in the old Villard house. Some consoling balm, though, flowed from the fact that Ruth Livingston's twin sister, Elizabeth, married the highly eligible and loftily connected English aristocrat William George Cavendish Bentinck. The Mills mansion, in time, attained a very special notoriety. As Clare Brandt reports: "Mrs. Mills' incessant house parties soon acquired a reputation for luxury, social intrigue and inflated stakes at the bridge table." It is no wonder, then, that in her 1905 novel, *The House of Mirth*, that gimlet-eyed surveyor of the social scene, Edith Wharton, used the mansion as the setting for an uncompromisingly lavish but hollow gathering. The "stairway in the Ogden Mills house at Staatsburg, New York," Louis Auchincloss observes in *Edith Wharton: A Woman in Her Time*, "suggested the one at Bellomont where Lily Bart paused to look down at the house party and to sense the futility of her life."

Among all the packing towns and steel towns and mill towns and mining towns that sent caravans of the new rich to Gotham in the 1880s and 1890s none could match the heady mix exported by Pittsburgh—with its Carnegies, Phippses, Fricks, and Thaws—and California. Among the most picturesque of the Californians was James Graham Fair, a penniless Irishman who became one of the four partners who shared in the $300 million bounty of the Comstock Silver Lode discovered in the 1850s. The lifestyle of "slippery Jim" was described by a colleague who served with him in the United States Senate as one of "gaudiness and irregularity." The irregularity must have been trying, for his wife, Theresa, divorced him and raised their two daughters with all the gentility that could be mustered by the progeny of a barber. One, Virginia,

The year that White completed enlarging the Mills mansion, he began designing Rosecliff in Newport for Mrs. Herman Oelrichs. Modeled on the Grand Trianon at Versailles, Rosecliff is faced with white glazed terra cotta.

"Birdie," would rise to the rarefied stratosphere of marrying Alva's son, William K. Vanderbilt, Jr., while the other, Theresa, "Tessie," would have a spectacular wedding in San Francisco to Herman Oelrichs, a German whose family organized and managed the illustrious North German Lloyd Steamship Company.

Tessie Oelrichs, her niece the writer Michael Strange commented, "was strongly addicted to Society." As Caroline Astor gradually lost her mind as well as her grip on her social sceptre, and settled for ruling over the imaginary dinner parties she gave in her Fifth Avenue mansion, Tessie, far less exclusive than Ruth Mills, was not only prepared to welcome those who were not of the "twenty families," but had no qualms about sharing the queenly throne with the two other female powerhouses, Alva Vanderbilt

Belmont and Mrs. Stuyvesant Fish, who made up the triumvirate which succeeded Mrs. Astor. To reign properly—even as one of a troika—required something more than Tessie's sumptuous Fifth Avenue mansion; it called for a "cottage" in summer society's holy city. Thus in 1897 Mrs. Oelrichs commissioned Stanford White to design what would prove to be one of the loveliest nests in Newport.

Constructed of ivory terra cotta from the Perth Amboy Terra Cotta Company—the architect's favored supplier—Rosecliff is an Edwardian version of Mansart's Grand Trianon at Versailles. With its paired columns, tall arched French windows, flowered swags, and graceful balustrade it is perhaps the most perfect Beaux Arts residence ever constructed in America. Inside, the hall's imperial

The grand salon or ballroom of Rosecliff is an enchanting evocation of eighteenth-century decor. Scenes for The Great Gatsby *were filmed in this sumptuous space. After several harrowing brushes with destruction, Rosecliff is now safely in the hands of the Preservation Society of Newport County.*

staircase, of an almost Art Nouveau fluidity, is one of Stanford White's supreme creations. Rosecliff's 40-by-80-foot ballroom, the largest in Newport, is a French *lanterne*, open on two sides, one with views of the formal garden, the other looking out over the Atlantic, which breaks upon the cliff below. From its perfect parquet floor, past its elegant fluted Corinthian pilasters, up to its richly molded plaster ceiling, this chamber reveals its architect's extraordinary ability to produce, when he thought it appropriate, a wondrously restrained opulence. In the ballroom at Rosecliff monochromatic white gives off the same wattage of glittering glamour that the one at Marble House required yards of gilding to produce.

So anxious was the energetic Tessie—she was known to wield a mop to improve the work of her maids—to enter the Newport lists that she moved into Rosecliff in 1900, a full two years before the pavilion was completed. But her most famous party, the "Bal blanc," was not held until August 19, 1904. For this legendary fete, all the decor, as well as the guests' gowns, was white, and because the United States Navy would not lend her its Great White Fleet, Tessie created her own. Elizabeth Lehr was present:

> Mrs. Herman Oelrichs was one of the hostesses who remained faithful to the stately traditions of Newport entertaining, for her

The Beaux Arts architects' perfect balance between classical style and modern materials is illustrated in the guest house and recreational pavilion which Stanford White designed in 1902 for Ferncliff, the John Jacob Astor IV estate at Rhinebeck, New York. While the façade is another variation on Mansart's Grand Trianon, the tennis court to the rear is boldly enclosed by metal parabolic arches and Guastavino tile vaults.

beautiful villa "Rosecliffe" lent itself to picturesque settings. Her lawn, with its white marble balustrade, looked right out over the sea, so she had a fleet of full-size skeleton ships of all types made, each brilliantly illuminated, anchored in front of the house to give the illusion of a harbour.

If the United States Navy was beyond her command, her architect was not. Three days before the "Bal blanc," Tessie telegraphed White, who had been fishing in Canada: "I expect you to stay with me. Thanks for salmon. Wire what train you are coming on."

Tessie spent her summers awing Newport, not only with her perpetual entertainments but also with what her niece said was her "racy and unfailingly amusing monologues and up-to-the-minute profanity." She ended her days much like Mrs. Astor, quite mad, passing her evenings in the glorious ballroom Stanford White had designed for her, inviting spectral guests to "take one more glass of champagne."

The Grand Trianon, this time in limestone, was used as the model, in a far more restrained manner very close to Mansart's original, in the guesthouse/squash court/swimming pool/tennis pavilion White designed between 1902 and 1904 for Mrs. Astor's son, John Jacob Astor IV, at his country house, Ferncliff, at Rhinebeck, New York. Astor, who was lost on the *Titanic* in 1912 while returning from Europe with his second wife, proved to be a most difficult client. John Jacob IV liked the façade and most of the interior facilities, but the tennis court, where the architect had covered the sensational parabolic vaults with Guastavino tile, proved to be an acoustical nightmare. The intelligent but eccentric millionaire, who, like most of the male members of his family, had great difficulty in communicating with his fellow beings, took the aural problem as a personal affront. White later said that he understood why Jack Astor was commonly known around town as "Jack Ass."

The architect again turned to the style of the *grand monarque* for the large country house, Harbor Hill, that he built between 1899 and 1902 for Mr. and Mrs. Clarence Mackay at Roslyn, New York. The 648-acre site, reputedly the highest spot on Long Island with views over Hempstead Bay, was as dramatic in its way as that of Rosecliff. Harbor Hill's style was the choice of both the architect

and Mrs. Mackay, the imperious Katherine Duer, a descendant of an ancient New York family, who had been a bridesmaid at the 1896 wedding in St. Thomas Church of Alva's lovely and intelligent daughter, Consuelo, to the despicable fortune-hunting ninth Duke of Marlborough. Katherine Mackay, who was, among other things, a devout suffragette, gave her instructions to White with an imperious ring. Richard Guy Wilson, in his *McKim, Mead & White Architects*, quotes this passage in a letter from patroness to architect: "I have decided to begin on these plans at once so you will express me as soon as you get this, some books about and drawings of Louis XIV Chateaux." Mrs. Mackay could afford such high-handedness, for her husband's father, John W. Mackay, had been a partner of "slippery Jim" Fair's in the bottomless Comstock Lode.

Fashioned of the finest pale gray Indiana limestone, Harbor Hill's exterior exemplified Mrs. Mackay's request for "a very severe house." It was, in fact, a simplified version of Mansart's Maisons-Laffite near Paris, with the chief decorative effect provided by the high mansard roofs which crowned the central section and the two flanking pavilions. An alluring hint of the luxury within was provided by the entrance, a masterful composition—inspired by the Hôtel de Montrescot at Chartres—of banded columns supporting a broken pediment which carried a bold cartouche embossed with a monarchal "M."

The interiors of Harbor Hill were, to say the least, not severe. The main hall, which measured 48 by 80 feet, was, like most of the rooms, filled with furnishings bought by Stanford White at the

The commanding site of Harbor Hill, the country house White created for Mr. and Mrs. Clarence Mackay overlooking Long Island Sound near Roslyn, New York, is evident in this watercolor and pencil drawing. Constructed between 1899 and 1902, the exterior of Harbor Hill was a virtuoso re-creation of a seventeenth-century French château.

STANFORD WHITE'S NEW YORK

request of Mrs. Mackay. Here among the various accoutrements was a complete set of choir stalls from an ancient French church. Harbor Hill also boasted the de rigueur white-and-gold Louis XV-style salon, a "Stone Room" with an antique ceiling, a Renaissance-style dining room, a billiard room, and a glass-and-iron conservatory which would not have been out of place in a public park. The skyrocketing cost of the house and its furnishings—some estimates run as high as $2,000,000—finally forced Mackay to caution both his wife and his architect. He must have been reassured when White replied that, when completed, Harbor Hill's only competitor for American country-house glory would be George Washington Vanderbilt's Biltmore, for later, to save a few fine trees, Mackay spent an extra $150,000 on a meandering driveway.

One of the high points in the life of Harbor Hill was the extravagant ball given there in 1924 for David, the peripatetic Prince of Wales. Curiously, after being shown through rooms crammed with priceless paintings, rare tapestries, and fantastic furniture, the one item which impressed the future Duke of Windsor was Gutzon Borglum's statue of old John Mackay. Fate was to play other tricks on Harbor Hill. After inheriting in 1902 a $500 million estate which included the Commercial Cable Company and the Postal Telegraph Company, which his father had founded with James Gordon Bennett, Clarence Mackay expanded these entities into the great worldwide Mackay communications system. In 1926, at the very peak of his success, one of Clarence and Katherine's daughters, Ellin, announced her intention to marry the songwriter Irving Berlin. The devoutly Catholic Mackay family not only objected to their proposed son-in-law's Jewish faith but were even more scandalized by the fact that he was much older than their daughter and had been divorced. Ironically, when, during the Great Depression of the 1930s, the Mackay communications system ran into serious difficulties, Irving Berlin quickly came to the aid of his father-in-law. At such a moment, *Town Topics'* description of Harbor Hill as a "delightful extravagance" must have rung strangely in Clarence Mackay's ears.

With its fine oak paneling, Ionic columns, and elaborate plaster ceiling the great entrance hall which swept across the front of the Mackay house signaled the grandeur which the visitor could expect to find throughout the mansion. Harbor Hill was demolished in 1947.

CHAPTER 11
SPLENDID DOMESTICITY IN GOTHAM

While life in the grand country houses during the decades bracketing the turn of the century was often brilliant, it rarely reached the wattage that illuminated the mansions and town houses of New York City. Consuelo Vanderbilt Balsan, in her bittersweet autobiography, *The Glitter and the Gold*, recalls luminous nights in her parents' Fifth Avenue domicile:

> . . . how gay were the gala evenings when the house was ablaze with lights and Willie and I, crouching on hands and knees behind the balustrade of the musicians' gallery, looked down on a festive scene below—the long dinner table covered with a damask cloth, a gold service and red roses, the lovely crystal and china, the grownups in their fine clothes.

This scene, of course, took place in the Richard Morris Hunt-designed château, where, on March 29, 1883, Consuelo's imperious mother, Alva, gave a costume ball for 1,000. Alva had appeared dressed as a Venetian princess with, just for additional snap, several

Starting in 1899, Stanford White began major renovations on two old houses, 125 and 127 East Twenty-first Street, which had been purchased by his friend the financial publisher Henry W. Poor. The first-floor hall of the Poor mansion was filled with furnishings and architectural elements purchased by White: an Italian silver sanctuary lamp, a brass menorah, antique Cippolino marble columns, a ceiling from Umbria, and black and gold silk velvet Portuguese portieres.

strands of priceless pearls which had belonged to Catherine the Great of Russia hanging from her batrachian neck, while her austere sister-in-law, Alice—Mrs. Cornelius Vanderbilt II—had surprised everyone by coming as an electric light bulb. The real purpose of the ball, though, was not to flaunt fantastic costumes, but to show off the $3,000,000 dwelling to prove just how rich the Vanderbilts were—which it did—and to get them into society—which it did too. Who would not be impressed with a family whose Francis I-style home encompassed a main hall 60 feet long and 20 feet wide, a fully equipped gymnasium, and a $50,000 bathtub carved from a single block of flawless black Italian marble? Hunt's Vanderbilt palace prepared the way for McKim, Mead & White's New York domestic work. In the evenings Charles McKim often strolled by 660 Fifth Avenue. His explanation: "I can sleep better knowing it's there."

In 1904 Stanford White was asked by Consuelo's brother Willie—William K. Vanderbilt Jr.—and his bride, Virginia Fair, to design a house for them next to the Vanderbilt château. In tribute to the deceased Hunt, the architect followed closely the general design of the original structure and thus produced one of his few creations with Gothic elements.

The unstinting magnificence of Stanford White's great New York houses coincides with an era of astonishing prosperity in the United States. Though the beginning of the 1890s had been marked in the country by a financial crisis which led to the failure of banks and businesses and manifested itself most clearly in the bitter Pullman Strike of 1894, New York felt the stress less than the rest of the nation. The reality was that much of the money made from the steel mills of Pittsburgh, the stockyards of Chicago, and the mines of the West had made its way to Manhattan. Mrs. John King Van Rensselaer, in her peevish social survey *The Social Ladder*, spelled out the new realities of New York society:

The West was yielding tremendous riches . . . Steel barons, coal lords, dukes of wheat and beef, of mines and railways, had sprung

The house that Stanford White created in 1904 for Mr. and Mrs. William K. Vanderbilt, Jr., at 666 Fifth Avenue, was adjacent to the French château which Richard Morris Hunt had designed in 1879 for William's parents. Though White matched Hunt's limestone and built in the same Francis I style, some critics found the dwelling less successful than its older neighbor because of the numerous windows in its façade. Both structures were demolished in the mid-1920s.

up from obscurity. Absolute in their own territories, they longed for fresh worlds to conquer. Newspaper accounts of the affairs of New York Society pictured this organization in colors that thrilled the newly rich of the West. In a great glittering caravan the multi-millionaires of the midlands moved up against the city and by wealth and sheer weight of numbers broke through the archaic barriers.

Typically, the Pittsburgh steel baron Andrew Carnegie, whose dollars would be a factor in the character assassination of Stanford White following his murder, had no difficulty in giving $2,000,000 for the completion of the concert hall on West Fifty-seventh Street which would bear his name. Carnegie, a Scottish-born near-dwarf, who concealed his avariciousness behind a façade of platitudes, such as "The man who dies possessed of millions ... dies disgraced," had attempted to speed construction of the edifice by purchasing a nearby Fifty-sixth Street tavern and closing it so that, after twelve hours on the job, his workmen could not have a drink. For Carnegie the high point of the May 5, 1891, opening of the hall was his brutal mimicry at a party afterward of the evening's guest conductor, the somewhat effeminate Peter Ilich Tchaikovsky. As Tchaikovsky recalled: he "expressed my greatness by standing on tiptoe and raising his hands up high, and finally threw the entire company into raptures by showing how I conduct." "Carnegie," a contemporary observed, "delighted in humiliating those who were in no position to respond."

With so much glitter being provided by Carnegie and other new arrivals in Gotham, it is not surprising that in the election of 1896, which pitted the Republican gold standard bearer, William McKinley, against the Democrats' silver-tongued supporter of silver coinage, William Jennings Bryan, New York came down heavily on the luteolous side. Though Stanford White, after hearing Bryan deliver his stirring campaign speech with its coda, "You shall not crucify mankind upon a cross of gold," at Madison Square Garden, flirted briefly with the Democrats, he quickly returned to his nominal Republicanism.

The boom that had been gathering force during the second half of the 1890s reached a crescendo by the end of the decade. With the just approved "Greater New York" charter placing the formerly independent boroughs of Brooklyn, Queens, the Bronx, and Staten Island under the governance of Manhattan's City Hall, with the city's population exceeding 4,000,000, and with one-half of all United States government revenues coming from customs duties levied at the Port of New York, the New York *Times* could, in its January 1, 1900, lead editorial, unhesitatingly announce: "The year 1899 was a year of wonders, a veritable annus mirabilis, in business and production . . ." and then go on to predict: "The outlook on the threshold of the new year is extremely bright."

For some the new year would be more than bright; it would be downright dazzling. During 1900, White's patron J. P. Morgan would organize the United States Steel Corporation with a capitalization of one billion dollars and in January 1901 would pay Carnegie $225,000,000 for his share of the Carnegie Steel Company. In 1900, the promoter Thomas Fortune Ryan—with the help of another White patron, William C. Whitney—was well on his way to the 1904 recapitalization of the American Tobacco Company at $180,000,000 after an original investment of little more than $50,000. These "bright" years marked the epoch when John "Bet-a-million" Gates cleared something like $15,000,000 from the American steel and wire trust and therefore could, with a calm mind, play poker with limits starting at $2,000 in private rooms at the Waldorf-Astoria; when Reginald Vanderbilt on the night that he became twenty-one and had thus inherited $75,000,000 could insouciantly drop $70,000 at Richard Canfield's gambling house at 5 East Forty-fourth Street; when banquets at Rector's featured tanks of live trout in the center of the table and guests like Nora Bayes and Nat Goodwin fished for their dinner after finding diamond favors wrapped in their napkins.

Nineteen hundred was particularly memorable as the year in which Leslie Stuart's smash hit, *Florodora*, opened at the Casino on Broadway at Thirty-ninth Street. Each evening pandemonium broke out as the Florodora Sextette, six florescent young women attired in long pink lace dresses and wearing large black picture hats, paraded onto the stage, where six handsome frock-coated young men knelt before them and sang:

Tell me, pretty maiden,
Are there any more at home like you?

Whereupon, deftly twirling their parasols, the Sextette coquettishly replied:

There are a few, kind sir,
But simple girls, and proper too.

Beginning in 1901, Stanford White regularly sent a Union Club cab to the Casino to fetch Florence Evelyn Nesbit after she had finished her bit part as a Spanish dancer. The cab carried her across the street to the Audubon Hotel, where the architect had taken a suite for the teenager with the lovely oval face, copper-colored hair, and hazel eyes and for her mother. White had been permitted this largess only after Mrs. Nesbit, at his invitation, had visited him in the offices of McKim, Mead & White and had pronounced the man who had befriended her daughter "charming."

There were those who did not approve of what came to be known as the "Naughty Nineties" and "Naughty Naughties." On a Sunday morning in February 1892, standing in the pulpit of his Madison Square Presbyterian Church, the Reverend Dr. Charles H. Parkhurst hurled a verbal thunderbolt at New York Mayor Hugh Grant, District Attorney De Lancey Nicoll, and the city's police commissioners. "Every step that we take looking to the moral betterment of this city has to be taken directly in the teeth of the damnable pack of administrative bloodhounds that are fattening themselves on the ethical flesh and blood of our citizenship . . ." Afterward Dr. Parkhurst was embarrassed when he could not prove his charges before a grand jury, but he was a determined man and, with the aid of a private detective, eventually got his evidence by personally visiting saloons, opium dens, and houses of female and male prostitution.

Dr. Parkhurst's charges led to the formation of an investigative committee chaired by State Senator Clarence Lexow. The Lexow Committee held its first meeting on March 9, 1894, and some 678 witnesses and 74 sessions later, reported that New York City was truly a cesspool of police bribery and official corruption. The indictment was so incontrovertible that New Yorkers did the almost unheard-of thing and elected an honest mayor, Republican William L. Strong, who promptly appointed Theodore Roosevelt to the new city Police Board. Roosevelt, with his typical energetic self-assuredness, immediately enforced every one of the city's blue laws. Thus he ordered the arrest not only of any saloonkeeper who sold a drink on Sunday but of any florist who proffered a bunch of violets, any iceman who delivered a block of ice, and any soda jerk who poured a root beer. Morality and reform were in the air. Theodore Dreiser's trenchant novel of life in Chicago and New York, *Sister Carrie*, was labeled pornographic and withdrawn from the city's bookstores. One of the casualties of this swing in sentiment would be Stanford White's reputation. Ironically, Dr. Parkhurst would give the architect the opportunity to design his favorite building.

"When Americans have luxuries," an English critic observed, "they tend to brood about them." Those for whom White designed his New York houses did not brood. These houses have a special quality which sets them apart from the residences—such as that for Chicago *Tribune* publisher Robert W. Patterson—which White designed in other cities for non-New Yorkers. The Patterson house, at the corner of Chicago's fashionable Astor Street and East Burton Place, is a handsome ochre-colored Roman brick mansion with an impressive Renaissance-style double loggia, but its unspectacular interiors reveal that it is the work of a superb architect, not of an intimate friend. White's New York houses were, on the whole, executed for those who were, if not friends, at least close acquaintances. Often they were for families—such as the Whitneys—for whom the architect had worked on a number of projects and thus intimately knew their tastes, their dislikes and likes. These dwellings became, in fact, show houses where, in order to create dazzling effects to convince others to employ him, the architect often made changes at his own expense. These New York houses were the chief beneficiaries of White's staggering collection of bits and pieces of architecture. As Channing Blake wrote in his article "Stanford White's New York Interiors," which appeared in *Antiques* magazine:

> White's monumental doorways and fireplaces were taken from an inventory of architectural and decorative fragments so large that a two-day sale was required to disperse it after his death. Although columns and pediments often did not match, White combined them sensitively to create the effects he desired. Occasionally he would complete the grouping with facsimiles.

In addition, White scoured Europe for antique rugs, tapestries, old velvets, paintings, and furniture for these residences. His taste and insatiable appetite made his office into a kind of universal clearinghouse for dealers and other scouts after artistic artifacts. The grand Paris dealer Fernand Robert writes: "The celebrated collection of the arms & armors belonging to the Duc de Dino could be bought, not at auction, but amicably, and all together . . ." While his friend Arthur M. Acton, father of the noted aesthete Sir Harold Acton, drops a line from Marseille reporting that "I have found here some fine panels—Watteau style and am getting the photos. They are seven and complete for a room . . ."

Stanford White's intimate involvement with his New York clientele is tellingly illustrated by the reconstruction and furnishing, beginning in 1899, that he did for the stockbroker and business publisher Henry W. Poor. The client's fortune was founded on his Railroad Manual, which had become an essential part of any investor's reading after 1884, when it had bluntly and correctly reported, in the words of Matthew Josephson, "that the entire capital stock of the railroads, then about four billions of dollars, represented water . . ." Poor was not only a close friend; he was the sort of patron who delighted the architect, a highly cultured businessman who could intelligently respond to White's subtle aesthetic suggestions and fully share a delight in the architect's far-flung discoveries, which here included a wall fountain picked up on the Isle of Capri. The history of the Poor house also reveals Stanford White's deep and tender feeling for his native city, particularly for its special enclaves, such as Greenwich Village and, in this case, Gramercy Park. When, at the end of the 1890s, 125 and 127 East Twenty-first Street, just across Lexington Avenue from his own residence, came up for sale, White was instrumental in convincing Poor to purchase them. And though the architect would have realized considerably more money had he encouraged Henry Poor to follow his first inclination and demolish the structures—which had fallen to the level of boardinghouses—and construct an entirely new dwelling, he instead advised him to preserve the buildings' charming exteriors while totally redoing their interiors.

These interiors are among the most exquisite Stanford White ever devised and show him to the fullest as the great interior designer he was. The library of the Poor house—crowned by a princely Venetian ceiling—was the thoughtfully opulent setting for a bibliophile who effortlessly read a dozen languages, including Greek, Latin, and Hebrew, and whose book collection ranked just below those of Morgan and James Lenox. But it is in the drawing room that White struck the new note of unconditional magnificence which is palpable in these late houses. Perfectly proportioned, with the walls left unadorned to better display tapestries and paintings, the room is ornamented with a massive Italian white marble mantelpiece and a doorway whose architrave is held up by Corinthian pilasters, but once again it is the palatial ceiling, found somewhere along the Grand Canal, which is the chamber's chief glory. Channing Blake makes an important point about White's use of these extravagant ceilings:

> The most impressive characteristic of the new style was the heavy emphasis on the architectural features of the rooms. On his trips to Europe he was always searching out ceilings, doorways, fireplaces,

and other architectural elements, that he could use in his installations. In fact, White and Isabella Stewart Gardiner of Boston exhausted the market in only a few years. Italian wooden ceilings were almost always used in White's houses, because of their mellow natural color and traces of polychrome decoration. However, more importantly, these imported ceilings demonstrated the function of joist and floor-board construction that is implicit in every roof, and they set the scale and proportions of every room.

The acquisition of such ceilings was not always easy. A letter written to White in 1903 by the famed Paris antiquaire Jacques Seligmann discusses the difficulties of procuring a particularly fine one from a titled Frenchwoman: "As far as the ceiling is concerned

In order to create a new entrance for the Henry Poor Mansion at number 1 Lexington Avenue— just across the avenue from his own house—White devised a charming street-level Ionic colonnade.

she is not yet decided to sell it as she fears that the castle would fall in if she takes the ceiling away."

These lambent spaces have been the object of scorn and disparagement by the critics who have followed the lead of the Midwestern minimalist Thorstein Veblen, whose Tin Pan Alley phrase "conspicuous consumption" is as catchy and as inaccurate as Mies van der Rohe's "less is more." Veblen's mind was as fixed upon the dollar sign as was John D. Rockefeller's; when he saw gilding he thought only of the gold. John Ruskin is a far better critic to look to for an understanding of what Stanford White was about: "... the glory of architecture," Ruskin wrote in *Mornings in Florence*, "is to be whatever you wish it to be,—lovely, or grand, or comfortable ..." These rooms wish to be lovely and grand, proclaiming in their way as surely as do the steel I beam and ferroconcrete the coming of age of America. These rooms are the memories of chambers seen by Americans on the Grand Tour, images of a high civilization which some of those Yankee pilgrims hoped the raw new republic would emulate. No one has more tellingly depicted the allure of these spacious compartments than did Henry James in *The Wings of the Dove* when he describes the sensuous delight experienced by Milly Theale after she has leased Venice's Barbaro Palace:

> ... she felt herself sink into possession; gratefully glad that the warmth of the Southern summer was still in the high florid rooms, palatial chambers where hard cool pavements took reflexions in their lifelong polish, and where the sun on the stirred sea-water, flickering up through open windows, played over the painted "subjects" in the splendid ceilings—medallions of purple and brown, of brave old melancholy colour, medals as of old reddened gold, embossed and beribboned, all toned with time ...

It was also Henry James who wrote in a letter of 1872: "It's a complex fate, being an American ..." White's glittering Renaissance interiors, reflecting a longing for tradition, are as integral a part of that fate as is Henry Ford's Model T or Louis Sullivan's Auditorium Building. In her perceptive memoir, *Roma Beata*, White's friend Maud Howe Elliott reported the remark of a fellow countryman in Rome: "When we Americans want beauty as much as we want rapid transit we shall get it." In his stunning New York rooms—all of which have vanished—Stanford White revealed that not every American opted for rapid transit.

White's ambition to bring splendid domesticity to New York found an enthusiastic backer in William C. Whitney. This attractive, rich, brilliant man was devoted to the good life in all of its aspects and had been Stanford White's boon companion on many a

The dazzling centerpiece of the Poor dining room was an extremely rare twelfth-century Italian altar tabernacle of white marble. Only one of the dining-room chairs was antique. White had found it in Italy also and had fourteen copies made. Unfortunately, Poor went bankrupt in 1907 and the contents of his glorious house were dispersed in a four-day sale in 1909. The tabernacle now graces the Cloisters. The house itself was demolished in 1930.

late-night carouse. Indeed, in 1906 it came out that Whitney had paid the oily Colonel William d'Aton Mann $10,000 to keep his name out of the colonel's scandalmongering *Town Topics*. Born in Massachusetts in 1841, Whitney graduated from Yale and went on to become an influential New York lawyer representing Vanderbilt and Carnegie interests. His marriage in 1869 to Flora Payne, sister of a college classmate, Oliver Hazard Payne, provided him with a beneficent connection to John D. Rockefeller's Standard Oil Company, for Payne was a major stockholder. These were the years when Henry Adams deemed William C. Whitney to be one of the patrician politicians who could be counted on to serve the country with disinterest. In this guise Whitney prosecuted New York's Tammany bosses, helped to organize a reform wing of the Democratic Party, and in 1885 was appointed Secretary of the Navy by his friend Grover Cleveland. After leaving that office Whitney suffered a sea change. Dixon Wecter recounted the details:

> Then upon his return to private life, after he had passed his fiftieth year, Whitney's love of wealth and luxury got the better of him. . . . Now he surrendered wholly to expedience, joined forces with Tammany, helped to organize the great Metropolitan Street Railway Company of New York in 1893, and garnered vast wealth from his virtual monopoly of street cars.

In less than ten years Whitney amassed a fortune estimated at $40,000,000.

William C. Whitney's drive to become rich was understandable. Possessing but a modest fortune, the one-time Secretary of the Navy's luxurious lifestyle was subsidized by his rich brother-in-law. Oliver Payne, a bachelor, doted on his sister Flora and on the muscular six-foot William. In the 1880s, Oliver purchased for more than half a million dollars the vast Frederick Stevens mansion at the corner of Fifth Avenue and Fifty-seventh Street and presented it to Flora. Oliver himself quickly took up residence there in a grand second-floor apartment. Between 1889 and 1890 Stanford White made important alterations to the red brick Whitney house. The chief undertaking was the creation of a larger ballroom for the party-loving Flora. By incorporating an adjoining salon and building an extension onto the house, White was able to double the chamber's size.

Following Flora's death from heart trouble in 1893 and his marriage in 1896 to Edith May Randolph, a sister of the Caroline May who had been engaged to James Gordon Bennett, Whitney gave the mansion to his elder son, Harry Payne. This marriage to a woman whom Flora had accused of flirting with William, transformed Oliver Payne from a fond friend into a fierce foe. With blatant promises of large gifts of money now and fabulous inheritances later on, Oliver Payne worked assiduously to turn the four Whitney children against their father. With two—William Payne, always known as Payne, and Pauline, who had married an impecunious Englishman, Almeric Hugh Paget—he succeeded. With the other two—Harry Payne, and the youngest, Dorothy, later Mrs. Willard Straight—he failed. The gift of the Fifth Avenue and Fifty-seventh Street house was, in part, a recognition of Harry's loyalty. Of course, William C. Whitney had no reason to fear that his elder son would ever suffer from a shortage of shingles over his head. Harry's wife was Gertrude Vanderbilt, whose parents, Cornelius and Alice, lived just across Fifty-seventh Street in New York's largest private dwelling, and who, in the summer, inhabited Newport's most spacious "cottage," The Breakers.

For his bride and himself Whitney purchased for $650,000 a four-story brownstone mansion at the northeast corner of Fifth Avenue and Sixty-eighth Street which had been designed in 1884 by William Schickel for the sugar magnate Robert L. Stuart. Now his immense fortune was used to transform 871 Fifth Avenue into a palace. It is estimated that by the time the work was completed in 1902, some $4,000,000 had been poured into 871. White gave to the entrance an inescapable grandeur by adding a high porte cochere, incorporating the gilded iron-and-bronze gates from Rome's Doria Palace, which provided a covered entryway to the vestibule and

In 1896, White began transforming the brownstone residence that Whitney had purchased at the northeast corner of Fifth Avenue and Sixty-eight Street into one of New York's truly princely palaces. It later became the home of Whitney's son, Harry Payne, and his wife, Gertrude Vanderbilt Whitney.

233

White's marble hall and grand stairway for the William Whitney mansion were particularly opulent. Animal pelts, such as that of the lion lurking beneath the marble bench, were the dernier cri of Gilded Age decor.

stair hall. This hall, as was typical of Stanford White's great houses of this period, struck the opening notes for the carefully orchestrated magnificence of the gala rooms above. In the Whitney hall one moved past rare Brussels tapestries to a grand marble stairway whose balustrade was so intricately carved that it might have been taken for ivory. Two of the palace's party rooms were particularly notable: the dining room, whose walls were completely covered by Italian Renaissance paintings that had been cut down to size, and the vast ballroom, which was paneled with elegant Louis XVI boiseries acquired from a château near Bordeaux.

William Whitney was delighted with what the New York *Times* proclaimed was a house "without rival in this country." When he opened it—still incomplete—at the beginning of 1901 with a party for the sacred number of 400, Ethel Barrymore exclaimed that the mansion left her "breathless." It is no wonder that Henry Adams, with his usual blend of sardonicism and savvy, wrote of Whitney:

After gratifying every ambition and swung the country almost at his will . . . [he] had thrown away the usual objects of political ambition like the ashes of smoked cigarettes; had turned to other amusements, satiated every taste, gorged every appetite, won every object that New York afforded, and not yet satisfied, had carried his field of activity abroad, until New York no longer knew what most to envy, his horses or his houses.

Even with clients like William C. Whitney and the fact that he received a 10 percent commission—his usual practice—on the estimated $1,000,000 worth of furnishings which he purchased for the Whitney mansion, Stanford White's financial position was steadily deteriorating. In 1901, already $300,000 in debt, the architect lost an additional staggering $400,000 in the stock market. Conditions soon reached the unpleasant state where local merchants were pounding on White's Gramercy Park door demanding immediate payment. Desperate, White borrowed money from Whitney and other clients, including Whitelaw Reid, and, in order to get another loan from Charles Barney, put up as collateral the furnishings of the Gramercy Park house, of Box Hill, and of his Madison Square apartment. Matters eventually reached the point where his partners were forced to draw attention to the fact that he had overdrawn his account at McKim, Mead & White by more than $75,000. The disconcerting task of facing McKim and Mead and having to negotiate terms of repayment were undoubtedly factors in a mood which led to what some in the White family refer to as "rumors of contemplated suicide."

Yet there is no evidence that the architect for a moment changed his manner of living. He continued to run up enormous bills for jewelry at Tiffany's, at Marcus & Co., at Black, Starr & Frost; for flowers at the fashionable florists Siebrecht & Wadley, where his account for one month in 1901 reached a hefty $2,500; and for private parties at Sherry's. Certainly one factor behind this ceaseless spending was White's liaison with Evelyn Nesbit, whom he had met in the summer of 1901. As Evelyn recalled in her autobiography, *Prodigal Days*, published in 1934, the sexual aspect

of the affair had begun in September after her mother departed for Pittsburgh to visit a suitor. White had asked Evelyn to come down to his offices to see the photographs which his friend Rudolph Eichemeyer had taken of her:

> After we had enthused over the pictures together, Stanford sent for Mr. McKim, his partner, introduced me and showed him the photographs.
>
> "This little girl's mother has gone to Pittsburgh and left her in my care," he explained.
>
> "My God!" said Mr. McKim.

Several nights later, in Stanford White's Twenty-fourth Street apartment, where they had supper and "several glasses of champagne," Evelyn was given a complete tour of the hideaway, including the bedroom:

> In one corner stood a four-poster canopied bed draped with gorgeous curtains that drew apart or together at the pull of a cord. The headboard of the bed, the dome of the canopy and the wall next to the bed were three solid mirrors. Adroitly hidden all around the top of the bed were tiny electric bulbs and within easy reach a series of buttons regulating the light effects. By pushing one button an amber glow was cast about the inverted mirror overhead. Another button produced a rose coloring, another a soft blue.

Afterward, though she was on the four-poster with a well-known man-about-town, Evelyn claimed that she was surprised to find, when she woke up, that they had had sex. She blamed it on "the unusual quantity of wine I had had." Later, though, when speaking of White, she admitted that "I was head over heels in love with him."

The lovers' special place was the tower of Madison Square Garden:

> Many nights or, I should say, mornings around three o'clock, Stanford and I would ride up in the elevator to its last stop, then climb the stairs to the top of the tower. Here one reached a narrow spiral stairway leading to the feet of Diana. I loved to climb to this high point and, holding tight to Diana's heel, gaze out over the city. . . . We could see in every direction. The Hudson to the west, with moving boats' lights etched clear. Southward, faint outlines of the city's highest spires. It was an especially enthralling sight on clear nights when the moon was full. Often we would stand there for a long time, holding hands and softly talking.

Though facing his own financial Waterloo, Stanford White was paying all of Evelyn and her mother's bills, and supplementing her small salary in *Florodora* with a $25 weekly allowance. His gifts for

Among the extravagant gala chambers on the *Whitney* mansion's second floor was the ballroom whose eighteenth-century boiseries came from a French château. It laid claim to being the largest private ballroom in New York. The lovely paneling went to a museum in Baltimore following the demolition of the *Whitney* palace in 1942.

Christmas 1901 included an oriental pearl on a platinum chain, a ruby-and-diamond ring, two diamond solitaire rings, and a set of white fox furs.

The architect's business relationship with the Whitney family did not end with the completion of work at 871 Fifth Avenue. Between 1900 and 1902 White was busy putting the finishing touches on William Whitney's large country house at Westbury, Long Island, and then designed a monument for the family in Woodlawn Cemetery. He was also in charge of erecting new gates and making other improvements at Oliver Payne's plantation, Greenwood, at Thomasville, Georgia.

After Whitney's sudden death from appendicitis in 1904, his Fifth Avenue palace eventually came into the possession of Harry Payne and Gertrude Vanderbilt Whitney. (Edith had already died, following a hideous riding accident.)

Though White advised the Whitneys on various changes in the furnishings of 871 Fifth Avenue, his next important commission from the family was the mansion that Oliver Payne gave his nephew Payne Whitney upon his marriage to Helen Hay, the daughter of John Hay, Secretary of State under both Presidents McKinley and Theodore Roosevelt. In a characteristically sensitive gesture, White, in order to make Helen Hay Whitney feel at home in her new house, consulted her father as to the marbles in the dwelling in which she had grown up. This had been one of the famous adjoining residences which the architect's old boss, H. H. Richardson, had designed for John Hay and Henry Adams in Washington:

Department of State
Washington

March 1, 1904

My dear Mr. White:—
I have your letter of the 26th of February.
I have no onyx mantel in the drawing room. The hearth is of Mexican onyx and the mantel is a pink marble, which was called by

The house Stanford White began in 1902 for Payne and Helen Hay Whitney was a wedding present from Payne's uncle, Oliver Payne. Located on Fifth Avenue between Seventy-eighth and Seventy-ninth streets, the gray granite bowfront dwelling, on the right in this picture, was built independently of the house to the north. Payne Whitney's house was sold in 1949 by his son, John Hay Whitney. It now houses the cultural services branch of the French embassy.

the dealer Aurore Pompadour. There are several other marbles of a rosy tint in the house which are all African. One I remember was called Boisé d'Orient. I have forgotten the name of the dealer of whom we bought them. It was a large marble shop pretty well up town, where Richardson and Mrs. Hay and I went and spent an afternoon looking for marbles. I am sorry the name escaped me, but it was at that time the principal place of the sort in New York.

I am sending this to Mrs. Whitney's care, and perhaps she may add something to the very scanty information it contains.

Yours faithfully,
John Hay

Begun in 1902, the house at 972 Fifth Avenue, between Seventy-eighth and Seventy-ninth streets, is a five-story light gray Vermont granite edifice whose inviting white marble doorway has flanking panels decorated with classical motifs designed by Adolph Weinman. There is an almost mannerist quality to the swell of the structure's bow front which is at once emphasized and controlled by its four boldly molded string courses and by its strongly profiled cornice. The sense of movement is further heightened by the tightly paired pilasters which rise through each story above the channeled base. The increasing cost of the project—it eventually reached $1,000,000—led White to write a letter of apology to Oliver Payne: ". . . the changes I have made in the treatment of the smaller rooms have added over a hundred thousand dollars to the price, and I have dreaded to speak to you about it until the house was far enough finished for you to see the result."

This uncharacteristic diffidence on the part of the architect may have sprung from the fact that Oliver Payne was regularly lending him money to cover his margin accounts and he thus did not wish to appear extravagant. White, for several reasons, need not have worried. When Oliver Payne died in 1922, he left an estate of $178,893,655, one of the largest ever recorded in the United States, and the smaller rooms in 972 Fifth Avenue—such as the multi-mirrored reception room—are among the most delightful of Stanford White's creations.

As with William C. Whitney's house, that of the Payne Whitneys received universal critical acclaim. The October 14, 1911, *Town & Country* went into raptures over its Italian treasures:

> The Whitney house stands as a triumphant blending of decorative art, old and new, a marvelous assembling of pictures, furniture, sculpture, tapestries, velvets, and wood carvings, which seem veritable voices of that ancient Italy of Leonardo da Vinci, of Benvenuto Cellini, and others of the Cinquecento.

If Stanford White's relationship with the Whitney family can be characterized as an *entente cordiale*, then that with Joseph Pulitzer

Among the forty rooms in the Payne Whitney house was the exquisite, mirrored first-floor reception room. The lavish interiors of the mansion were used for a number of scenes in the film, Rebecca.

might be called an armed truce. But then almost everything about the great publisher's life was a curious contradiction. Born in Hungary in 1847 to a Roman Catholic mother and a Jewish father, Pulitzer, like August Belmont, turned eventually to the comfortable bosom of the Protestant Episcopal Church; and though he served in the Union Army during the Civil War, in 1878 Pulitzer married a cousin of Jefferson Davis, President of the Confederate States of America; finally, the man who was the prescient editor-publisher of the St. Louis *Post-Dispatch* and of the New York *World* was, for a large part of his life, almost totally blind. In *Reminiscences of a Secretary*, Alleyne Ireland makes an astute assessment of Pulitzer's character:

> That he was arbitrary, self-centered, and exacting mattered little to me; it was a combination of qualities which rumor had led me to expect in him, and with which I had become familiar in my acquaintance with men of wide authority and outstanding ability. What disturbed me was that his blindness, his ill health, and his suffering had united to these traits an intense excitability and a morbid nervousness.

Stanford White would, in time, attest to the accuracy of Ireland's words.

The architect's introduction to Pulitzer came through their mutual friend William C. Whitney, for Pulitzer too was a reform Democrat and a Cleveland supporter. In 1887 the publisher had purchased from Charles T. Barney—whose wife, Lilly, was Whitney's sister—his house at 10 East Fifty-fifth Street following Barney's move to more magnificent quarters on Park Avenue. Undoubtedly one of the factors that led to Pulitzer's interest in the dwelling was his devotion to the number 10. As he constantly reiterated, he had been born on April 10, had arrived in St. Louis on October 10, 1865, had taken control of what became the *Post-Dispatch* on December 10, 1878, had acquired possession of the *World* on May 10, 1883, and had ordered that the cornerstone of the gold-domed *World* Building at 59–63 Park Row be laid on October 10, 1889.

White undertook considerable renovations in the Barney house for the publisher, and in the 1890s added a forty-foot-square, four-story granite tower to Chatwold, Pulitzer's summer residence at Bar Harbor, Maine. The tower—with its heated basement swimming pool, its magnificent ground-floor library/dining room, and its bedrooms for Pulitzer and his five male secretaries—was, according to Ireland, "designed with a view to securing complete quietness." As Pulitzer's health deteriorated, the publisher's determination to avoid anything that might be described as "noise" became an obsession. Aboard his 300-foot yacht, *Liberty*, everyone was required to wear rubber-soled shoes, and when Pulitzer was asleep that portion of the deck over his bedroom was roped off. White's work at Bar Harbor evidently pleased his client, for he wrote: "Let me both compliment and thank you and say specifically that I am much more than satisfied with the result . . ."

At the beginning of the century, 10 East Fifty-fifth Street, along with Pulitzer's collection of fine furniture and art objects, was destroyed by fire, and in 1901 he asked White to design him a much larger house farther uptown. Pulitzer's numerological faith led to the location, which took in numbers 7, 9, 11, 13, and 15 East Seventy-third Street. His biographer James Barrett explained the intricate calculations this way: "Seven plus nine, plus eleven, plus thirteen, plus fifteen, equals fifty-five; and five plus five equals ten. Also, seven plus three equals ten." Because of his client's near-blindness, White provided him with models of a French Renaissance château in the manner of the William K. Vanderbilt mansion and of a Florentine palazzo not unlike Charles McKim's University Club. Since both were summarily rejected, the architect must have realized that these comparatively smooth-surfaced structures lacked the articulation necessary for Pulitzer's fingers to feel the reality of their façades. Though McKim, Mead & White were quite capable of making scale models of their projects, the elaborate maquettes Stanford White wanted for the Pulitzer house may well have come from the workrooms of the Fifth Avenue establishment of the English art dealer Joseph Duveen. In *The Proud Possessors*, Aline

Joseph Pulitzer, the often irascible publisher of the New York World, *had the distinction of being one of the few clients Stanford White had difficulty pleasing.*

Saarinen points out that White's relationship with the man who would become Baron Duveen of Milbank was an interesting one:

> The galvanic redheaded architect would dash into the galleries of the art dealer Duveen and, darting from object to object, indicate "This tapestry for William C. Whitney's house—that statue for the dining-room of Senator Clark." Duveen's was paid $25,000 for making scale models of clients' prospective palaces. They were exquisite little doll houses, complete to hand-woven tapestries in miniature replica and tiny electric-lighted chandeliers. Nor did White find inappropriate the miniatures of the expensive old masters the dealer chose to include.

Searching for a surface which his client could, as it were, grasp, Stanford White turned to the baroque palazzi of the seventeenth-century Venetian architect Baldassare Longhena, the creator of the unforgettable Santa Maria della Salute at the entrance to the Grand Canal. The Pulitzer mansion is a subtle combination of the channeled ground floor and the entrance of Longhena's Palazzo Rezzonico, while its placement of columns—a rhythmical two, one, two, one, one, two, one, two—is taken from that of the Palazzo Pesaro. White wished to have the columns of pale green cipollino marble, but Pulitzer balked at the $8,000 per shaft cost. The architect's letter of August 23, 1901, to his client shows that this was no mere copybook construction:

> It was because we have this feeling about the columns ourselves that we wished to have them in polished granite of marble. If they are single columns of the same stone as the building they would have a weak look . . .

The columns, alas, are of limestone, the material used for the rest of the façade.

The interiors of the Pulitzer mansion were to give White endless problems, but his solutions, at least in one case, resulted in one of his finest rooms. At the very beginning of the project the publisher had stated:

The limestone Venetian palazzo on East Seventy-third Street that White created for Pulitzer between 1900 and 1903 is one of the architect's most impressive dwellings. The Pulitzer house is now divided into luxurious apartments.

SPLENDID DOMESTICITY IN GOTHAM   245

No ballroom, music room, or picture gallery under any disguise . . .
There must be no French rooms, designed or decorated to require
French furniture . . .

After reading this letter White is said to have exclaimed, "What sort
of man is this anyway!" He was particularly astonished regarding
the stricture about the music room, for music was a passion which
Pulitzer and White shared. Royal Cortissoz, who worked as an
office boy for McKim, Mead & White in the 1880s, and whose
career, first as a music critic and later as the art critic of the New
York *Herald Tribune*, owed much to White, wrote: "I wish I could
bring back to you a living, breathing impression of Stanford White
when the musical mood was on him. I wish I could help you to see
how inspiring he then was, how endearing. I have heard the sym-
phonies of Beethoven played by many great orchestras; but when I
think of them there is no memory that returns more poignantly than
the memory of White, whistling the slow movement from the
Pastoral." In a similar vein, Pulitzer had once brought the entire
New York Philharmonic to Chatwold, and every evening before he
went to sleep, had one of his secretaries play on the piano the
"Liebestod" from Wagner's *Tristan and Isolde.*

Beginning his campaign with the music room, Stanford White
used all of his extraordinary charm, knowledge, and tact to convince
Joseph Pulitzer and his equally demanding wife, Kate, that they
should have interiors to match their residence's marvelous façade.
An accurate understanding of this process may be gained from the
portrayal of the architect, Seymour, in William Dean Howells's
novel *The Rise of Silas Lapham*, for Howells, who was not only
Mead's brother-in-law but a correspondent with White's father,
most likely based his fictional architect on White. Here is Seymour
in the act of persuading Lapham to do the "correct" thing in his new
house in Boston's Back Bay:

"I presume," he said, "you'll have the drawing-room finished in
black walnut?"

"Well, yes," replied the architect, "if you like. But some less expensive wood can be made just as effective with paint. Of course you can paint black walnut too."

"Paint it?" gasped the Colonel.

"Yes," said the architect quietly. "White, or a little off white."

Lapham dropped the plan he had picked up from the table. His wife made a little move toward him of consolation or support.

"Of course," resumed the architect, "I know there has been a craze for black walnut. But it's an ugly wood; and for a drawing-room there is really nothing like white paint. We should want to introduce a little gold here and there. Perhaps we might run a painted frieze round under the cornice—garlands of roses on a gold ground; it would tell wonderfully in a white room."

After what seemed an endless altering of plans, the architect was able to convince Pulitzer to have a music room, as well as a ballroom and even some French decor and furniture, which were employed in one of the mansion's most pleasing chambers. The publisher's phobia concerning noise during mealtime—he would not accept a dinner invitation unless the hostess assured him that he would be seated between two women with soft voices—led White to position the breakfast room, where Pulitzer intended to take most of his meals, so that it would have no contact with the cacophony of the outside world. This pale green circular room once more demonstrates the genius of the Beaux Arts school. Daylight, without sound, was provided for the enclosed space by a state-of-the-art overhead walkway constructed of the most modern materials, glass block and steel, which was placed close to a large sealed window. At the same time, the room's beauty came from its refined Louis XVI-style decoration carried to an appropriate conclusion by a trellis-work dome which created no barrier to the light pouring down into the space. Here indeed is the *beau idéal* of form following function!

But White failed to make the entire East Seventy-third Street dwelling soundproof and a constant source of irritation was the pump needed to control a spring beneath the house. When Pulitzer was still dissatisfied after the notable Harvard acoustics expert

Professor W. C. Sabine was brought in, the usually unflappable Mead exclaimed: "... nerves are his trouble and that is not part of an architect's business to supply the client with a proper set of nerves." Eventually Pulitzer turned to another firm—Foster, Ade & Graham—to build him a bedroom at the rear of his mansion. "In the bedroom," Alleyne Ireland wrote, "with its triple window and its heavy double-door closed, J.P. enjoyed as near an approach to perfect quietness as it was possible to attain in New York." After Pulitzer's death aboard the *Liberty* in 1911, a long-suffering secretary, responding to a reporter's question about how his master had died, answered, with a touch of irony, "Quietly."

A year before his death, one of Pulitzer's sons, Ralph, published *New York Society on Parade*, a deliciously sardonic glimpse of Gotham's smart set. One of the vignettes in Ralph Pulitzer's book depicts a grand ball thrown in a Fifth Avenue mansion:

> When enough arrivals have gathered to give one another moral support, they begin their advance. Across the hall they wend their way with stately tread and dignified composure. Then up the majestic stairs the climbing cortege winds, its full-flung trains draping the steps with glory, and, having gained the summit, in glittering array sweeps slowly toward the hostess. In a great doorway, her triumphal arch, flanked by her married daughter, she stands, an imposing figure, instinct with formality and power. The still lines of her satin dress, the steady glitter of her diamonds, the rigid coiffure of her pale hair, the tautened crispness of her skin (the victory of massage over matter), her straight carriage, all show the born leader of women. Her guests file past her with the air of sumptuous gladiators crying: "Hail, Hostess!"

This passage vividly illustrates the signal significance, in New York's Gilded Age mansions, of the grand stairway, for it was nothing less than the tribune upon which the chatelaine stood to receive her guests' obeisance. Indeed, it was the desperately felt need for such a stairway that brought Stanford White one of the most diverting of all his clients.

The Stuyvesant Fishes, like the Whitneys, were an impressive

The circular Louis XVI–style breakfast room in the Pulitzer residence owed its form to the publisher's acute sensitivity to sound, for the chamber had no contact with the outside world.

In 1890, the Stuyvesant Fishes abandoned the makeshift grandeur of their Gramercy Park house for the buff brick mansion Stanford White designed for them at the northwest corner of Madison Avenue and Seventy-eighth Street. The Renaissance residence has been converted into offices.

combination of impeccable lineage—this time Knickerbocker New York—and newly made wealth, though on a far more modest scale than the Whitneys. There is a ring of truth to Mrs. Fish's bosom buddy Harry Lehr's shout when, at a Newport party, the Stuyvesant Fishes rose to depart: "Sit down, Fishes, you are not rich enough to be the first to leave!" Fish was president of the Illinois Central, nicknamed, because it was a favorite investment of New York grandees such as the Goelets, Astors, and Cuttings, the "Society Railroad." Fish himself, due to his blondness, his girth, and his physical awkwardness, was known as "the White Elephant." His wife, Marion—"Mamie" to her friends—was the holy terror of New York Society, quite capable of relieving the monotony of upper-crust crushes by insisting that the guests at one of her balls come dressed as characters out of Mother Goose rhymes, with their hostess attired as old Mother Goose herself. Monotony was most certainly not something Mrs. Fish tolerated. She reduced the interminable eight-course society banquet to a briskly served fifty-minute dinner, invited people just because they were amusing or attractive, and, in a move which may be seen as a foretaste of 1920s Café Society, replaced the large orchestra at her soirees with dance bands playing tunes from Broadway musicals. If she got bored or felt that the party had gone on too long, Mamie Fish would instantaneously instruct the conductor to strike up "Home, Sweet Home."

In the late 1880s, as Mrs. Fish positioned herself to challenge Mrs. Astor's regnancy over social New York, she concluded that the various red-brick Federal and Italianate brownstone houses which the Fish family owned were not suitable pads from which to launch her societal rocket. Thus, in 1887, the Stuyvesant Fishes bought 20 Gramercy Park, an 1850s Greek Revival dwelling with faintly Parisian addenda. Mamie Fish inspected the alterations which White was currently making at the nearby Players Club and asked the architect to conjure up an appropriate setting for her Astorian campaign. The $120,000 spent on 20 Gramercy Park was used to carve out a new ground-level entrance and to construct a fittingly magnificent stairway upon which Mrs. Fish could perch to proclaim her defiance of Caroline Webster Schermerhorn Astor. Mr. Fish, Elizabeth Lehr observed, was often astonished upon his return from an inspection tour of the IC to find his house filled with strangers. "It seems I am giving a party," was his invariable comment.

The patchwork palatialness of 20 Gramercy Park satisfied Mamie Fish for only a decade; by then she had joined Alva and Tessie upon the late Mrs. Astor's suzerain sofa. Commissioned in 1897 and completed in 1900, the Stuyvesant Fish mansion at the northwest corner of Madison Avenue and Seventy-eighth Street is constructed, not in the opulent masonry manner of the Joseph

The architect and "Mamie" Fish both attended the notorious James Hazen Hyde ball of February 1905. White is standing third from the right in the rear. Mrs. Fish is the lady seated on the right. It is not difficult to see what wags meant when they said that her malicious wit made up for her lack of beauty.

Pulitzer and Payne Whitney palaces, but in the economical brick-and-terra-cotta mode of the house that White did for his brother-in-law Prescott Hall Butler at 22 Park Avenue in 1895 and the one he had designed five years earlier for the city's Parks Commissioner, J. Hampden Robb, at 23 Park Avenue. Some idea of the bottom-line difference of the two approaches may be gathered from the fact that a major stone window cap took two men up to six months to carve and cost $1,700, while the stone capital of a pilaster required one man ten months to carve and cost $1,500. By using terra cotta these elements could be quickly mass-produced for a few hundred dollars.

There is, though, an enormous difference between the Butler and Robb houses and that of the Fishes. In both of the former, the two-tiered entrance loggia, which advertises the dignity of the dwelling and the architect's familiarity with Renaissance design, is placed on the façade as though it were, as was indeed the case with the Players Club, a structural addition. Neither loggia is fully integrated into the body of the building. While the Butler and Robb houses are handsome, they are essentially a gathering together of exquisite elements not yet brought into a compositional unity. This sense that the sum of the parts is greater than the architectural whole has vanished by the time of the Stuyvesant Fish mansion. Here the entrance and the windows, with their banded pilasters and consoles and pediments, have been correctly subordinated to the powerfully restrained façade which rises, without misstep, in four stories of buff Roman brick above its strong masonry base. With its superb interpretation of Roman classicism, the Stuyvesant Fish mansion is a worthy heir to the work of Giulio Romano at Mantua and of certain palaces by Andrea Palladio in Vicenza. At Madison Avenue and Seventy-eighth Street, Stanford White reveals that masterful sense of closed composition, without any extraneous details, which marks his last great buildings.

The wonderful Seventy-eighth Street façade of the mansion is, as it were, a Potemkin palace, a stage set designed to impress the arriving partygoer, for the Fish house is but two windows deep. Mamie Fish put her money where it mattered, into her white marble hall, her splendid stairway, and an all-white ballroom which vied with that of the Whitney house for the title of New York's largest. Mrs. Fish, unlike Pulitzer, loved her new circumambience, but it was not long before her sharp tongue brought her husband's railroad career to an abrupt terminus. It all came about because Mary Harriman told her husband, rail tycoon Edward H. Harriman, that at a tea party Mamie had called her something worse than the toad which she had said Alva Vanderbilt resembled. Harriman, a small nervous man, snapped, "I'll make those people suffer." And he did, by pushing Stuyvesant Fish out of the presidency of the Illinois

Central. Mamie Fish doesn't seem to have minded the skirmish very much. Until her death in 1915 she went merrily on leading revels in her mansion, which she announced, with some regularity, was "an uncomfortable place for anyone without breeding."

If Stanford White had a competitor for the laurels of New York's "leading man-about-town" at the turn of the century it was Charles Dana Gibson. Cleveland Amory quotes Mrs. Chester Burden, a social arbiter par excellence, in speaking of eras past: "Then people were different. They were fascinating and charming—men like Dana Gibson . . . He was the most attractive man, bar none, I've ever met . . ." Gibson was not only attractive and charming; he was also the talented creator of the Gibson Girl, that frightfully healthy, perfectly profiled, shirtwaisted all-American goddess whose image in the original *Life* magazine and *Collier's* and in innumerable books set the fashion for women from Montauk Point to Puget Sound. Dana Gibson was a close friend of White's, a buddy at the Players, a companion at the cheerful parties Edwin Austin Abbey threw in his studio in the White-designed Judge Building on Fifth Avenue, and one of the artists the architect had encouraged by paying $1,000 for a group of drawings to decorate his Garden City Hotel. Gibson had another string to his bow. He was married—White had attended his wedding in Richmond—to Irene, one of the inimitable daughters of the Virginian Chiswell Dabney Langhorne. Another daughter was the irrepressible Nancy Astor. Dana and Irene Gibson were one of the Gilded Age's memorable love matches. Rennie Martinuzzi, a great-niece, in an interview with Frederick Eberstadt, declared: "My Uncle Dana was certainly a romantic . . . He was absolutely crazy about his wife and she was crazy about him. This was evident up until the day he died. They really were a romantic couple in the old sense of the word." The presence of Gibson at parties such as the Pie Girl Dinner throws several pails of cold water on allegations that anything truly scandalous took place.

Though in 1902, when White designed his house at 127 East Seventy-third Street, Gibson was being paid the impressive sum of $500 a drawing, he was certainly far nearer the cash class of William

The town houses White worked on in 1891–92 for David H. King, Jr., the contractor in charge of Madison Square Garden, were a highly successful experiment in providing well-designed dwellings for those who were not rich. Located in Harlem on West 139th Street, the dwellings, in their use of thin Roman brick and in their spare but deft employment of classical details, bear a marked design relationship to White's aristocratically reserved Fish mansion. Cherished by Harlem's black community, the King houses were part of what was once known as Strivers' Row.

For his close friend, the artist
Charles Dana Gibson, White
designed a charming, but
economical Federal-style residence
on East Seventy-third Street. In
contrast to the more than
$370,000 cost of the Pulitzer
mansion, the bill for the Dana
house was less than $50,000.

Merritt Chase than to that of the Whitneys or even the Fishes. Thus his red-brick Georgian-Federal town house, like Chase's Shinnecock shingle cottage, has no hints of the palazzo about it, but reaches back for inspiration to an earlier, simpler moment in American history. The Gibson house, with its highly refined ambience, is a precursor of the chaste brick clubhouses White would design for the Lambs in 1904 and for the Colony in 1906.

The lovely entrance to the house consists of a pair of Doric columns supporting an undecorated architrave which carries an airy iron balustrade of the type common on Boston's Beacon Hill, while the doorway itself is a graceful combination of flanking reeded Ionic columns, side lights, and a rectangular Federal-style fanlight. The principal or parlor floor is indicated by a composition as brilliant as any of Edwin Lutyens's fanciful essays on the classical. White has dissected a Palladian window and then recomposed it by moving the flat-topped side windows out from the large central arched one. This act is underscored by the witty placement of limestone rectangles over the side windows, while a delicate limestone keystone, without any relating voussoirs to justify it, has been set above the central arch. White emphasized the playful game again by putting another limestone rectangle above the flat-headed center window of the third floor. The Gibson house concludes with a frankly romantic, steeply peaked roof with three dormers which recalls the old houses of Paris's Left Bank, a highly appropriate crown for the residence of an artist.

The spare ivory-colored interiors of the Gibson house, with their simple paneling, fluted pilasters, and delicate Adamesque fireplaces, were a conscious evocation of the Colonial interiors of Irene Langhorne's native Virginia. Both of the Gibsons were enchanted by their new home. "The beauties of the front," Dana Gibson wrote to the architect, "occupies my whole attention." The Charles Dana Gibson house would be a prototype for the restrained, well-mannered Upper East Side New York town houses designed by Delano & Aldrich, Mott B. Schmidt, and others in the generation after McKim, Mead & White.

The delicate interiors of the dwelling, completed in 1903, delighted both Charles Dana Gibson and his wife, Irene, the original model for "The Gibson Girl." These refined rooms are now used for offices.

There was another intimate link between Stanford White and Charles Dana Gibson. The illustrator had, in fact, met Evelyn Nesbit a few months before the architect. The chain of events which carried her to posing before Gibson's drawing board began in 1884 in Tarentum, a village near Pittsburgh, Pennsylvania. Evelyn's father, whom she always claimed was a lawyer, died when she was eight, leaving her mother with scant means to raise her and her younger brother, Howard. Mrs. Nesbit set about doing this in a way not unusual for the time; she moved to Pittsburgh and opened a boardinghouse. The stratagem eventually failed, and in 1899 the Nesbits migrated to Philadelphia, where they all found employment at Wanamaker's department store: "Mamma as a saleswoman," Evelyn wrote, "Howard as a cashboy, and me as a stockgirl."

The fourteen-year-old was already developing into a beauty. Acquaintances commented on her lovely skin—which had just a touch of olive—and on her luxuriant hair. Evelyn's break came when the family met at their Arch Street boardinghouse the sister of the respected Philadelphia painter John Storm. Soon she was being paid to pose, not only for Storm and other Philadelphia painters but also for the stained-glass artist Violet Oakley, who used her as the model for an angel in a window she was making for a suburban church. Though Evelyn's posing fees were a welcome addition to the family income, Mrs. Nesbit had doubts about the propriety of her daughter's career as a model. She was also weary of her work at Wanamaker's and bored with Philadelphia. Thus, after a year in the City of Brotherly Love, she announced one morning: "All right, let's try New York," and carried Evelyn and Howard off to a modest boardinghouse on West Twenty-second Street.

Mrs. Nesbit tried desperately but unsuccessfully to find work. It was only after she had run through her small savings that she permitted Evelyn to make use of the letters of introduction from Storm and others to various New York artists. One such letter was to James Beckwith, who immediately engaged her, and before long Evelyn was posing for the distinguished painter Frederick S. Church and for the sculptor George Grey Barnard, who portrayed her in marble as "Innocence." It was at this point in her career, just before an agent saw her photographs in a theatre magazine and offered her a bit part in *Florodora*, that Dana Gibson met Evelyn. He sketched her in profile, her wonderful hair curled over her shoulders to form a question mark. For Gibson, Evelyn Nesbit represented Woman, "The Eternal Question."

About 1902, Charles Dana Gibson portrayed Evelyn Nesbit as "The Eternal Question."

CHAPTER 12

THE NEW

FIFTH AVENUE

"In spite of Mr. White's designs for the Washington Arch and Madison Square Garden, he has been known until recently more as a decorator than as an architect," Gurdon S. Parker wrote in the *Architectural Record* shortly before Stanford White's murder. "Yet in the little group of buildings between Thirty-fourth and Thirty-seventh Streets, on Fifth Avenue, he combined the possibilities as an architect and decorator." This "little group of buildings," the Knickerbocker Trust, designed in 1901, and the Gorham and Tiffany buildings, designed in 1903, reveal, as Trinity Church Boston did and Madison Square Garden, the constant unfolding of White's genius, that ability to conjure up spectacular new edifices upon the foundations of previous work, which is the mark of the true artist. These three buildings, with their light color, their employment of the classical repertory upon commercial structures, and their perfection of design, were to change the face of Fifth Avenue.

The profundity of this change may be gauged by the

Stanford White's Corinthian-columned Knickerbocker Trust building, at the northwest corner of Fifth Avenue and Thirty-fourth Street, was only a year old when this photograph was taken in 1905 looking north from Thirty-third Street. The colossal structure on the left is the original Waldorf-Astoria, which vanished in 1929.

raconteur-historian Albert Steven Crockett's description, in his *Peacocks on Parade*, of midtown Fifth Avenue at the turn of the century:

> Mid-town New York, physically speaking, had undergone really very few changes during the last seven years of the nineteenth century. Above Thirty-fourth Street, Fifth Avenue had developed little during that time. Indeed, it was not until the old reservoir . . . began to be demolished that the transmogrification actually started of what, except for a sprinkling of consequential structures such as the Vanderbilt houses, the C. P. Huntington mansion and that of A. T. Stewart . . . and a few churches among the monotonous brownstone fronts, was hardly more imposing than the show street of any big town.

The demise of midtown's musty brownstone Fifth Avenue had been unmistakably signaled that day in late 1894 when the noted New York photographer Joseph Byron had been summoned to document for posterity the art gallery and ballroom of Caroline Astor's legendary mansion at the southwest corner of Fifth Avenue and Thirty-fourth Street. Early in the new year, after one last formal dinner whose interminable three-hour length and mediocre catered food were somewhat offset by a river of solid-gold plate and a rain forest of pink and mauve orchids, the social bastion fell before the new Astoria Hotel.

Behind the demolition of Caroline Astor's domicile lay what may be truly described as a blood feud. During the early years of her marriage to William Backhouse Astor, Caroline had been frustrated because, as the wife of the younger of the two Astor brothers, she was denied the right of being styled *the* Mrs. Astor. That honor went to Charlotte, consort of the elder brother, John Jacob III. But after Charlotte's death in 1887, Caroline struck, and by means of balls where the guest lists included President and Mrs. Benjamin Harrison, a prime box at the Metropolitan Opera, and the blinding flashes given off by her diamond-studded stomacher, usurped the title of *the* Mrs. Astor from its rightful owner, Charlotte's daughter-in-law, Mrs. William Waldorf Astor. Furious, the William Waldorf

Astors soon decamped for England, and, in an act which nicely combined financial acumen and personal revenge, commissioned Henry J. Hardenbergh to design a 13-story, 530-room hotel where their house had stood at the northwest corner of Fifth Avenue and Thirty-third Street. After the Waldorf opened on March 13, 1893, it was soon clear that the Teuton-style caravansary had achieved both goals sought by the William Waldorf Astors. It was making money and it was also casting a dark shadow over Aunt Caroline's abode. Caroline quickly got the message, moved up to a French château she had Richard Morris Hunt design for her at Fifth Avenue and Sixty-fifth Street, and four years later the Waldorf was joined by the $9,000,000 17-story Astoria built on the site of her old ballroom. Thus was born what knowing New Yorkers always referred to as "the Hyphen."

The essence of the gargantuan Waldorf-Astoria was to be found in Peacock Alley, that amber-marble-lined corridor stretching from the carriage entrance near the main lobby to the foyer and the grand restaurant. Here out-of-towners flocked hoping to glimpse a real live Vanderbilt or Fish or Belmont, and though they were often disappointed in this, they could always count on a good look at fashionable Gothamites marching past in the *dernières nouveautés* in frocks, hats, and baubles. The chorus of a song made famous by Dan Daly in the new smash hit *The Belle of New York* might well have been dancing through the heads of the proud passing natives:

> *Of course, you can never be like us:*
> *But be as like us as you're able to be.*

The magnetism of all this opulent glamour would quickly prove too insistent to be withstood by the shops of the old Ladies' Mile.

Just across Thirty-fourth Street from the Waldorf-Astoria the members of the Manhattan Club, New York's Democratic wigwam, were increasingly unhappy with the chilly marble splendors of the A. T. Stewart mansion into which the club had moved in 1890. The members, who boasted: "More famous drinks have been invented at the Manhattan than at any other place in the country," complained that not even a dozen Manhattan cocktails could warm up the mansion's parvenu pomp and had christened it "the Whited Sepulchre." In addition, even with dues payers of the stamp of William C. Whitney, Thomas Fortune Ryan, Perry Belmont, and Frederic Coudert, the club was having increasing difficulty paying its $40,000-a-year rent to the A. T. Stewart estate. It was with a Democratic sigh of relief that the Manhattan was able in 1899 to break its lease and move into more cozy quarters in the former Leonard Jerome mansion at the southeast corner of Madison Avenue and Twenty-sixth Street.

The site, though, seemed an ideal one for the Knickerbocker Trust Company, whose president was Stanford White's close friend Charles T. Barney. In 1901 Barney and a group of associates commissioned the architect to design a 13-story structure with the Knickerbocker bank occupying the first three floors and the upper stories containing hotel rooms or apartments, much like the plan the architect had devised for the Sherry Building at Fifth Avenue and Forty-fourth Street. Soon afterward, Barney's associates, perhaps becoming unsure of a project under the direction of a bank president who was more and more given to manic-depressive mood swings, withdrew. But though the structure was now reduced to the bank's three stories, Barney insisted on its being constructed so that the original plan could be carried out at some future time. White proceeded accordingly and reported that he was completing "the masonry walls, the iron work, and all the constructional work, the elevator wells, the feeds, and all necessary chases, and everything which would enable the balance of the stories to be built..." Surprisingly, the almost always optimistic White doubted that the additional stories would ever be constructed. In time they were, but above a mutilated base.

Fully aware that a building on such a pivotal corner would soon be surrounded by towering neighbors, White did what Cram, Goodhue & Ferguson were later to achieve in the new St. Thomas

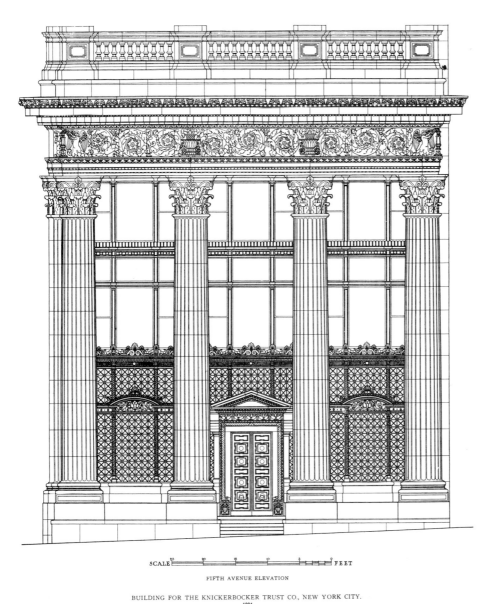

SCALE |⎯⎯⎯⎯⎯⎯⎯⎯⎯⎯⎯⎯⎯| FEET

FIFTH AVENUE ELEVATION

BUILDING FOR THE KNICKERBOCKER TRUST CO., NEW YORK CITY.
1904

The luxuriant beauty of the Knickerbocker Trust, with its white Vermont marble 3-story columns and rinceau frieze, is evident in this drawing of the Fifth Avenue façade. The structure was first shorn of its columns and then, in the 1920s, became the base of a tall office building.

Church at the corner of Fifth Avenue and Fifty-third Street, and designed a structure which, by the sheer brilliance of its presence, held and dominated the site. Though he had but three stories and a high attic to work with, White gave to the bank's 75-foot Fifth Avenue façade a sense of nobility by composing it of nothing but four three-story Roman Corinthian columns. He then turned the corner with panache by the striking device of breaking the architrave, the cornice, and the balustrade—a marble equivalent of the

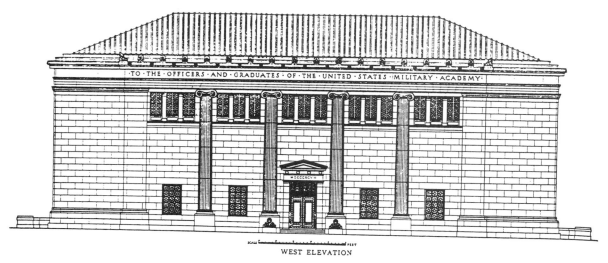

WEST ELEVATION

disappearing steel corner of Mies van der Rohe's Seagram Building—and leading the viewer to the row of six giant Corinthian pilasters which made up the 125-foot Thirty-fourth Street façade. Montgomery Schuyler, writing in the May 1904 number of the *Architectural Record*, saw a relationship between the Knickerbocker Trust, the architect's Cullum Hall at West Point, and Paul-René-Léon Ginain's building for Paris's Faculté de Médecine. Schuyler particularly liked the fact that the bank's columns—with their steel cores—truly held up the attic and roof, while the non-load-bearing spaces between them were clearly expressed by the light screen wall of metal—from Tiffany & Co.—and glass. The Knickerbocker's "front is one of the most impressive visual objects in Fifth Avenue," the critic wrote, "or indeed in the street architecture of New York, and we ought to feel very much obliged to the architect for giving us something so good to look at."

The virtuoso building was completed in 1904, but it was to serve the firm which commissioned it scarcely three years. By that time White was dead. It was a blessing that he did not witness the sordid end of the man he had enthusiastically put up for membership in the Players, the man for whom he had designed two residences, the man who had the financial oversight of the new Bronx campus he created for New York University, the man who had asked him to decorate the interiors of his luxurious yacht, *Invincible*.

In October 1907 a pool of traders attempted to corner the stock in copper, but one of those in on the deal sold out and the corner was smashed. Barney, word on the Street soon had it, without the knowledge of his bank's executive committee, had lent millions to those involved in the copper scheme. As a consequence, the New York Clearing House refused to clear Knickerbocker Trust checks and, on Tuesday, October 21, 1907, White's marvelous building was the center of one of the city's most spectacular financial panics. John K. Winkler, in *Morgan the Magnificent*, describes the scene:

> . . . a long line formed at the door of the trust company, at Fifth Avenue and Thirty-fourth Street. A messenger from the Night and Day Bank was first in line. He bore a thick portfolio. Millions of dollars were withdrawn in two hours. The vaults were soon empty. Amid scenes of furious anger, with men and women struggling desperately at the doors and squads of police fighting to maintain order, the Knickerbocker suspended business.

Not long afterward Charles T. Barney shot himself and died in the arms of his wife.

The flow of the aristocratic aspects of commerce up Fifth Avenue was given added impetus by the parallel movement of more modest establishments up Broadway to Herald Square just a block west. "Bennett's newspaper gave the square its name, but Isidor and Nathan Straus gave it an identity," David Dunlap notes in *On Broadway*. "R. H. Macy & Company, which they owned, was doing business at the turn of the century in a jumble of buildings east of Sixth Avenue. . . . The store needed a new home, but the Strauses did not want to build in the Union Square area, as the retail district had already shifted as far north as Twenty-third Street, leaving the future of Fourteenth Street in doubt. They decided to bypass the Twenties and go to Herald Square." Macy's colossal red-brick, limestone-trimmed Georgian-style building by De Lemos & Cordes, which opened in 1902, was soon joined by Saks & Company, making Herald Square the hub of New York's middle-level merchandising. The carriage trade, though, was on Fifth Avenue, and two structures by Stanford White proclaimed its breaching of the Thirty-fourth Street line.

The architect's relationship with the Gorham Company, particularly with its superb bronze foundry, had been a long one. He had specified Gorham bronze for numerous important commissions, including Cullum Hall at West Point, and in the 1890s had the firm execute a number of bronze tables. Just how much Gorham had gotten into the swing to the Italian Renaissance is made clear from a book the firm published in 1905: "Since the establishment many years ago of its Foundry the Gorham Company has endeavored worthily to carry on the traditions of those *Cinque-Cento* goldsmiths and silversmiths to whose artistic devotion we owe such masterpieces as the Florentine gates of Ghiberti . . ." Thus in 1903, when the company decided to abandon its picturesque Queen Anne-style premises at Broadway and Nineteenth Street and move to the southwest corner of Fifth Avenue and Thirty-sixth Street, it inevitably chose Stanford White as its architect and the Renaissance as its style.

The architect handled the ordering and decoration of this eight-story limestone structure with masterful finesse. The street-level display windows and mezzanine of Gorham's shop were treated as a closed arcade springing from graceful granite Ionic columns in a manner directly related to the open arcade of Madison Square Garden. Above this the four stories of offices are of marked severity. This section is topped by a two-story temple of attached Corinthian columns whose interstices are filled with metal and glass in the manner of the Knickerbocker Trust which contained the firm's workrooms. The building is surmounted by a stupendous Florentine-inspired copper cornice, cantilevered eight feet over the pavement, which set a style for Fifth Avenue's commercial structures until well into the 1930s.

At the Gorham Building, White brilliantly employed decoration to draw attention to the top and bottom of the composition, thus compacting it and visually reducing its height to that of a traditional Florentine palazzo. The underside of the cornice was

brightly colored and gilded, while the spandrels of the lower arcade
held images of the craft of the silversmith—the metier for which
Gorham was best known—by Andrew O'Connor, the sculptor
who had recently collaborated with Daniel Chester French on the
tympanum of the central portal of the Cornelius Vanderbilt Memo-

rial at St. Bartholomew's Church and had sculpted the New and Old Testament friezes linking the three entrances of White's majestic construction. Russell Sturgis had criticized O'Connor's figures as being too realistic, of having "too much of Rodin" about them, but Augustus Saint-Gaudens had risen to their defense and announced: "O'Connor's work is a revelation to me."

Saint-Gaudens's approbation at this time was undoubtedly both welcome and touching to White, for though the two old friends had, between 1894 and 1897, joined forces on the memorial to Peter Cooper just south of the famed school he financed, the sense of artistic compatibility, so remarkable in the Farragut, seems to have lessened. The reality is that, as Stanford White moved toward the status of New York's most famous architect, he insisted on his contribution to any collaboration being given more and more prominence. This architectural overkill led to the placement of the somewhat shaggy Cooper within an elegant classical granite-and-marble ciborium. The resulting rather ridiculous memorial has about it the air of some self-made Victorian paterfamilias posing on the set of a photographer's studio. Saint-Gaudens had been profoundly dissatisfied with the Cooper project, and though there was no actual break with White, the sculptor's three-year stay in France, which began just after the completion of the memorial, and his decision after he developed cancer in 1900 to remain most of the time at his home and studio in Cornish, New Hampshire, kept the two apart. But in the spring of the year in which he was killed, White proposed to come up with McKim to Cornish to see the sculptor. On May 7, 1906, Saint-Gaudens replied: ". . . we are having the worst spring that ever occurred (the roads are in awful condition) . . ."

White, on May 11, with the tender gusto he so often displayed, answered: "Beloved!!! Why do you explode so at the idea of Charlie and myself coming up to Windsor? If you think our desire came from any wish to see any damned fine spring or fine roads you are not only mistaken, but one of the most modest and unassuming

Gorham's main floor was a commercial space made inviting by columns and walls of artificial Caen stone and an ornamental plaster ceiling.

men . . . We are coming up to bow down before the sage and seer we admire and venerate. So weather be damned, and, roads, too!"

Andrew O'Connor also designed the standing lions flanking the cartouche bearing a "G" and an anchor, symbol of Rhode Island, Gorham's corporate base, just above the building's office section. Unfortunately, the sculptor, whom White had employed on a number of projects, seems to have had great difficulty in getting paid. While working on the Gorham Building decorations, O'Connor wrote the architect a desperate letter:

84 Boulevard Garibaldi
Paris, January 4, 1905

Dear Mr. White,

I am entirely without money here and nobody will send me any for all the work I've done. Won't you make your office pay for either the,

Whitney house carving	$3,000.
Columbia Library fountain	300.
Knickerbocker Trust model	50.

White had expended a great deal of time on the Gorham project and was highly pleased with the result. In 1936, Lawrence Grant White, then head of McKim, Mead & White, writing to the president of Russek's, which then occupied the Gorham Building, confirmed his father's satisfaction. It was, Lawrence White said, "one of the very finest designs ever produced by our firm."

Stanford White's relationship with the Tiffany family stretched back to his joint effort with Louis Tiffany in Newport at the beginning of the 1880s on the dining room of Kingscote. Tiffany's jewelry mart, located since 1870 in a cast-iron Italianate edifice on the west side of Union Square, was also well known to the architect. It was his favorite place to buy the oriental pearls he said were perfectly set off by the olivaceous cast of Evelyn Nesbit's skin. Pearls were not the only gifts that White was presenting to the seventeen-year-old ingenue. In 1902, when he moved Evelyn and her mother to the new Wellington Hotel on Seventh Avenue, the

For the sculptural decoration on the façade of the Gorham Building, Stanford White turned to Andrew O'Connor. One reason he began using younger sculptors rather than Augustus Saint-Gaudens was that they were more readily available. Another reason was that Saint-Gaudens had not been pleased with the setting White had designed for his statue of Peter Cooper, completed in 1897, in Cooper Square.

architect designed and furnished their apartment. Evelyn described her bedroom in detail:

> My bedroom was in red and white—white satin walls, red velvet carpets, a huge white bearskin on the floor, ivory-white furniture, the bed draped in ivory satin ending in a huge crown from which protruded five thick white ostrich plumes.

It was in this apartment that the well-known producer George Lederer offered Evelyn the part of a gypsy in his new musical—which he claimed to have named after her—*The Wild Rose*. The show, whose theme "My Little Gypsy Maid" was the Tin Pan Alley hit of 1902, was a smash and launched Eddie Foy on his great comic career. The apartment might well have been the setting for more than a Broadway audition. On the day that *The Wild Rose* opened, Mrs. George Lederer sued her husband for divorce and named Evelyn Nesbit as corespondent. Evelyn brushed the accusation aside and announced that in 1902 she had already been proposed to by no fewer than six millionaires, including cute Bobby Collier, son of the publisher of *Collier's* magazine, who, for some unfathomable reason, wanted to send her to art school in Paris. Bobby, Evelyn pointed out, was one of the group of boys she palled around with who were members of the exclusive Racquet Club, males she liked because they were "more my age than Stanford."

For more than five weeks in the summer of 1902, White was fishing at the elite Restigouche Salmon Club on Quebec's Gaspé Peninsula, of which he was a member, and for part of that time Bessie and Larry were with him. While he was out of town Evelyn had something that was more than a mere sexual affair with an admirer she had met at one of White's Madison Square Tower parties. In Evelyn's eyes he was "a handsome young man . . . Ethel Barrymore's young brother, Jack, then a cartoonist on the *Evening Journal*." The affair became so intense, and due to their regular suppers at Rector's, so public, that it made the gossip columns of the *Morning Telegraph*. Twenty years later Evelyn's recollection of John

The marble Tiffany & Co. Building at Thirty-seventh Street, completed the same year as the Gorham Building, was a Venetian palace transformed into an emporium for New York's most prestigious jeweler. Though the glorious palazzo survives, Tiffany's has been located at Fifth Avenue and Fifty-seventh Street since 1940, and the first floor of its old store has been divided into small shops.

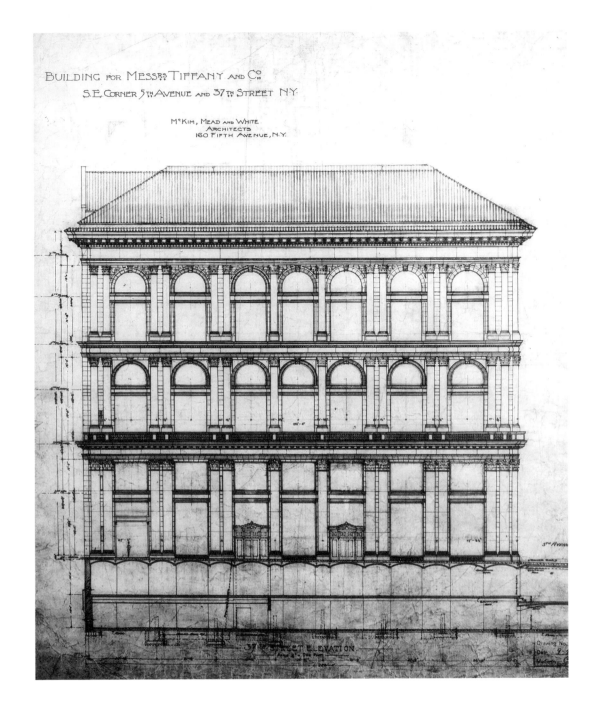

BUILDING FOR MESSRS. TIFFANY AND CO.
S.E. CORNER 5TH AVENUE AND 37TH STREET N.Y.

McKIM, MEAD AND WHITE
ARCHITECTS
160 FIFTH AVENUE, N.Y.

Barrymore was still tinged with the passion she had felt for him: "The girls think he's good-looking today; adore his famous profile. They should have seen him then—when he was about twenty-two!"

After he returned from Canada and learned of the liaison,

White was, in Evelyn's words, "tight-lipped," but when her mother told him that she feared Evelyn might be pregnant, it was White who took her to a doctor. Afterward, he sent for Barrymore to meet with Evelyn and him at his Tower apartment. There Barrymore proposed. "What would you live on?" the architect queried. When the future embodiment of Hamlet answered, "Love," Evelyn quickly lost interest. With gloriously unselfconscious narcissism, she described the moment in her memoirs: "In a mirror across the room I could see myself sitting in a chair, the soft glow from a hidden lamp overhead falling across my hair and heightening all its coppery tones, so that I seemed to be wearing a burnished tiara."

In 1903, Tiffany's—where they sold real tiaras—decided, like Gorham, to leave the Ladies' Mile and move uptown to be near its customers. The site selected, the southeast corner of Fifth Avenue and Thirty-seventh Street, was not far north of Gorham's. The Tiffany Building is another outstanding example of White fitting perfectly a structure's form to its function. Whereas for the Century clubhouse he had turned to Sanmicheli's Palazzo Canossa in Verona, the architect now studied Sanmicheli's Palazzo Grimani on Venice's Grand Canal of 1556. While the comparatively flat surface of the Canossa suited the narrow dark street where the Century stood, a street offering scant opportunity for chiaroscuro effects, the deep articulation of the Grimani was the ideal surface to catch the strong afternoon sunlight which so often bathes the east side of Fifth Avenue. In addition, since none of the six floors of Tiffany's Fifth Avenue frontage were to be used for offices, but were to be devoted to the display of emeralds, rubies, and diamonds, of bronze statues, of deeply cut crystal and eggshell-thin porcelain, and to studios for the polishing of gems, the engraving of silver, and the crafting of gold, the architect had to provide as great an expanse of light-giving glass as possible.

The white marble building contains six floors and an attic behind three horizontal divisions emphasized by rows of paired Corinthian pilasters and columns topped by a cornice of the same white South Dover marble. The design clearly expresses the struc-

TIFFANY & CO.

Fifth Avenue and 37th Street, New York

Gold and Jeweled Bangles

Bangles and Bracelets quoted are in 14-karat gold

Open work scrolls and rosettes, burmese finish,
with seven amethysts, - - - - - each $38

Oval band, richly chased, Roman finish, with eight
torquoise matrix, - - - - - - each $44

Open work, burmese finish, with eight peridots,
- - - - - - - - each $50

Carved scrolls, and open work, burmese finish, with
six oblong amethysts, - - - - each $55

Rosettes and open work, burmese finish, with seven
aquamarines, - - - - - each $65

Renaissance scrolls, open work, burmese finish, with
six Montana sapphires, - - - - each $80

Double wire bracelet, with diamonds and seven
Montana sapphires set in platinum - - each $95

Double wire bracelet, with diamonds and baroque
pearls set in platinum, - - - - each $95

Plain Gold Bangles and Bracelets

Gold bangles, - - each $13.50, $15.50, $17, $20

Gold chain bracelets, each $15, $17, $20, $25, $35

Gold engagement bracelet, with permanent locking
catch, - - - each $18.50, $27, $28, $36

Photographs of above or richer bracelets sent upon request

Fifth Avenue New York

Tiffany & Co. always welcome a comparison of prices

A *Tiffany advertisement shortly after the firm moved into its new Fifth Avenue home.*

ture's steel frame, which White further underscores—in order to flood the interior with sunlight—by boldly cutting away most of the wall and glazing it. The architect's always enthusiastic embracing of new materials found full expression in the Tiffany Building. The top-floor storage room was covered by a vast vault of Guastavino tile which permitted at its center a 20-by-60-foot skylight, while the roof, though it appeared to be of tile, was, in fact, fabricated of tile-patterned, fireproof metal made by the Meurer Brothers of Brooklyn. White deliberately left the building's façade devoid of sculpture and, instead, placed upon it the ancient wooden composition of Atlas holding up a clock which had embellished the front of Tiffany's Union Square shop.

The interior of Tiffany's was one of New York's most elegant retail spaces. A veritable forest of pale purple German marble columns rose up to a coffered ceiling, while the cages of the elevators were said by *Architects & Builders* magazine to be "the finest piece of artistic steelwork in this country." This modern Renaissance palace opened in 1906, the very year that the United States Congress finally followed Tiffany's example and made English sterling the standard for American silver. When Henry James saw the new emporium he found a rare reason to rejoice in the architecture of his native city:

> I found myself observing, in presence of so distinct an appeal to high clearness as the great Palladian pile just erected by Messrs. Tiffany on one of the upper corners of Fifth Avenue, where it presents itself to the friendly sky with a great nobleness of white marble. One is so thankful to it, I recognize, for not having twenty-five stories, which it might easily have had, I suppose, in the wantonness of wealth or of greed, that one gives it a double greeting, rejoicing to excess perhaps at its merely remaining, with the three fine arched and columned stages above its high basement, within the conditions of sociable symmetry.

The "sociable symmetry" of the Tiffany and Gorham buildings, and of the Knickerbocker Trust even if it had been built to its full height of thirteen stories, was no accident. McKim, Mead & White were profoundly opposed to structures of more than fifteen stories. This conviction sprang both from the teachings of the Ecole des Beaux-Arts and from the fact that a high proportion of the firm's designs grew out of the Italian Renaissance. It was, in fact, in the Renaissance, following the publication in 1485 of Leone Battista Alberti's *De Re Aedificatoria*, that for the first time in the modern Western world architects created planned cities with carefully worked-out perspectives. The director of planning studies at Yale, Christopher Tunnard, in his challenging book *The City of Man*, clearly states the historical sequence: "If, as is generally believed, modern perspective stems from Alberti, it was developed by the painters into a real instrument of civic design. Before Laurana's panels at Urbino it is hard to find paintings in which whole buildings and streets appear as complete compositions; formerly interiors, loggias, or arches were used but now the city begins to appear; a dream city, of course, but soon to be translated into reality."

The chief architectural element in this dream city become reality were the literally eye-catching cornices that were used first in that mother of the Renaissance, Florence, and then in all the principal cities of Italy. These powerful projections served to control the streetscape and directed the eye of the viewer to some prearranged physical or psychological vanishing point. It was the uniformly mandated cornice line which gave to Chicago's 1893 Fair its sense of harmony and unity though the buildings were by a multitude of architects. Thus the low horizontality of White's edifices just north of Thirty-fourth Street, emphasized by their magnificent and bold cornices, was an attempt to bring a similar harmony to Fifth Avenue. Stanford White and Charles McKim's "sociable" structures—the Knickerbocker Trust, the Gorham Building, the Tiffany Building, the University Club, and the Metropolitan Club, as well as edifices by other Beaux Arts architects such as the New York Public Library—created an American rue de la Paix of pleasing variety and benign unity. Paul Goldberger, writing in the New York *Times*, January 7, 1990, succinctly expressed its essence:

> Fifth Avenue from 34th Street to Central Park has always embodied the most endearing side of Manhattan's ability to satisfy haute bourgeois fantasies: a street of grand shops, fine department stores, churches, and a smattering of banks, clubs, hotels and office buildings, all organized to make a coherent, though hardly repetitive, whole.

But of course White's Fifth Avenue architecture has also been peppered with unfavorable criticism. In *Space, Time and Architecture*, one of the most influential books in the field in the first half of the twentieth century, the Swiss critic Sigfried Giedion sounds the alarm concerning these structures:

> American architecture came under many different influences during the nineteenth century, but none was so strong or came at such a critical moment as the rise to power of the mercantile classicism developed in the East.

Giedion's "mercantile classicism" has been expertly decoded by Christopher Tunnard:

> A conditioned hatred and envy of wealth, which extends into the ranks of our intellectuals, has enveloped the names of Saint-Gaudens, McKim, White and Burnham with a miasma of suspicion based largely on their crime of subservience to the Robber Barons.

Sigfried Giedion is of the school of those who, like Henry Steele Commager, scent an "undemocratic" odor about Stanford White's architecture.

Interestingly, Giedion in his book goes on to quote approvingly the conversation Frank Lloyd Wright claims to have had with Daniel Burnham, the Chicago architect who championed the 1893 Fair's classicism and who went on to design, among other things, New York's Flatiron Building. When Burnham offered Louis Sullivan's young protégé four years at the Ecole des Beaux-Arts, Wright replied, "I've been too close to Mr. Sullivan. He has helped spoil the Beaux Arts for me, or spoiled me for the Beaux Arts, I guess I mean." Following this "oh, shucks" answer Frank Lloyd Wright went on to build his American "democratic" architecture far from hoi polloi—in the sylvan suburbs of Oak Park and Riverside, Illinois; in the exclusive hills above Los Angeles; and upon the sanitary sands of the Southwest.

When Wright did consider the city, his proposed mile-high skyscraper was a missile aimed at the heart of urban amenities. In contrast, White, picking up the note from McKim, adored and adorned the city. His firm's conscious choice in the matter of the tall building was given a not to be forgotten social interpretation in 1906 by Herbert Croly in his seminal review of the work of McKim, Mead & White:

> The only explanation is that McKim, Mead and White have been disinclined to be closely identified with the design of such buildings. . . . They have probably hoped that the time would come when the laws would place restrictions on the skyscraping tendency of business structures, and they have consciously avoided the design of façades whose height was badly proportioned to their frontages and to the width of the streets on which they were situated.

If "democratic" be the test of architecture, what choice should be made between Wright's topless tower and White's Gorham Building, whose shop windows delight the passersby, whose ornament cheers the heart, and whose "sociable symmetry" does not rob the populace of sunlight and sky?

CHAPTER 13

DYNAMOS EARTHLY AND CELESTIAL

While completing the Gorham and Tiffany buildings, White began designing a clubhouse for a coterie quite different, at least in one essential aspect, from those that had commissioned the Century, the Players, the Harmonie, and the Metropolitan clubs. The genesis of the Colony Club goes back to the summer of 1900 when, at Newport's select Bailey's Beach, in the words of Anne F. Cox in *The History of the Colony Club*, "a group of five women discussed forming a club in New York City that would have enough space for a lawn tennis court (that was the most important consideration) and comfortable rooms and accommodations for rest and relaxation." The roof of the old Plaza Hotel was considered, but that idea had to be abandoned when the club's organizers were informed that the structure was about to be demolished and replaced by Henry Hardenbergh's grand new Plaza. Thus on January 20, 1903, the lots from 120 to 124 Madison Avenue near Thirtieth Street were purchased and Stanford White was selected as architect. The choice was almost inevitable, for White was well

In the first years of the twentieth century, Stanford White was again carrying out commissions around Madison Square, where, so many decades earlier, he and Saint-Gaudens had raised the Farragut monument. White's most important twentieth-century commission on the square was the Madison Square Presbyterian Church, seen in this 1910 photograph just to the north of the Metropolitan Life Insurance Company's skyscraping campanile.

known to several founding Colonists, including Anne T. Morgan, Gertrude Vanderbilt Whitney, Helen Hay Whitney, and Ava Willing Astor, for whose fathers or husbands he had executed major commissions. He was also undoubtedly chosen because of the ingenuity of his planning in such complicated projects as Madison Square Garden and the deluxe 300-room Hotel Imperial he had designed for the Goelets at Broadway and Thirty-second Street. The range of facilities to be packed into the clubhouse was indeed formidable. In addition to lounges, bedrooms, and a ballroom, there was to be a swimming pool, a gymnasium circled by a forty-nine-yard running track—the pet project of J. P. Morgan's athletic daughter Anne—as well as a "parking room" where members could leave dogs weighing less than eight pounds.

The founders of this, New York's first social club for women, also felt that in White they had an architect sympathetic to their cause. This was of no small importance. In the social world in which the Colony pioneers moved, the only career open to a woman was marriage; after that newsworthy event days were passed in shopping, pouring tea, and, according to one club member, "senseless visiting." As a result, the mere thought of a club like the Colony brought down upon the organizers the wrath of what to some passed for God. When it became known that this was to be a place where a woman could stay overnight without her husband and a place where she could exercise, newspapers proclaimed that the Colony was "the swan-song of the American home." Even former President Grover Cleveland joined the chorus of carpers and pontificated: "Women's clubs are harmful. The best and safest club is a woman's home. A life retired is well inspired." And when White wrote about the Club to Charles Barney, whose daughter Helen was a founding Colonist, he got, in February 1905, this sharp reply:

> In regard to the Women's Club, I really do not know what to say. They seem to have difficulty in getting members and I do not know whether they can incur more expenditure or not. My own judgement would be they had better sell their lots, pay up and shut up. This, I suppose, for four hundred feminines will be impossible.

It took all the brilliance and perseverance of the Colony's first president, Mrs. J. Borden Harriman, to steer the group's incorporation through a balky New York State legislature and to ignore her banker husband's warning: "Daisy, I don't think you can make it pay."

Stanford White's affection for the Federal style, which had found such sparkling expression in the Charles Dana Gibson house, and his sense that its delicate scale and domestic ambience was appropriate, led him to employ it again at the Colony. His immediate inspiration was Charleston's Nathaniel Russell house, an elegant circa 1809 Adam-inspired Federal residence on Meeting Street. White was particularly fond of the aristocratic old South Carolina city, and when he and Bess had visited there, he wrote to his mother:

> We are both wild over Charleston. It is the most lovely old city, with about the swellest old houses I have ever seen this side of the water. The Battery is almost as pretty as ours must have been.

Thus the Colony Club is a thread in that Southern strand in White's oeuvre, a strand linking the Palladian library of New York University's Bronx campus, the rebuilding of Jefferson's Rotunda at Charlottesville, the Breese house, and the interiors of the Gibson house.

The façade of the Colony Club is one of New York's finest examples of brickwork. Built of specially made Harvard brick with a rough texture resembling that of a woven fabric, it is constructed of the ends, or "headers," of the bricks, which wits announced fit perfectly the unconventional constitution of the Colony itself. The beauty of the façade is enhanced by diaper patterns in darker brick, while, within the high arched recesses above the parlor floor windows, the bricks are laid in a strikingly unusual diagonal pattern.

To carry out the decoration of the interior, Stanford White turned to a recently retired thirty-nine-year-old actress who, in the drawing-room dramas in which she had appeared, had excited far more interest by the smart gowns she wore than by her thespian talents. Elsie de Wolfe had attracted a flutter of attention and a few requests to "do up" friends' residences when, after reading Ogden Codman and Edith Wharton's 1897 manifesto *The Decoration of Houses*, she had dramatically transformed the dollhouse she shared with Elizabeth Marbury at the corner of Irving Place and Seventeenth Street. Almost overnight Elsie had banished all Victorian clutter, and by the prodigal application of white paint on furniture and woodwork, the hanging of pale striped wallpapers, and the scattering about of a few real French objects, had created the illusion of Louis XVI panache.

In these bright rooms Elsie and her friend Elizabeth Marbury, who was not only well connected socially but, in the words of Elsie's biographer Jane S. Smith, "the foremost theatrical agent in the world," carried on what one Frenchman called a *salon d'esprit*. These gatherings—where one might encounter Miss Marbury's famous clients, such as Oscar Wilde, J. M. Barrie, and George Bernard Shaw, or friends like Sarah Bernhardt, Nellie Melba, and Henry Adams—delighted White, who was frequently at Irving Place. "You never know whom you are going to meet at Bessie's and Elsie's," William C. Whitney observed, "but you can always be sure that whoever they are they will be interesting . . ."

Before White took the memorable step of recommending Elsie de Wolfe for the Colony commission, he had had ample opportunity to analyze her taste and to see that it was very much like his own. A note written by Elsie to the architect just before the Colony project reveals that the feeling was mutual. In a previous letter the fledgling decorator had told White that she wanted him to have a "very fine" Louis XVI marble mantelpiece which would not fit into the room for which she had intended it. Elsie then reports that she and Miss Marbury were having differences concerning the treasure:

122, Seventeenth Street East

Dear Stanford
Please pardon delay but I am trying to convince E.M. that she cannot use the mantel in the dining room, and that takes time and an

expert opinion. I feel sure she will come to the same conclusion in the next 48 hours, and I will telephone you so that you may send for it.

Stanford White not only proposed Elsie de Wolfe for the Colony commission but, ironically, had to help her overcome the opposition of the club's female Board of Governors, who questioned whether a woman had the experience to manage such a project. The architect's pronouncement: "Give it to Elsie and let the girl alone!" was quickly repeated in New York drawing rooms. White's championing of Elsie de Wolfe at the beginning of her career was a far from unique episode; indeed it climaxed a lifetime in which he showed a quick willingness to accept and to promote the abilities of women. Typically, after her intense affair with John Barrymore, White, with her mother's approval, sent Evelyn Nesbit to a private school run by Cecil B. De Mille's mother in Pompton Lakes, New Jersey, to study music and literature. But on a far more disinterested level, Stanford White was a serious patron of Candace Wheeler, the textile designer who worked with Louis Tiffany's Associated Artists; he was the first to encourage Gertrude Vanderbilt's career as a sculptor and attempted to convince Daniel Chester French to accept her as a pupil; he commissioned the watercolorist Julia Brewster to portray his projects; and in 1903 he tried to get his firm to hire Christine Darrow as its first female draftsman, only to have Mead send him a curt memo: "We don't employ Lady draughtsmen!"

White also played a key role in the career of the dancer Ruth St. Denis. He first met Ruth Dennis—as she was then named—in 1895, when she was sixteen, and quickly introduced her to important friends of his in the theatre, including Melba and Nordica, and sent her to a number of producers. After a theatrical engagement fell through and the architect had lent Ruth and her mother money, Mrs. Dennis wrote him a letter of thanks:

And now I must say a word about the prompt and delicate way in which you responded to my letter—it shows us that God still lives—and I am not at all unconscious of the unselfishness in which you have acted toward Ruth without exacting any return from her. Most men are not so. It only increases her respect and affection for you, for although she is a child in some things she is not in others and has the intuitions and perceptions of a divine woman.

Perhaps the most revelatory comment on the architect's welcoming openness to the talents of women appears in *Modeling My Life*, the autobiography of the Indiana-born sculptress Janet Scudder. She first met White in Paris at the studio of MacMonnies, with whom she was studying, but it was in New York during the winter of 1905/06 that the architect recognized Scudder's artistic abilities:

> If I were making a diagram of my career with marks to indicate the most important points—milestones—I should certainly indicate in red letters the day on which Stanford White bought my Frog Fountain . . . To have him buy my first really important piece of work meant much more to me than I even realized myself. It was months later that the effect of this purchase began to loom up as the dominating factor in my career.

White paid Miss Scudder $1,000 for her fountain.

The check was most likely drawn on his account at the Knickerbocker Trust, where Charles Barney permitted him overdrafts of up to $20,000. The overdrafts, though, were the least of Stanford White's financial woes. A note which came due on February 23, 1905, at the Trust was for $100,000 and carried an additional $4,000 in interest. There was also the possibility that he would be evicted from 121 East Twenty-first Street, for by 1904 he was six years in arrears on his rent and owed his landlord, Henry A. C. Taylor, more than $50,000. The architect's letter of May 24, 1904, to Taylor's agent, E. J. Hancy, shows the desperation of White's plight:

> In regard to your request that I should send you a check for half the amount of my note of $20,000 to Mr. Taylor, or a substantial payment on the same, I can only say that I will do this the moment it is possible for me to do it. The only resources I have for the payment

of my indebtedness are my income and my life insurances, and the personal property, which I have assigned to Mr. Charles T. Barney, for the benefit of my creditors.

In addition, he was in trouble with his partners. In an agreement drawn up in June 1903, White had admitted that he had overdrawn his account at McKim, Mead & White by $75,000 and agreed that a part of his yearly income accruing from the firm's profits should go toward paying off this debt. But by May 1905, matters had gotten much worse. With his overall debt soaring to some $700,000, he was anxious to protect McKim, Mead & White from both embarrassment and liens and submitted to an entirely new arrangement with the firm. In consequence, his financial rights as a partner were relinquished and he was placed on a $1,000 monthly salary. Thus, in an ironic twist, Stanford White, at the apex of his career with his transcendent structures rising along the avenues of New York, had ceased to be a partner in McKim, Mead & White.

Stanford White had another problem. He was being tailed by detectives hired by Harry Kendall Thaw of Pittsburgh. To describe Harry Thaw as a lunatic would be charitable. His memoir, *The Traitor*—the title refers to one of Thaw's attorneys, not to White—published in 1926, is filled with passages which seem to have sprung from *Alice in Wonderland*:

> Then London. The dances there are tiresome. If Royalty comes, worse. You see rows and rows of girls, most tied to each chair. But as the Queen died the new King allowed a very few dances, and very small, and that year they were very different. I went to half of them, I think; Mrs. Bentinck, Mrs. Ramsey and Mrs. Jefferson, and every debutante was there, less than fifty older women and lots of men, so no one had to dance.

Born in Pittsburgh in 1871, he was the son of William and Mary Copley Thaw. His father was a member of the gang made up of Alexander J. Cassatt, G. B. Roberts, Frank Thompson, Andrew

Carnegie, and others, who systematically bribed the morally som-
nolent members of the Pennsylvania legislature to give the Pennsylvania Railroad choice rights-of-way and other privileges. When
he died in 1893 William Thaw left his heirs, among other treasures,
$40,000,000 in Pennsylvania Railroad bonds.

Early in 1901 Harry Thaw began spending most of his time in
New York, where the tall, dark-haired millionaire quickly gained a
reputation as a "loony" playboy. Curiously, his obsessive hatred of
Stanford White antedated Thaw's introduction to Evelyn Nesbit.
Not long after his arrival in the city he told Frances Belmont, one of
the Florodora Sextette, that he would rent a private room at
Sherry's and throw a party to which he would invite a group of
well-heeled men if she would invite some of her theatrical lady
friends. Frances Belmont, not one to pass up a lively good time,
readily agreed. But on the night before the planned festivities, she
and her current beau, Frank Crowninshield, the future renowned
editor of *Vanity Fair*, walked into Sherry's and came upon Thaw and
some of his society chums. When Frances greeted him, Thaw
turned away. It was obvious that the Pittsburgh millionaire didn't
wish to be seen talking to someone who might be considered
demimondaine. Frances Belmont, not surprisingly, was furious, and
the following night she shepherded her fair friends to one of
White's Madison Square Tower frolics, leaving Thaw and his male
guests to sip their champagne without the companionship of the
"weaker sex." When *Town Topics* ran the line: "Florodora beauties
sing for their supper in White's studio, while Thaw's orchestra
fiddles to an empty room at Sherry's," the would-be cosmopolite
was incensed. It was only some months later, in December 1901,
that Thaw—who had seen Evelyn on the stage—persuaded a
mutual acquaintance to arrange a meeting. The event was not a
success. "There was some indefinable quality about his whole
personality that frightened and repulsed me," Evelyn remembered
in *Prodigal Days*.

Having little success with the daughter, Harry Thaw eventually managed to ingratiate himself with the mother. When Evelyn had an appendicitis attack at the De Mille school in April 1903, it was Thaw who drove Mrs. Nesbit to Pompton Lakes.

After her affair with Barrymore and the persistent appearance of Thaw on the scene, Evelyn's attitude toward Stanford White slowly altered. Underlying this change was the fact that she had never been able to understand White's continued devotion to his wife or to accept his gallantry to other women friends: "My own unreasonable jealousy and Stanford's attitude in the Barrymore tangle had ended our love affair." Perhaps, too, Evelyn knew far more than she ever revealed about the calamitous state of White's financial balance sheet, for suddenly the new protector of Evelyn and her mother was none other than the recently despised Harry Thaw. It was Thaw, during Evelyn's convalescence in New York following her appendectomy, who had her meals prepared by Oscar of the Waldorf and presented her nurse with a diamond brooch. And it was Thaw who suggested that, to complete her recovery, Evelyn and her mother accompany him to Europe. In one of his typically generous gestures, just before the S.S. *New York* sailed in May 1903, Stanford White came to the ship and presented Evelyn with a $500 Cook's letter of credit. He remarked that it might come in useful in case of an emergency.

Evelyn's five-month stay in Europe was to be a kind of Grand Guignol grand tour. The Nesbits' first surprise came in Paris, where, instead of being lodged in a hotel as they had been promised, mother and daughter found themselves sharing an apartment on the posh Avenue Matignon with Thaw and his valet. This too cozy arrangement disturbed Mrs. Nesbit far more than it did Evelyn, who was dining at Voisin and Lapérouse, assembling a new wardrobe at couturiers like Doucet, and attending the brilliant Sunday-afternoon gatherings at the house Elsie de Wolfe and Elizabeth Marbury had rented in Versailles. The second surprise affected Evelyn much more directly. Harry Thaw, she soon discovered, was possessed of a truly terrifying jealousy:

If he observed any man looking at me with frank admiration there was bound to be a rumpus. He would make a mad dash for the unfortunate fellow and start a fight. But if the man did battle, Thaw would back out at once and want to shake hands. He was an abject coward.

If Stanford White was mentioned, as happened one evening in a café when an American girl innocently dropped the architect's name, the rumpus became a rampage: "A bombshell could not have thrown Thaw into a more violent rage," Evelyn recalled. "He threw over the tables, smashed dishes and glassware, flung silverware."

It was not long before Thaw began pestering Evelyn with constant marriage proposals and her negative response "upset, flabbergasted him." Harry Thaw was not a man to accept rejection rationally, and while demanding that Evelyn give him a reason why she would not marry him, he kept the Nesbits virtual prisoners in the Avenue Matignon apartment. Mrs. Nesbit wanted to use Stanford White's $500 to flee to America, but her warning that "there's something wrong with this man" only drew from Evelyn the response that they had not yet seen London or Berlin or Vienna, all of which had been promised.

Day after day, Thaw kept up his endless proposing and questioning. Finally, one night, worn down by the demented cross-examination as to why she continued to reject his suit, a weary Evelyn, who still hoped for more travel and presents and thus did not want to say outright that it was because she found him loathsome, coyly hinted that it all had to do with something in her past. Harry, at once springing to the bait, asked, "Are you a good girl? Pure?" Evelyn had hoped that this would end the siege, but it only spurred Harry on. For three more days and nights he asked her time and again, "Are you a virgin?" When Evelyn hinted that he was near the crux of the matter, her captor suddenly queried, "Was it Stanford White?" The exhausted young woman answered, "Yes."

"The beast!" the triumphant Thaw cried. "The filthy beast!" Then he wept hysterically.

Mrs. Nesbit at once sensed the danger. "You have made a mistake. You should have never told Harry Thaw your secret!"

The trio next moved to London, where Evelyn, staying at Claridge's, began again having a wonderful time, particularly when Thaw dashed into Tiffany's and presented her with "four lovely diamond brooches, flawlessly matched and graduating in size." One day, without warning, Harry Thaw announced that Mrs. Nesbit—who was so appalled by the whole affair that she had almost stopped speaking to her daughter—was returning to America and that he and Evelyn would go back to the Continent. He promised Evelyn a suitable chaperon, endless luxuries and travel. The suitable chaperon failed to materialize, and their travels soon took them to Schloss Katzenstein in the Austrian Tyrol, where the ensuing scene would not have been out of place in the Marquis de Sade's *Justine.* There, in the isolated castle, while Evelyn slept, a naked Harry Thaw, whom she already knew to be a cocaine addict, entered her bedroom and beat her so viciously with a dog whip that it took several weeks for the welts to heal. "Every bit of humanity had gone out of him; he was a monster, a fiend, a demon." Thaw, it would appear, had a penchant for abusing persons of either sex. In 1917 he was indicted for kidnapping after he had enticed nineteen-year-old Frederick Gump from a soda fountain in Long Beach, California, and took him to New York's McAlpin Hotel. In the course of the investigation, it came out that on Christmas Eve 1916, while Gump was in bed, Thaw entered his room and beat him unconscious using the same type of whip that he had wielded with such devastating effect upon Evelyn. To hush up the incident, Thaw's mother paid Gump's parents $25,000. After the nightmare of Schloss Katzenstein, Harry apologized, and when Evelyn was well enough to appear again in public, they returned to Paris. In October, Evelyn, in the company of Elsie de Wolfe and Elizabeth Marbury, sailed for New York. Harry Thaw, for the moment, remained in Europe.

At seven o'clock one evening three days after Evelyn Nesbit's return to America, there was an insistent knocking on the door of

The powerhouse which White designed on Eleventh Avenue and Fifty-ninth Street for the Interborough Rapid Transit Company flawlessly fitted a classical envelope over the generators which produced the electricity to run the system's subway trains. When completed in 1904, the structure's tall smokestacks tied it visually to the ocean liners on the nearby Hudson River. The IRT powerhouse still serves its original purpose, but its stacks have been reduced to one and its handsome cornice has been removed.

the suite she had taken at the Savoy Hotel. When Evelyn opened the door, she was wearing one of the costly Paris ensembles and the four diamond Tiffany brooches Harry Thaw had bought her in London. The visitor was Stanford White:

> There he stood, eyebrows uplifted, studying me in my gorgeous Rue de la Paix outfit, the Tiffany brooches glittering on my gown!

After surveying the scene for a moment and undoubtedly perceiving what all the luxury implied, White murmured, "Kitten, where have you been? What have you been doing? You wrote me only one letter."

That was indeed the sad sum of her epistles to her onetime lover and old friend. The affair between Stanford White and Evelyn Nesbit was, as she noted in *Prodigal Days*, emphatically finished:

> And while the sentimental relations between myself and Stanford were severed, there remained between us a deep attachment which nothing, nobody could ever destroy.

In the last chapter of his masterpiece, *Mont-Saint-Michel and Chartres*, Henry Adams notes that whereas the great medieval theologian Thomas Aquinas thought of God as a prime motor, a kind of dynamo producing all of the energy in the universe, modern man, with his increasing scientific skill, has created his own power-producing dynamos and now, more and more, looks to them, not to God, for the force to run the world. Two creations of Stanford White's final, supreme design phase prove that he could provide magnificent housing for dynamos both earthly and celestial. Each reveals what John La Farge meant when he said that White was "animated with a passion for the beautiful."

The Interborough Rapid Transit Company was incorporated in the spring of 1902 with a charter which, among other things, mandated construction of a fourteen-mile subway stretching from Park Row near City Hall to Kingsbridge in the Bronx. One of the directors of the new entity was the ubiquitous Charles T. Barney,

who lobbied for Stanford White to be given the lucrative contract to design a power station on Eleventh Avenue at Fifty-ninth Street where coal could be converted into steam to produce the electricity to drive the IRT's subterranean transportation system. Where one might have expected another unsightly or, at best, unremarkable industrial building, the architect produced a paradigm of economical elegance and practical perfection. Standing upon a base of pink granite which marks the level of the water table, the severely august buff brick structure rises in bays delineated by vigorously rusticated pilasters accurately echoing the internal steel girders which support the gargantuan coal hoppers that feed the power station's steam

engines. If the Woolworth Building is a Cathedral of Commerce, this is a Palace of Power. In a dazzling coda, White transfigured the six 162-foot chimneys by constructing them with an entasis, that swelling which the ancient Greeks gave to the columns of their temples to deceive the eye into thinking they were straight. Seen from a distance the stacks of White's powerhouse might belong to a lordly liner, the *Deutschland* or the *Caronia*, riding upon the hard-by Hudson. Looking at them shortly after their completion in 1904, Charles Baldwin saw them in yet another light: "The chimneys seem almost elegant, with the grace of Lombardy poplars." Encapsulating the nobility of Roman architecture, the IRT power station

In 1903 White designed a showroom for the Havana Tobacco Company on the first floor of the St. James Building, located on the southwest corner of Broadway and Twenty-sixth Street. (The St. James is the tallest structure in this 1899 view looking up Broadway from Twenty-third Street.) The commission was a favor from Oliver Payne, an important shareholder in the Pierre Lorillard Tobacco Company, which owned the shop. With its white marble coolness, its tropical palms, and its murals of Cuban scenes by Willard Metcalf, the showroom was an effective advertisement for the fine Cuban tobacco the company used in its cigars. The shop has vanished as completely as the smoke of the cigars it once purveyed.

ranks with the rear elevation of Carrère and Hastings's New York Public Library as one of Manhattan's unheralded evocations of the essentials of classical architecture.

Stanford White's last building was to be his personal favorite. For some years the congregants of the Madison Square Presbyterian Church, housed in a gloomy Gothic sanctuary dating from 1854, had been aware that the Metropolitan Life Insurance Company coveted their site for expansion. The church's location on the northern half of the block on Madison Avenue between Twenty-third and Twenty-fourth streets effectively stifled any building plans of the Metropolitan, which occupied the southern half of the same block. Fortuitously, the Presbyterians, flourishing under the distinguished pastorate of the Reverend Charles H. Parkhurst, D.D., of, among other organizations, the Society for the Prevention of Crime, had had thoughts for some time of a more gracious earthly home. In October 1902, the narrow gap between those believing in predestination and those whose faith was founded on actuarial tables was bridged. For a lot at the northeast corner of

Madison Avenue and Twenty-fourth Street plus a cash sum of $325,000, the Presbyterians moved north across Twenty-fourth Street. A building committee, which included Louis Comfort Tiffany, was quickly formed, and within three weeks Stanford White was put in charge of designing the new church.

The architect was faced with an enormous challenge. Because of the soaring Venetian campanile Napoleon LeBrun was erecting on the site of the old church, a structure which would dwarf anything near it, White had to design a house of worship which would have visual impact without the aid of spire or belfry. His solution was a temple of perfection in both scale and design. The exterior of the new Madison Square Presbyterian Church was an architectural wreath fashioned of the pantheons of Paris and Rome, of Andrea Palladio's sixteenth-century *tempietto* at Maser, and of Thomas Jefferson's Rotunda at the University of Virginia. Built of his beloved thin buff-colored Roman brick with moldings of terra cotta in a polychromatic array of ochre, blue-gray, and moss green, the Greek-cross body of the church had a splendid crispness about it.

For the Madison Square Presbyterian Church, White turned for inspiration to early Christian sources, particularly to Constantinople's Hagia Sophia. The architect began working on the project in 1903 and the church was dedicated four months after his murder in 1906. In the photograph opposite, the edifice's pediment has not yet received the ornamentation depicted in the drawing at right. Alas, the remarkable house of worship survived its creator a mere thirteen years.

·FRONT ELEVATION·
·MADISON SQVARE PRESBYTERIAN CHVRCH·
·SCALE ¾ INCH EQVALS ONE FOOT·

The colored terra cotta was a delightful serendipity for the architect. White had long been urging the Perth Amboy Terra Cotta Company to make the material in various hues, but it was only in 1903 that the firm had achieved the difficult breakthrough. In order to make an inescapable statement on Madison Square itself, White gave the church a slightly outscale portico, consisting of six 30-foot pale green granite Corinthian columns supporting a pediment ornamented with cream and blue terra-cotta reliefs in the manner of Della Robbia designed by the sculptor Adolph Weinman and the painter H. Siddons Mowbray. (The architect had tested the ability of the company to produce the effect he wanted by having it copy a Della Robbia in his collection.) The radiant composition was capped by a low green tiled dome carrying a golden lantern 113 feet above the street. The interior of the structure harks back to the early years of the Christian Church, for its shimmering Tiffany gold mosaic dome, encircled by a necklace of arched windows and resting upon four sharp pendentives, recalled that of Constantinople's Hagia Sophia.

Though White's decision not to build in the expected Gothic style was fully supported by Dr. Parkhurst, it led to an outcry on the part of some members of the congregation. White's answer to the dissenters was a disarming combination of knowledge and wit:

> The style of architecture of the Madison Square Presbyterian Church is that of the early Christians, with a modified Byzantine treatment in the interior. It is, to a certain extent, a protest against the idea so prevalent among laymen that a building, to be church-like, must be built in the Medieval Style. The style of architecture known as Gothic has nothing to do with the simple forms of early Christian religion; or with that of the Reformation; or with the style of architecture which prevailed in our own country when it had its birth as a nation. All these, which belong to the Protestant religion and to us, have no affiliations whatsoever with Gothic, but with the classic style. Gothic, or Medieval form of architecture . . . belongs absolutely and only to the Roman Catholic Church . . .

When it was completed in 1906, shortly after the architect's death, the edifice was immediately hailed as one of New York's most glorious buildings. "It was like a Byzantine jewel," John Jay Chapman wrote, "so concentrated, well-built and polished, so correct, ornate and lavish that a clever Empress might have had it built." In 1919, when, after an all too brief life, the church was demolished, the anonymous writer of *The Nation*'s "In the Driftway" mourned for it and for White's Knickerbocker Trust building, which had recently been shorn of its majestic Corinthian columns:

> It was all on account of the Madison Square Church. That had been Stanford White's masterpiece.... It carried Rome and the Renaissance on toward the ultimates. It took five thousand years to achieve that church ... and they demolished it in a week ... another grievance—a bank on Fifth Avenue that had been compelled to take down its splendid columns because they intruded a foot or two onto the legal sidewalk. In Paris the state would have bought the building if necessary to save those columns. In America the orthodox number of inches for a sidewalk, or the declining number of Presbyterians below Times Square, was enough to scrap a thing of beauty. What were Presbyterians and sidewalks on the scale against beauty?

CHAPTER 14

RENDEZVOUS

During the construction of the Madison Square Presbyterian Church, White had reached the difficult decision to settle some of his massive debt by auctioning off his immense collection of antique marble statues, museum-quality Gobelin tapestries, old master paintings, gilded eighteenth-century Venetian furniture, and his Ali Baba's cave of precious bibelots. To facilitate this plan, in the spring of 1904 he began removing items from his own houses and apartments, from various storerooms, and from the residences of dozens of friends to whom he had loaned pieces and brought all of the collection together in a space he had rented on the top floor of a six-story building on West Thirtieth Street. As in some divine retribution, some playing out of the theme of a Greek tragedy, this glittering boodle was to become nothing but sticks to feed a bonfire of the vanities. On the afternoon of February 13, 1905, faulty electrical wiring on another floor set ablaze the building housing White's treasure and with terrible swiftness almost everything was

Stanford White about 1905.

303

destroyed. The full extent of the loss was summed up in a letter that White wrote to a friend on April 29:

> I had my things stored in a large loft, preparatory to the sale, in order to catalogue them, at 120 West 30th Street. My sale was postponed from February until May, and just previously I had transferred about $150,000 worth of things from my house. These things, as I suppose you know, all burnt up, but the misfortune was a double one because the insurances had run out and I did not renew them, and I did not transfer the insurances on the things from my house, and I therefore, not only lost my things, but the realization of about $350,000 which I expected to use in partially paying off my debts.

Though White was devastated, his first concern was for Bess, then traveling in Italy. He immediately wrote to his son, who had entered Harvard the previous year at the age of sixteen, not to worry and not to bother his mother. White's letter to his wife reveals the closeness which always existed between them:

> February 17, 1905
>
> My darling Bess,
> I have just got your letter from Palermo and cable from Rome. I sent you a cable every week and have written three times a week so far, and am glad you are having so good a time. I have been having a pretty tough one. Long before you receive this I suppose you will have seen in the Paris edition of the New York *Herald* an account of the fire which destroyed the storage warehouse. . . . The floors fell in, and sheets of water were poured over everything, which froze in a solid mass, and it will be quite a while before they unearth the debris and I find out exactly what is saved or lost. This misfortune is certainly a hard blow after all the others, but after all there are so many, many worse things that could have happened that I suppose I should not be too disheartened, so I am grinning and going back to work as hard as I can. Do write, my dearest.
>
> Stanford

One debt which White had hoped to be able to repay from the proceeds of the sale, a debt which profoundly disturbed him, was the $100,000 he owed to Bessie. Confirmation of the architect's warm familial relationship with his wife and son comes from Janet Scudder, who visited Box Hill in the last months of the architect's life:

> During the spring and summer, when I was invited by Mrs. White to their summer home at St. James, I began to see another side of this great man. In the midst of his family, in a delightful house, filled with treasures from Italy and Spain, surrounded on all sides by the beautiful gentle country of the north shore of Long Island, I learned to know him, not as a rushing, business-distracted architect, but as a thoughtful host who was always gay and animated and amusing.

This was the Stanford White whom Bessie, who lived until 1950, remembered, cherished, and spoke of to her numerous grandchildren. It was the memory shared by Larry White, whose journal is filled with recollections of his father's pleasure in surprising family and friends with one of the first motion-picture projectors in a private house, of journeys with his parents up the Nile, of visits to the 1893 Chicago World's Fair to see McKim, Mead & White's vast Agricultural Building, of Canadian fishing expeditions and canoe trips, of the 1900 International Exposition in Paris when his father took him to Saint-Gaudens's studio to view the superb Robert Louis Stevenson relief, and to Sargent's studio in London, "where I distinguished myself by putting my finger on the wet paint of a portrait." There is also this stark entry in Lawrence Grant White's journal: "My father's tragic death at the end of my sophomore year changed all our plans . . ."

When Evelyn Nesbit returned to New York she had "determined to break every bond with Thaw," but that was not easy, for she received daily cablegrams from Paris, and when Thaw came back to the city, though Evelyn moved to another hotel leaving no forwarding address, his detectives soon tracked her down.

*E*velyn Nesbit in 1902, dressed
for her role as a gypsy in the play,
The Wild Rose.

Eventually, Evelyn consented to see him, for, as she said, "I was not
one to nurse a grievance." Behind this decision undoubtedly lay the
fact that though White continued to be friendly, she knew that their
affair was over and must have known too that his financial situation
had worsened. In addition, she was now totally estranged from her
mother, who was again living in Pittsburgh. Thaw offered security
and the luxurious lifestyle Evelyn clearly craved.

In June 1904 the pair once more sailed for Europe, a trip that
included endless gambling by Harry in Monte Carlo, the gift of a
triple strand of pearls, and once, when Stanford White's name came
up, the display of a fully loaded revolver. They were back in New
York for the winter of 1904/05 and once more Harry laid siege to
Evelyn to become his wife. This time, though, he brought on a Big
Bertha, his mother, whom Evelyn remembered as "stout . . . an

*H*arry K. Thaw in 1902, soon
after he met Evelyn.

Amazon type." Mrs. Thaw made it patently clear why she wanted
Evelyn to accept Harry as her husband:

> My son is very much in love with you, Evelyn, and I wish you
> would marry him. He has always been a trial to me, a cause of
> anxiety, but I have renewed hope for him now that he has found a
> girl he can love.

That is Evelyn's recollection of the interview, but there is undoubtedly a good deal of truth in the tale, for otherwise Mary Copley
Thaw would never have let her precious child marry an actress.

On April 5, 1905, in the parsonage of Pittsburgh's upper-crust
Third Presbyterian Church, Evelyn Nesbit became Mrs. Harry
Kendall Thaw. A significant aberration during the couple's wedding

Evelyn in Pittsburgh in 1906, shortly after her marriage to Harry K. Thaw.

trip West was that, while in Chicago, the newlyweds did not stay at the elegant Palmer House or Grand Pacific Hotel, but at the rather dowdy Virginia, whose name had drawn Harry to it. "Alone in our suite at the hotel," Evelyn observed, "he kept harping gleefully on the reactions Stanford White would be subject to when he read about us in the newspapers and saw that we were stopping at the Virginia." Ever since that night in Paris when Evelyn had foolishly confessed her "secret," Thaw had revealed his obsession with the concept of virginity. After their honeymoon the Harry K. Thaws returned to Pittsburgh to reside for the winter with mother Thaw at her estate, Lyndhurst. Life at Lyndhurst was so boring that the bride reported:

Only once did I see any animation at Mother Thaw's table; that was when she suffered a heart attack from eating too much mince pie and ice cream!

There was no lack of animation, though, about Harry. Evelyn grew increasingly alarmed at his target practice with a pistol and more than once found herself exclaiming, "Listen, Harry, now that we're married, the least you can do is act like a normal human being."

Early in the spring of 1906 Mary Thaw announced that she would go to Europe in June and Harry said that he and Evelyn would accompany her. Shortly after the beginning of June, the three traveled to New York and took two suites on separate floors at the Lorraine Apartment Hotel at Fifth Avenue and Forty-fifth Street. Mother Thaw had already informed them that she would sail on June 23 aboard the *Minneapolis*, a less than grand vessel which also carried cattle and other cargo. Harry, much to Evelyn's relief, refused to join her on the bovine bark and said that they would follow shortly on a first-class, deluxe liner. During the day Thaw concentrated on his whist game—or so he told Evelyn—while in the evenings the couple went to the theatre and to the flashy restaurants frequented by the Broadway crowd: Delmonico's, the Café Martin, and Louis Bustanoby's Café des Beaux Arts, which featured bands of strolling Hungarian gypsies. Harry was not short of money with which to indulge himself, for mother Thaw—who still controlled her husband's fortune—had him on a hefty annual allowance of $70,000. During their New York stay Thaw forbade Evelyn to visit most of her old friends and forced her to promise to report any chance encounters with Stanford White. She did, in fact, see the architect once on the street, but they did not speak. When she informed Harry, he snapped that he would have found out whether she had told him or not. "The significance of that remark was lost upon me," Evelyn commented later. "I should have realized that I was being followed by detectives . . ."

Harry Thaw seems to have taken a puerile pleasure from prying into other people's lives. Two years before, he had gone to the dingy Nassau Street office out of which Anthony Comstock ran the Society for the Suppression of Vice and informed the city's supreme snoop as to what he said were the facts his hired sleuths had ferreted out concerning the goings-on in Stanford White's Madison Square Tower apartment. According to Thaw, the architect and his cohorts regularly used the premises to drug underaged virgins and then take advantage of them. White, Thaw announced, had "ravished three hundred and seventy-eight girls." In *Anthony Comstock: Roundsman of the Lord*, Heywood Broun noted that after an unusually exhaustive investigation "there was not enough evidence to secure his arrest."

That Thaw should have made common cause with Comstock shows that his bizarre behavior was in some way connected to that peculiarly American mix of prudery and reform which, as it will from time to time, was then rapidly surfacing. On October 9, 1905, Comstock himself had managed to have Bernarr Macfadden arrested for publicizing his "Mammoth Physical Exhibition" in Madison Square Garden with posters that daringly showed twelve young women clad in what appeared to be white union suits. That same year Comstock could also be credited with forcing the distinguished art dealer William Macbeth to remove Bryson Burroughs's painting "The Explorers" from his Fifth Avenue window because the five small children depicted on the canvas wading in a brook were unclothed. And when New York's Appellate Court, by a narrow margin of two to one, allowed George Bernard Shaw's *Mrs. Warren's Profession* to be performed even though the usually liberal *World* had attacked it as "tainted drama" for discussing prostitution, Anthony Comstock had been a leader of the chorus of disapproval which greeted the decision.

There was indeed a change in popular mores taking place. Gambling, formerly tolerated in spots such as Frank Farrell's just west of the Waldorf, which, after White had given it a $500,000 face-lift and installed an Italian Renaissance portal, became known as "The House of the Bronze Door," was suddenly verboten. Even the once sacrosanct precincts of Richard Canfield's casino, where the exceptional art collection included sculptures by Saint-Gaudens and paintings by James McNeill Whistler, was raided. And in an era when George Kessler, representing Moët et Chandon, and Mannie Chappell, representing Mumm's, would enter Rector's and begin sending competing bottles of champagne to tables occupied by "Diamond Jim" Brady and Stanford White, the drive toward the "Noble Experiment" of prohibition was already underway. It was indeed often difficult, if not impossible to separate the prudery from the reform. After witnessing a New York automobile race sponsored by Cornelius Vanderbilt, the Calvinist president of Princeton University, Woodrow Wilson, announced that "nothing has spread socialist feeling in this country more than the use of the automobile" because it is "a picture of the arrogance of wealth, with all its independence and carelessness."

Nothing, though, indicated more clearly which way the new wind was blowing than the unexpected reaction to the costume extravaganza thrown on January 31, 1905, by James Hazen Hyde, the twenty-eight-year-old heir to a large chunk of the $260,000,000 assets of the Equitable Life Assurance Company. The bill for transforming two floors of Sherry's into a fair facsimile of Versailles, providing the 600 guests with dance music by Naham Franko's society orchestra, entertainment in the form of the great French tragedienne Madame Réjane, and slaking the assembled throng's thirst with rare wines and its appetite with caviar, lobster, and pheasant, came to $200,000. Though Whitney Warren was in charge of the lavish decorations, White undoubtedly had a hand in them, for Elizabeth Lehr saw him "hard at work with an army of painters and sculptors transforming Sherry's into a replica of the court of Louis XVI." He attended the ball along with old friends such as James Hyde's sister, Mrs. Sidney Dillon Ripley, who appeared as Princess Victoire, a daughter of Louis XV; Mrs. Clarence Mackay, whose silver-and-turquoise dress had a train held up by two pages; Mrs. Stuyvesant Fish, all in pink and white with a rare lace bertha; and Elsie de Wolfe, who followed the host's orders to come in eighteenth-century French costume by wearing a white satin dress copied stitch for stitch from one in a Jean-Marc Nattier portrait. Reports of the glittering gala filled the press for days preceding and following the affair. But in place of the awed wonder they would have elicited a few years earlier, the intemperate extravagance quickly led to a New York State investigation into the finances of insurance companies and the equally quick departure of James Hazen Hyde to the country of his original inspiration, France.

Stanford White spent the weekend of June 23–24, 1906, at Box Hill with Bessie and Lawrence. Summer in New York had officially begun, as the advertisements and social columns in the newspapers made abundantly clear. B. Altman, located at Nineteenth Street and Sixth Avenue, offered Paris dresses of thin white muslin with embroidery and lace for $25, and announced that it would be closed Saturdays from twelve noon for the duration of the season. The Lilliputian Bazaar of Best & Co., 60–62 West Twenty-third Street, promoted girls' and misses' summer hats, including sunbonnets in a variety of colors. Lord & Taylor, Broadway and Twentieth Street, suggested men's cambric robes at 50 cents for warm summer nights, while Simpson Crawford Co., Sixth Avenue between Nineteenth and Twentieth streets, had ladies' cool kimonos at 98 cents. The smart straw boater every well-dressed man needed to complete his summer attire was being reduced from $5.00 to $1.95 by Saks & Company, Broadway between Thirty-third and Thirty-fourth streets. For summer reading, at home or on vacation, McClure's suggested its new collection of short stories by O. Henry, *The Four Million.*

Summer social notes included the information that while Clarence Mackay had sailed for some weeks of deer stalking in Scotland, Mrs. Mackay and her children had taken off for the hills of Lenox, Massachusetts. So many people were rushing to Saratoga, where the Boston Symphony Orchestra was playing at the United States Hotel, that extra daily trains had to be put on to carry the vacationing throngs to the grand old spa. In Newport, Mr. and Mrs. E. J. Berwin had opened their cottage, The Elms, for the season, while the Oliver H. P. Belmonts' Belcourt was being readied for its

*B*essie *White dressed for a*
costume ball about 1905.

*L*awrence White (left) and a
friend, Frederic R. King, as
sophomores at Harvard College in
1905. Lawrence had entered
Harvard in 1904 at the age of
sixteen. After graduation, he
studied architecture at the Ecole
des Beaux-Arts and eventually
became head of McKim, Mead &
White. Lawrence White died in
1956. Frederic King, who also
became an architect, was the
brother of LeRoy King, a guest at
Box Hill the weekend before
Stanford White was killed.

owners' imminent arrival. The Whites' Long Island was most certainly not left out of the social swim. The New York *Times* noted that at Southampton the Meadow Club was once again proving to be the center of social life despite the "continued low temperature," while under the heading "Pastimes in Patchogue" the newspaper detailed an exceptionally lively party at the Clifton Hotel. Another *Times* headline reassuredly reported: "Westhampton Awakens." Just to show that the Episcopal Church was not asleep to the realities of the season, Bishop Henry Codman Potter used the pulpit of St. Bartholomew's to rather alarmingly warn parishioners that if

Stanford White and a chauffeur in White's Mobile steamer at Box Hill in 1902. The steamer, according to Lawrence White, "used to burn out its boiler every few days." The architect was enthralled by automobiles and became so knowledgeable that friends, such as Charles McKim, regularly asked his advice before purchasing one.

New York City rectors were not given long vacations they "will go mad!"

The Whites had two weekend guests at Box Hill, LeRoy King, a classmate of Larry's at Harvard, and Laura Chanler, the daughter of White's friend Mrs. Winthrop Chanler. Laura would eventually become Larry's wife. White spent some of the weekend working on details of the monument he was designing for Brooklyn's Fort Greene Park to commemorate the more than 11,000 Americans who had perished during the Revolution in British prison ships anchored in Wallabout Bay. One afternoon he drove over to Southampton in his new Rainier automobile—the cost of which would have given Woodrow Wilson Presbyterian paroxysms—to consult with the Breeses about certain still incomplete details at The Orchard.

Early Monday morning, June 25, Stanford White returned to New York by automobile. The weather was predicted to be mild, with clouds and a chance of rain. The two boys and Laura Chanler came back to the city in the afternoon. The architect had a busy day. Though Dr. Parkhurst was already conducting services in his new kirk, White was still working on some of the decorative elements of the Madison Square Presbyterian Church and he had a conference at the Players with Saint-Gaudens concerning a memorial they were planning for Whistler at West Point. All day White had been debating whether or not to take the late train to Philadelphia, where he had a business meeting the next day. But he hesitated to go, for with Mead abroad and McKim suffering from one of his recurrent bouts of nerves he was the only partner in the office. At the last moment he decided to remain in New York. Shortly after seven that evening, White, Larry, and LeRoy King drove from the Gramercy Park house to the Café Martin, the rather raffish restaurant which occupied Delmonico's old quarters on Twenty-sixth Street between Fifth Avenue and Broadway. White led the way to the restaurant's Broadway side, which Louis Martin had converted into a Parisian café with marble-topped tables, banquettes, and supplies of French newspapers and illustrated journals. Evelyn, Harry, and two of

The spacious terrace of the Café Martin, located on Twenty-sixth Street between Fifth Avenue and Broadway, was one of New York's popular turn-of-the-century hot weather dining spots. On June 25, 1906, this terrace, on the restaurant's Broadway side, was the setting for Stanford White's last meal. This photograph was taken shortly before that event.

RENDEZVOUS

Thaw's friends, Thomas McCaleb and Truxton Beale, were seated at a table in Martin's main dining room, a cream-and-gold Edwardian showplace lit by enormous chandeliers. Martin's was the right place for White to take two young men out on the town, but an extremely odd place to take one's wife, for the restaurant's Broadway foyer was frequented by smartly turned-out females who were not loath to accept invitations from single males to have a flute of champagne or a bit of pheasant under glass. Thaw's back was to the room, but Evelyn saw Stanford White making his way to the café and "determined to play fair with Harry, I asked for a piece of paper and pencil—since I couldn't speak of it before McCaleb and Beale—and wrote: 'The B. was here but has left.'" This rather unnecessary action, which Evelyn reported in *Prodigal Days*, fits into a pattern which indicates that the now twenty-one-year-old woman was systematically using the architect to stimulate her husband's jealousy and, perhaps, his interest. Not long before this she had spread the totally false rumor that Stanford White had told a friend that he intended to win her back.

After dinner, White drove his son and LeRoy King to the New Amsterdam Theatre on West Forty-second Street, where they had tickets for *The Governor's Son*, a farce written by and starring George M. Cohan which was playing in the "Aerial Garden" on the theatre's roof. They might have gone to see the new smash-hit revival of Shakespeare's *Twelfth Night* with E. H. Sothern and Julia Marlowe at the nearby Academy of Music, but undoubtedly the feast of "Song, Parodies and Comedy" promised by the Cohan offering had more attractions for two boys just down from Cambridge. After dropping them off, White headed to the Madison Square Roof, as the Garden's open-air theatre was formally called, to see *Mamzelle Champagne*, a musical by Edgar Allan Woolf and Cassius Freeborn. It was the first night of the production that had been billed as the "Best, Brightest, Breeziest Show in Town," and White was an investor. He had told the boys, who were staying at the Gramercy Park house, not to wait up for him. The architect planned, as he often did, to work late in his Tower apartment.

The theatre on the roof of Madison Square Garden where Stanford White was shot while watching a performance of Mamzelle Champagne. The play had originally been a Columbia College varsity show. At Columbia, because Mamzelle Champagne had an all-male cast, lines such as "I'm a good girl—you can't insult me" had elicited howls. When spoken by real actresses, though, they fell flat. The publicity engendered by White's murder kept the vapid review running for sixty performances and seats at his table near the stage sold at a premium.

It could well have been sheer coincidence that the Thaws and Stanford White were at the Café Martin that evening, but it is certainly suspicious that Harry and Evelyn should have been going to see *Mamzelle Champagne*, not because of the play—they often attended first nights—but because of the location. Evelyn had been dumbfounded when Harry had told her where they were headed. "I could scarcely believe that Thaw had so reconciled himself to things that he would even set foot in the Garden, with which Stanford White's name and my seduction were so immutably linked. Incredible!" Employing no fewer than four detectives to shadow White, Harry Thaw most certainly knew that a table had been reserved for the architect on the Garden's roof that night. Thaw was, in fact, stalking White. Several friends had warned the architect of the mad millionaire.

The theatre on the roof of Madison Square Garden was essentially a cabaret, with a small stage, seating arranged around tables, and, overhead, vines and red, yellow, and blue electric lights. The Thaws' table for *Mamzelle Champagne* was three-quarters of the way back from the stage. Harry, who attracted considerable attention because he was wearing a heavy black overcoat on a warm June night, quickly left the table and began moving restlessly about. Stanford White—he had most likely stopped off at the Manhattan Club just south of the Garden—did not arrive until late in the production, just as the male lead, Harry Short, was singing "I Could Love a Thousand Girls." For a time, Harry Stevens, Madison Square Garden's official caterer, joined the architect at his table near the stage. Afterward, White sat alone. The show, even when the voluptuous Viola de Costa in the title role sprang out of a papier-mâché champagne bottle, had little of the brightness or breeziness promised by the producer. Evelyn, McCaleb, and Beale were frankly bored, and when Thaw returned to their table, though the play had not ended, they immediately rose to leave. As the party neared the elevator, Harry suddenly dashed away.

Thaw's objective was Stanford White. He moved within three feet of the architect and, whipping out a pistol from beneath his overcoat, fired three point-blank shots. One entered White's left eye and came to rest at the base of his brain, one lodged in a nasal passage, and one struck him in the shoulder. The time was 11 P.M.

Mamzelle Champagne was limping toward its finale, which featured chorus girls dressed in tights holding aloft épées while they sang "I challenge you to a duel . . ." At first the audience thought the pistol play was part of the musical, but as the realization dawned that what they had witnessed was not dramaturgy, the panicked playgoers rushed for the exits. The music died away, the chorus ceased singing, and no amount of cajoling on the part of the conductor could make the musicians resume playing. A waiter covered White's powder-burned face with a tablecloth.

Thomas McCaleb, who had been watching Thaw, turned to Evelyn and cried, "He's shot a man! He has killed somebody! My God, what it is to be crazy!"

When a fireman took the pistol out of Thaw's hand, Harry's comment was "He deserved it." Passing Evelyn, he said, "It's all right, dear. I have probably saved your life."

Officer Debbs of the Tenderloin station placed the murderer under arrest. As they were about to enter an elevator to descend to the street, Harry Thaw handed Debbs ten dollars. "Here's a bill, Officer," he explained. "Get Carnegie on the telephone and tell him I'm in trouble."

On Tuesday, Bessie White, who had come into New York and was at the Gramercy Park house, told the press that her husband's funeral would be held on Thursday at St. Bartholomew's Church at Madison Avenue and Forty-fourth Street. Bessie held up well, but the architect's mother, after being informed of his murder, had collapsed. On Wednesday, with the story of the killing splashed across the front page of almost every American and European newspaper, and reporters, acquaintances, sensation seekers, and artists besieging 121 East Twenty-first Street, where White's body lay before an antique Roman statue of Venus, it was announced that the funeral would be held on Long Island.

At eight o'clock Thursday morning—an hour earlier than the

time given to the press—the casket, accompanied by floral tributes, was ferried across the East River and placed in the first car of a special four-car funeral train at Long Island City. When the train pulled out shortly after 9 A.M., more than two hundred of the Whites' relatives and friends were aboard, including William Rutherford Mead—just back from Europe—Peter Cooper Hewitt, and James Breese. Also aboard was a distraught Charles McKim, who, when the New York *Times* had telephoned him at 11:45 Monday evening with word of the murder, had exclaimed, "I cannot conceive of such an awful thing. It is a horrible nightmare." McKim's own health was precarious, made worse daily by the gargantuan task of designing what would be his masterpiece, New York's Pennsylvania Station.

The funeral was held at St. James Episcopal Church, a white frame country chapel not far from Box Hill for which the architect had designed three stained-glass windows. More than three hundred people packed the small structure. The traditional service for the dead from the *Book of Common Prayer* was conducted by the rector of St. James, assisted by the Reverend Dr. Leighton Parks, rector of St. Bartholomew's Church, with music provided by a choir from the New York parish. Among the hymns was one with these well-known words:

> *Now the laborer's task is o'er;*
> *Now the battle day is past;*
> *Now upon the farther shore*
> *Lands the voyager at last.*
>
> *There the tears of earth are dried;*
> *There its hidden things are clear;*
> *There the work of life is tried*
> *By a juster judge than here.*

It was noon when the service ended. Stanford White was buried in the cemetery behind the little church. He was only fifty-two. "Vogue la Galère" had been the motto of the great triumvirate. For one indeed, as the hymn said, the ship had reached shore. Charles McKim would design a stone to mark the spot.

By the time of Stanford White's funeral, the *Herald* and the *World*, both of whose publishers had been friends and patrons of the architect, were in captious competition to print the most scandalous story about the murdered man. A typical example of the press's cavalier regard for the truth was the fact that when some of White's friends, quite correctly, refused to discuss either the killing or the architect's relationship with Evelyn Nesbit, the *World* announced that "Stanford White's intimate friends did not rally to the defense of his memory." The facts were otherwise. McKim and Mead never wavered in their loyalty to their slain partner, while Cass Gilbert, John Carrère, Whitney Warren, Richard Watson Gilder, Janet Scudder, Charles Dana Gibson, among others, all openly expressed their admiration for the architect. A letter written by Augustus Saint-Gaudens on July 6 to Alfred Garnier, a friend from the sculptor's Ecole des Beaux-Arts days, expressed what many of White's acquaintances must have felt:

Dear Old Man:
    You have no doubt read in the newspapers of the death of White by an idiot fool who imagined himself wronged, wronged because of a woman. A stupid vengeance, an instantaneous death in a theatre right at the foot of one of his best works! . . . An idiot that shoots a man of great genius for a woman with the face of an angel and the heart of a snake!

And in an article in the August 4 issue of *Collier's*, White's friend the ace journalist Richard Harding Davis declared:

In New York it is impossible for the poor man, the rich man, the man of taste and the man with none, to walk abroad without being indebted to Stanford White . . .

The White-Nesbit-Thaw case proved to be a bonanza for the fourth estate. Within a week of the murder the *World* boasted that its readership had jumped 100,000. Even the usually conservative New York *Times* was caught up in the yellow-journalism frenzy of inaccuracy and innuendo. On the very first day after the murder, Tuesday, June 26, the *Times* reported that "he [White] it was who put Miss Nesbit, now Mrs. Thaw, on the stage," and quickly followed this with the news that "Mr. and Mrs. White have not been living together recently," while calling the architect's Tower flat his "pleasure house." By Friday, June 29, the *Times* was running front-page headlines to the effect that White had "drugged, ruined and insulted Mrs. Thaw" and implied that perhaps the murder was not of much consequence, for the coroner's physician had declared that White was suffering from Bright's disease, incipient tuberculosis, and fatty degeneration of the liver and did not have long to live anyway. On Saturday, June 30, the *Times* reported that Evelyn would be active in her husband's defense and noted that, among his other sins, the architect was $500,000 in debt. The *Times* was also one of a dozen newspapers to carry the claim by Anthony Comstock that he had filing cases of incriminating material concerning White's life, though later, when asked to produce it, the head of the Society for the Suppression of Vice, suppressed it.

It is little wonder that Richard Harding Davis wrote of the dead architect:

> Speaking as one who has been in the newspaper business for fifteen years, I have never known an attack made upon anyone as undeserved, as unfair, as false as that made upon him.

The tone of the popular mood molded by this massive and unrelenting character assassination may be gained from the comment of the Reverend Charles A. Eaton, minister of Cleveland's Euclid Avenue Baptist Church, the sanctuary of the Rockefellers: "It would be a good thing if there was a little more shooting in cases like this." The newspapers did not report whether the Reverend Mr. Eaton drew any moral lessons from the fact that on Friday, June 22, President Theodore Roosevelt had announced that the Rockefellers' Standard Oil Company would be prosecuted for flagrant antitrust activities.

Thaw's frantic plea for help to Andrew Carnegie had not gone unheeded. Indeed, the Carnegies were undoubtedly relieved that the murder had overshadowed the news that the Monongahela Railroad was suing the Carnegie Steel Company's Union Railroad for usurping its right-of-way. By the time that the case of "the people v. Harry K. Thaw" opened on January 23, 1907, in the Criminal Court Branch of the New York State Supreme Court, the Thaws' fortune and the influence of brother-in-law George Carnegie, nephew of the steel mogul, had begun to work their magic to keep Harry out of the electric chair. Mother Thaw, who was at sea when the shooting occurred, had rushed home and hired a battery of the best attorneys that money could buy, including the French-born Californian Delphin Michel Delmas, a noted orator famed for his brilliance in cross-examination. And when on Thursday, January 24, Evelyn's mother, now Mrs. Charles J. Holman of Pittsburgh, was reported "prepared to go to the stand to prove as far as she can that Thaw had never had the feelings of a husband towards her daughter," and it was stated that she possessed letters which would clear White's name and reveal Harry Thaw for what he was, one of mother Thaw's attorneys rushed to Pittsburgh and with $50,000 relieved Mrs. Holman of the letters as well as the urge to testify. There was, to use the New York *Times*'s phrase, such an "ocean of scandal" surrounding the killing that as District Attorney William Travers Jerome rose to conduct the prosecution, one would have thought that White, not Thaw, was in the dock.

The story was copy catnip. Extra seats for the press were placed in Judge James Fitzgerald's courtroom, and Western Union established a special office to handle the expected flow of verbiage. The company was not disappointed. The Kentucky humorist Irvin S. Cobb, who covered the trial, wrote in *Stickfuls*:

> Nobody ever took the pains to figure out how many hundreds of columns of the proceedings the New York papers printed, nor how many square miles of pictures they carried. I know that there were between seventy-five and eighty reporters, special writers and artists in constant attendance.

The crowds attempting to get into the courtroom were the largest in the history of New York jurisprudence, at one point numbering more than 10,000.

Evelyn, whom Cobb described as "Evelyn Nesbit Thaw in her navy blue school girl costume, 'her testimony clothes,'" gave the stellar performance of her dramatic career. She parroted perfectly every line the defense fed her, painting White in the darkest of colors, while suppressing the sable side of Thaw's character. When it came to the question of why she had hesitated to marry Harry, for example, Evelyn never mentioned the repulsion she felt toward the "loony" playboy, but made everything hinge on her relationship with the architect:

> I told him several times after that even if I didn't marry him the friends of Stanford White would always laugh at him and make fun of him. I said marriage would not be a good thing—that I had been on the stage and that I had been to a great many apartments with Stanford White.

On April 8, Delmas, brushing aside any suggestions of insanity, summed up the case for the defense by demanding a total acquittal:

> . . . if Thaw is insane it is with a species of insanity known from the Canadian border to the Gulf. If you expert gentlemen ask me to give it a name, I suggest that you label it *Dementia Americana.* It is that species of insanity that inspires every American to believe his home is sacred.

In response, District Attorney Jerome asked the jury, "Will you acquit a cold-blooded, deliberate, cowardly murderer because his lying wife has a pretty girl's face?" The question obviously stumped the jurors, for on April 12 they informed the court that they were hopelessly deadlocked.

By the time of Harry Thaw's second trial for murder, which began on January 6, 1908, the stories circulating concerning Stanford White were so lurid and William Travers Jerome's prosecution so uneven that after the case reached the jury on January 29 it took the twelve men just twenty-four hours to announce that they had "found that this defendant is not guilty of the murder of Stanford White on the ground of insanity." The court then ruled that Harry Kendall Thaw should be sent to the Asylum for the Criminal Insane at Matteawan, New York. When Thaw arrived at Grand Central Terminal to board a train for Matteawan, he was cheered by a large crowd of well-wishers and hailed as a genuine American hero. Seven years later, in July 1915, Harry Thaw, after a hearing, was declared sane and acquitted of all the charges against him. One of his first acts as a free man was to begin divorce proceedings against Evelyn.

The denigration of Stanford White following his murder and the glorification of Thaw, however brief, was but the froth upon the surface of a soundless sea. It was, in fact, the acting out upon a courtroom stage, with the press providing the playbill, of the popular conception of the drama considered appropriate to the life of an artist in America. The theme of this morality play—which still finds popular acceptance—is that the price of creativity is misery springing from alcoholism, sexual debauchery, and debt. The stark reality of Stephen Collins Foster's deliriumed death in a New York charity hospital, of Poe's poverty-stricken end, of Louis Sullivan dying in a cheap Chicago hotel without a decent suit to clothe his corpse, of Scott Fitzgerald's boozy frustrated finale beneath a blazing Hollywood sun, of Hemingway pressing the double-barreled Boss shotgun to his forehead, so peoples the pages of America's cultural history that it is difficult to say whether the singers created the song or the song the singers. This is not, though, the essential myth of the artist in Italy or France, not even in Germany or England. Perhaps it was nurtured by America's romance with democracy. It is as though by their dazzling brilliance artists surpass the democratic norm, by the liberty of their creation they challenge an essential fraternity. Harry K. Thaw's quip, after seeing a florid Palm Beach villa designed by Addison Mizner, that "I shot the wrong architect," still reaps smiles. If the victim had been a doctor or an

One of Stanford White's last projects was the Prison Ship Martyrs' Monument in Brooklyn's Fort Greene Park. The architect began working on the memorial in 1904, but due to delays caused by fund-raising problems it was not completed until 1909, three years after his death. To commemorate the more than 11,000 Americans who perished during the Revolution in the holds of British prison ships anchored in nearby Wallabout Bay, White created an ensemble of studied dignity. Three broad flights of stairs rise to a 143-foot-tall Doric column bearing a bronze tripod by Adolph Weinman which once cradled a perpetual flame.

engineer or a bank president, it is likely that the reaction would have been very different. White, like Icarus, had flown too near the sun and thus he should not have been surprised if his cunning and beautiful wax wings melted from the heat. There was too, for White, an additional burden. The architect was so urban, so cosmopolitan, so New York, that he was a ripe target for the envy and malice of those who, either in their mind or in their domicile, were provincial.

Fortunately, the essential reality of Stanford White, particularly in New York, is not his death but his life. If in this vast vertical metropolis New Yorkers have become, in the words of Lewis Mumford in *The City in History*, " 'strangers and afraid,' in a world they never made: a world ever less responsive to direct human command, ever more empty of human meaning," then Stanford White's creations are a salubrious anodyne of communality and joy. They strike the senses with the force of the warm perfume of lilacs across a still-cold spring field: the campanile of the Judson Memorial Church rising like a gracious rebuke to the uncivilized modern chapel next to it; the buoyant limestone spring of the Washington Arch launching Fifth Avenue on its northward course; the Church of the Ascension's chancel wall of quarried honey; the waves that break with visible sound over the dolphins on the base of Madison Square's Farragut Memorial; the Tiffany Building's becolumned impeccability; the Charles Dana Gibson house's brilliantly calculated reticence; the august Doric column in Brooklyn's Fort Greene Park manifesting the resting place of the bones of martyred patriots. Yet these great works carry not only communality and joy; they also serve to remind Americans that this land is not a ship adrift at sea or an isolated island, but is part of a consecrated continuum, which, like a golden chain, stretches back, link by link, through the Ecole des Beaux-Arts and Thomas Jefferson, to Paris and Rome, and to the very embryo of Western civilization, that high hill in Athens, that Acropolis, where Stanford White first fell in love with the Erechtheum.

A SELECTIVE BIBLIOGRAPHY

ADAMS, HENRY. *Democracy.* New York: Henry Holt and Company, 1880.

ADAMS, HENRY. *The Education of Henry Adams.* Boston and New York: Houghton Mifflin Company, 1918.

ADAMS, HENRY. *Monte-Saint-Michel and Chartres.* Boston and New York: Houghton Mifflin Company, 1913.

AMORY, CLEVELAND. *The Last Resorts.* New York: Harper & Brothers, 1952.

AMORY, CLEVELAND. *Who Killed Society?* New York: Harper & Brothers, 1960.

ARMSTRONG, DAVID MAITLAND. *Day Before Yesterday.* Edited by Margaret Armstrong. New York: Charles Scribner's Sons, 1920.

ARMSTRONG, HAMILTON FISH. *Those Days.* New York: Harper & Row, 1963.

AUCHINCLOSS, LOUIS. *Edith Wharton: A Woman in Her Time.* New York: The Viking Press, 1971.

BAKER, PAUL R. *Stanny: The Gilded Life of Stanford White.* New York: The Free Press, 1989.

BALDWIN, CHARLES C. *Stanford White.* New York: Dodd, Mead, 1931.

BALSAN, CONSUELO VANDERBILT. *The Glitter and the Gold.* New York: Harper & Brothers, 1952.

BARRETT, JAMES W. *Joseph Pulitzer and His World.* New York: The Vanguard Press, 1941.

BIGELOW, POULTNEY. *Seventy Summers.* New York: Longmans, Greene & Co., 1925.

BLACK, DAVID. *The King of Fifth Avenue: The Fortunes of August Belmont.* New York: The Dial Press, 1981.

BOURGET, PAUL. *Outre-Mer: Impressions of America.* New York: Charles Scribner's Sons, 1895.

BRANDT, CLARE. *An American Aristocracy: The Livingstons.* Garden City: Doubleday & Company, Inc., 1989.

BRISTED, CHARLES ASTOR. *The Upper Ten Thousand.* New York: Stringer & Townsend, 1852.

BROOKS, VAN WYCK. *New England: Indian Summer, 1865–1915.* Cleveland and New York: The World Publishing Company, 1946.

BROUN, HEYWOOD C. *Anthony Comstock, Roundsman of the Lord.* New York: A. C. Boni, 1927.

BROWN, HENRY COLLINS. *Brownstone Fronts and Saratoga Trunks.* New York: E. P. Dutton & Co., Inc., 1935.

BURDEN, SHIRLEY. *The Vanderbilts in My Life.* New Haven and New York: Ticknor and Fields, 1981.

CHAMBERS, JULIUS. *The Book of New York.* New York: Book of New York, Co., 1912.

CHANLER, MARGARET. *Roman Spring.* Boston: Little, Brown and Company, 1934.

COMMAGER, HENRY STEELE. *The American Mind.* New Haven: Yale University Press, 1950.

COREY, LEWIS. *The House of Morgan.* New York: G. Howard Watt, 1930.

CORTISSOZ, ROYAL. *John La Farge.* Boston: Houghton Mifflin Company, 1911.

COX, ANNE F. *The History of the Colony Club.* New York: The Colony Club, 1984.

CROCKETT, ALBERT STEVENS. *Peacocks on Parade.* New York: Sears Publishing Company, 1931.

DAVIS, RICHARD HARDING and LANG, ANDREW. *The Great Streets of the World.* London: J. R. Osgood, McIlvaine & Co., 1892.

DE KOVEN, ANNA FARWELL. *A Musician and His Wife.* New York and London: Harper & Brothers, 1926.

DE WOLFE, ELSIE. *After All*. New York: Harper & Brothers, 1935.

DOCTOROW, E. L. *Ragtime*. New York: Random House, 1975.

DOWNING, ANTOINETTE F. and SCULLY, VINCENT J. *The Architectural Heritage of Newport, Rhode Island*. Cambridge: Harvard University Press, 1952.

DREISER, THEODORE. *Sister Carrie*. New York: Doubleday, Page & Co., 1900.

DREXLER, ARTHUR, editor. *The Architecture of the Ecole des Beaux-Arts*. New York: Museum of Modern Art, 1977.

DRYFHOUT, JOHN H. *The Work of Augustus Saint-Gaudens*. Hanover and London: University Press of New England, 1982.

DUNLAP, DAVID W. *On Broadway: A Journey Uptown Over Time*. New York: Rizzoli International Publications, Inc., 1990.

EDEL, LEON. *Henry James: 1901–1916: The Master*. Philadelphia and New York: J. B. Lippincott Company, 1972.

ELLIOTT, MAUD HOWE. *Roma Beata*. Boston: Little, Brown, and Company, 1904.

ELLIOTT, MAUD HOWE. *This was My Newport*. Cambridge: Mythology Company, 1944.

ELLIS, EDWARD ROBB. *The Epic of New York City*. New York: Coward-McCann, Inc., 1966.

FERREE, BARR. *American Estates and Gardens*. New York: Munn and Co., 1906.

GIEDION, SIGFRIED. *Space, Time and Architecture*. Cambridge: The Harvard University Press, 1944.

HARLOW, ALVIN FAY. *Old Bowery Days*. New York and London: D. Appleton and Company, 1931.

HITCHCOCK, HENRY-RUSSELL. *The Architecture of H. H. Richardson and His Times*. New York: Museum of Modern Art, 1936.

HOFFMANN, DONALD. *The Meanings of Architecture: Buildings and Writings by John Wellborn Root*. New York: Horizon Press, 1967.

HOWELLS, WILLIAM DEAN. *The Rise of Silas Lapham*. Boston: Ticknor Co., 1885.

HOYT, EDWIN P. *The Whitneys*. New York: Weybright and Talley, 1976.

IRELAND, ALLEYNE. *Joseph Pulitzer: Reminiscences of a Secretary*. New York: Mitchell Kennerley, 1914.

JAMES, HENRY. *The American Scene*. New York: Harper & Brothers, 1907.

JAMES, HENRY. *The Wings of the Dove*. New York: Charles Scribner's Sons, 1902.

JOSEPHSON, MATTHEW. *The Robber Barons*. New York: Harcourt, Brace and Company, 1934.

JULLIAN, PHILIPPE. *Prince of Aesthetes: Count Robert de Montesquiou, 1855–1921*. New York: The Viking Press, 1968.

KOCH, ROBERT. *Louis C. Tiffany, Rebel in Glass*. New York: Crown, 1964.

LA FARGE, JOHN. *The Manner is Ordinary*. Garden City: Image Books, 1957.

LAWRENCE, WILLIAM. *Life of Phillips Brooks*. New York and London: Harper & Brothers, 1930.

LEHR, ELIZABETH DREXEL. *"King Lehr" and the Gilded Age*. Philadelphia: J. B. Lippincott Company, 1935.

LONGFORD, GERALD. *The Murder of Stanford White*. Indianapolis: Bobbs-Merrill, 1962.

LOWE, DAVID GARRARD. *Lost Chicago*. Boston: Houghton Mifflin Company, 1975.

LOWE, DAVID GARRARD. *Three St. Bartholomew's: An Architectural History of a Church*. New York: The Victorian Society, 1983.

MCALLISTER, WARD. *Society As I Have Found It*. New York: Cassell, 1890.

MCKIM, MEAD & WHITE. *A Monograph of the Work of McKim, Mead & White, 1879–1915*. 4 vols. New York: Architectural Book Publishing Co., 1915.

MAYER, GRACE. *Once Upon A City*. New York: The Macmillan Company, 1958.

MOONEY, MICHAEL MACDONALD. *Evelyn Nesbit and Stanford White*. New York: William Morrow and Company, Inc., 1976.

MOORE, CHARLES. *The Life and Times of Charles Follen McKim*. Boston and New York: Houghton Mifflin Company, 1929.

MOORE, MARGARET. *End of the Road for Ladies' Mile?* New York: The Drive to Protect the Ladies' Mile District, 1986.

MUMFORD, LEWIS. *The Brown Decades*. New York: Dover Publications, 1955.

MORRIS, LLOYD. *Incredible New York*. New York: Random House, 1951.

MOUNT, CHARLES MERRILL. *John Singer Sargent*. London: The Cresset Press, 1957.

MUMFORD, LEWIS. *The Brown Decades*. New York: Dover Publications, 1955.

NESBIT, EVELYN. *Prodigal Days*. New York: J. Messner, Inc., 1934.

O'GORMAN, JAMES F. *H. H. Richardson and His Office*. Boston: David R. Godin, 1974.

PORZELT, PAUL. *The Metropolitan Club of New York.* New York: Rizzoli International Publications, Inc., 1982.

PULITZER, RALPH. *New York Society on Parade.* New York and London: Harper & Brothers Publishers, 1910.

ROTH, LELAND M. *McKim, Mead & White, Architects.* New York: Harper & Row, 1983.

RUGGLES, ELEANOR. *Prince of Players: Edwin Booth.* New York: W. W. Norton & Company, Inc., 1953.

RUSKIN, JOHN. *Mornings in Florence.* London: G. Allen, 1899.

SAARINEN, ALINE B. *The Proud Possessors.* New York: Random House, 1958.

SAFFRON, MORRIS H. *The Harmonie Club.* New York: The Harmonie Club, 1977.

SAINT-GAUDENS, AUGUSTUS. *The Reminiscences of Augustus Saint-Gaudens.* Edited by Homer Saint-Gaudens. 2 vols. London: Andrew Melrose, 1913.

SCHUYLER, MONTGOMERY. *American Architecture and Other Writings.* Edited by William H. Jordy and Ralph Coe. Cambridge: Belknap Press, 1961.

SCUDDER, JANET. *Modeling My Life.* New York: Harcourt Brace, 1925.

SEITZ, DON CARLOS. *The James Gordon Bennetts Father and Son.* Indianapolis: The Bobbs-Merrill Company, 1928.

SHOPSIN, WILLIAM G. and BRODERICK, MOSETTE. *The Villard Houses.* New York: The Viking Press, 1980.

SILVER, NATHAN. *Lost New York.* Boston: Houghton Mifflin Company, 1967.

SIMMONDS, EDWARD. *From Seven to Seventy.* New York and London: Harper & Brothers, 1922.

SINCLAIR, DAVID. *Dynasty: The Astors and Their Times.* New York: Beaufort Books, Inc., 1984.

SMITH, JANE S. *Elsie de Wolfe: A Life in the High Style.* New York: Atheneum, 1982.

SULLIVAN, LOUIS. *The Autobiography of an Idea.* New York: Press of the American Institute of Architects, Inc., 1924.

SULLIVAN, LOUIS. *Kindergarten Chats.* Lawrence, Kansas: Scarab Fraternity Press, 1934.

SWANBERG, W. A. *Whitney Father, Whitney Heiress.* New York: Charles Scribner's Sons, 1980.

SYMONDS, JOHN ADDINGTON. *Renaissance in Italy.* London: Smith, Elder & Co., 1904.

THAW, HARRY KENDALL. *The Traitor.* Philadelphia: Dorrance and Company, 1926.

TUNNARD, CHRISTOPHER. *The City of Man.* New York: Charles Scribner's Sons, 1953.

VANCE, WILLIAM L. *America's Rome.* 2 vols. New Haven and London: Yale University Press, 1989.

VANDERBILT, ARTHUR T. *Fortune's Children: The Fall of the House of Vanderbilt.* New York: William Morrow and Company, Inc., 1989.

VAN RENSSELAER, MAE KING. *The Social Ladder.* New York: Henry Holt and Company, 1924.

VAN RENSSELAER, MARIANNA GRISWOLD. *Henry Hobson Richardson and His Works.* Boston: Houghton, Mifflin & Company, 1888.

VEBLEN, THORSTEIN. *The Theory of the Leisure Class.* New York: The Macmillan Company, 1899.

WALL, E. BERRY. *Neither Pest nor Puritan.* New York: The Dial Press, 1940.

WATTERSON, HENRY. *History of the Manhattan Club.* New York: The De Vinne Press, 1915.

WECTOR, DIXON. *The Saga of American Society.* New York: Charles Scribner's Sons, 1937.

WEITENKAMPF, FRANK. *Manhattan Kaleidoscope.* New York: Charles Scribner's Sons, 1947.

WHARTON, EDITH. *A Backward Glance.* New York and London: D. Appleton-Century Company, Inc., 1934.

WHARTON, EDITH and CODMAN, OGDEN. *The Decoration of Houses.* New York: Charles Scribner's Sons, 1897.

WHARTON, EDITH. *The House of Mirth.* New York: Charles Scribner's Sons, 1905.

WHITE, RICHARD GRANT. *The Fate of Mansfield Humphries.* Boston and New York: Houghton, Mifflin and Company, 1884.

WHITE, RICHARD GRANT. *National Hymns.* New York: Rudd & Carlton, 1861.

WHITE, RICHARD GRANT. *Words and Their Uses.* Boston: Houghton, Mifflin and Company, 1880.

WHITE, STANFORD. *Sketches and Designs by Stanford White with an Outline of His Career by His Son Lawrence Grant White.* New York: The Architectural Book Publishing Co., 1920.

WILSON, RICHARD GUY. *McKim, Mead & White, Architects.* New York: Rizzoli International Publications, Inc., 1983.

WINKLER, JOHN K. *Morgan the Magnificent.* New York: The Vanguard Press, 1930.

WODEHOUSE, LAWRENCE. *White of McKim, Mead and White.* New York and London: Garland Publishing, Inc., 1988.

ILLUSTRATION CREDITS

FRONTISPIECE: The New-York Historical Society. PAGE 2: The Library of Congress. PAGE 7: Peter White. PAGE 8: Private Collection. PAGE 16: Boston Public Library. PAGE 17: Mr. and Mrs. Robert White. PAGE 24: Private Collection. PAGE 26: Trinity Church. PAGE 30: Mr. and Mrs. Robert White. PAGES 30–31: The Bostonian Society. PAGE 32: Boston Public Library. PAGE 33: Boston Athenaeum. PAGE 34: Boston Athenaeum. PAGE 35: Peter White. PAGE 36: Peter White. PAGES 38–39: Boston Athenaeum. PAGE 42: Roger-Viollet. PAGE 43: Mr. and Mrs. Robert White. PAGES 44–45: Roger-Viollet. PAGE 46: Mr. and Mrs. Robert White. PAGE 47: Roger-Viollet. PAGE 49: Roger-Viollet. PAGE 51: Mr. and Mrs. Robert White. PAGES 52–53: Roger-Viollet. PAGE 53: Mr. and Mrs. Robert White. PAGE 54: Private Collection. PAGE 55: Private Collection. PAGE 56: Museum of the City of New York. PAGE 57: United States Department of the Interior, National Park Service, Saint-Gaudens National Historic Site. PAGES 58–59: Roger-Viollet. PAGE 60: Private Collection. PAGE 61: Roger-Viollet. PAGE 62: The Augustus Saint-Gaudens Memorial. PAGE 70: Private Collection. PAGE 71: Peter White. PAGE 73: United States Department of the Interior, National Park Service, Saint-Gaudens National Historic Site. PAGE 74: Private Collection. PAGE 76: Private Collection. PAGE 77: Private Collection. PAGE 78: The Newport Historical Society. PAGE 79: International Tennis Hall of Fame. PAGE 80: The Newport Historical Society. PAGE 81: John T. Hopf. PAGE 84: The Seventh Regiment Fund, Inc. PAGE 85: Private Collection. PAGE 86: Museum of the City of New York. PAGE 87: Avery Architecture and Fine Arts Library. PAGE 89: Private Collection. PAGE 90: Peter White. PAGE 94: Peter White. PAGE 96: Mr. and Mrs. Robert White. PAGE 98: Peter White. PAGE 99, top: The New-York Historical Society. PAGE 99, bottom: Peter White. PAGE 100: The New-York Historical Society. PAGE 101: Peter White. PAGE 102, top and bottom: Peter White. PAGE 103: Peter White. PAGE 104: Private Collection. PAGE 105: Photograph by Esther Bubley. PAGE 106: Museum of the City of New York. PAGE 109, top: Brown Brothers. PAGE 109, bottom: Private Collection. PAGES 112–113: The New-York Historical Society. PAGES 114–115: Museum of the City of New York. PAGE 116: Private Collection. PAGE 117: The New-York Historical Society. PAGE 118: Private Collection. PAGE 120: Church of the Ascension. PAGE 122: Church of the Ascension. PAGE 124: The Paulist Fathers. PAGE 127: The Library of Congress. PAGE 128: Museum of the City of New York. PAGE 135: The New-York Historical Society. PAGE 137: The New-York Historical Society. PAGE 138: Brown Brothers. PAGE 139: Avery Architecture and Fine Arts Library. PAGE 141: Private Collection. PAGE 144: Brown Brothers. PAGE 145: Private Collection. PAGE 148: The New-York Historical Society. PAGE 152: The Hampton-Booth Theatre Library at the Players Club. PAGES 154–155: The New-York Historical Society. PAGE 157: Private Collection. PAGES 158–159: Private Collection. PAGE 161: The New-York Historical Society. PAGE 164: Private Collection. PAGE 165: Private Collection. PAGE 166: The Brook Club. PAGE 167: The New York Public Library. PAGE 168: Private Collection. PAGE 169: The New-York Historical Society. PAGE 170, left and right: Brown Brothers. PAGE 171: Brown Brothers. PAGE 172: New York University. PAGE 174: New York University. PAGE 175: Private Collection. PAGE 177: The New York Public Library. PAGE 178: Avery Architecture and Fine Arts Library. PAGE 179: Frank Hall. PAGE 180: The New-York Historical Society. PAGE 181: Private Collection. PAGES 182–183: Museum of the City of New York. PAGE 185: The New-York Historical Society. PAGES 188–189: The New-York Historical Society. PAGE 189: Private Collection. PAGE 190: Private Collection. PAGE 192: Museum of the City of New York. PAGE 195: Museum of the City of New York. PAGES 196–197: Museum of the City of New York. PAGE 200: Peter White. PAGE 201: Peter White. PAGE 203: Private Collection. PAGE 204: The New-York Historical Society. PAGE 205: Private Collection. PAGE 207: Mills Mansion State Historic Site. PAGE 208: Mills Mansion State Historic Site. PAGE 210: John T. Hopf. PAGE 211: Private Collection. PAGES 212 and 213: The New-York Historical Society. PAGE 215: The New-York Historical Society. PAGE 216: The New-York Historical Society. PAGE 218: Private Collection. PAGE 220: Private Collection. PAGE 227: Private Collection. PAGE 228: Avery Architecture and Fine Arts Library. PAGES 232–233: Museum of the City of New York. PAGE 233: Private Collection. PAGE 234: Avery Architecture and Fine Arts Library. PAGE 236: Avery Architecture and Fine Arts Library. PAGE 239: Avery Architecture and Fine Arts Library. PAGE 241: Avery Architecture and Fine Arts Library. PAGE 243: Brown Brothers. PAGE 245: Private Collection. PAGE 249: The New-York Historical Society. PAGE 250: Private Collection. PAGE 252: Private Collection. PAGE 254: The New York Public Library. PAGE 256: The New-York Historical Society. PAGE 258: The New-York Historical Society. PAGE 259: Private Collection. PAGE 260: The New-York Historical Society. PAGE 265: Private Collection. PAGE 266: Private Collection. PAGE 269: The New-York Historical Society. PAGE 271: Museum of the City of New York. PAGE 273: Private Collection. PAGE 275: The New-York Historical Society. PAGE 277: Private Collection. PAGE 282: The New-York Historical Society. PAGE 295: Avery Architecture and Fine Arts Library. PAGE 296: The New York Public Library. PAGE 297: Private Collection. PAGE 298: Private Collection. PAGE 299: The New-York Historical Society. PAGE 302: Private Collection. PAGE 306: Private Collection. PAGE 307: Private Collection. PAGE 308: Private Collection. PAGE 313: Peter White. PAGE 314: Peter White. PAGE 315: Peter White. PAGE 317: Private Collection. PAGE 318: Avery Architecture and Fine Arts Library. PAGES 328–329: The New-York Historical Society.

INDEX